# Building a Project-Driven Enterprise

# Building a Project-Driven Enterprise

## How to Slash Waste and Boost Profits Through Lean Project Management

**Ronald Mascitelli**

**TECHNOLOGY** PERSPECTIVES

Northridge, CA

*Editorial and Sales Offices*: Technology Perspectives
18755 Accra Street, Northridge, California 91326


Publisher's Cataloging-in-Publication
*(Provided by Quality Books, Inc.)*

Mascitelli, Ronald.
  Building a project-driven enterprise : how to slash
waste and boost profits through lean project management /
Ronald Mascitelli. -- 1st ed.
  p. cm.
  Includes bibliographical references and index.
  LCCN 2001132364
  ISBN 0-9662697-1-3

  1. Project management. I. Title

HD69.P75M37 2002              658.4'04
                           QBI01-201471


10 9 8 7 6 5 4 3 2 1
First Edition

## Dedication

To Renee and Misty

*Two of the best friends a guy could have . . .
human or otherwise.*

# CONTENTS

## PART III
### The "Special Case" of New Product Development

**CHAPTER SEVEN**

## PART IV
### Building a Project-Driven Enterprise

**CHAPTER EIGHT**

**CHAPTER NINE**

# *Acknowledgements*

I am pleased to extend my appreciation to the many individuals whose contributions have made this book possible. First in line for thanks are those people who took the time to review and provide valuable comments on early drafts of this work, including Randy Karg, Marcelo Miranda, Gary Marves, Marty Wartenberg, John Hidahl, Adi Choudri, and Tyler Jensen. The excellent cover design, graphics, and typesetting of the text are the achievements of Shannon Bodie of Lightbourne. My lovely wife, Renee, combed through every word of this book for possible improvements and thereby polished the text immeasurably.

Although I must take credit (and blame) for the words on these pages, the ideas behind them are derived from myriad sources, including scholars, practitioners, and students. My References section is brimming with contributors whose insights have enriched this work. Two individuals, however, stand out among this august group: James Womack and Don Reinertsen. James Womack, and his collaborators at the Lean Enterprise Institute, deserve a round of applause for defining value and waste in a way that is fundamental, understandable, and easily extensible to the world of project management. I hold Don Reinertsen in the highest regard, both for his pragmatic and experience-laden writing, and his willingness to look in some unlikely places to find ways to accelerate product development. A very large pillar in the support structure of this book has these gentlemen's names engraved on it.

Finally, I'd like to acknowledge and thank the several thousand students that I have enjoyed learning from (yes, you read that right) over the past five years. The material in this book has been filtered, honed, enhanced, and validated by the audiences that have attended my *Lean Project Management* and *Lean Product Development* workshops. It is their practical perspectives and hands-on insights that make this book worth its price.

# A Note to the Reader

> *"I'm working to improve my methods, and every hour*
> *I save is an hour added to my life."*
> —Ayn Rand

What could be more valuable to a project team than saving time? Imagine that you were suddenly imbued with wizard-like powers over the temporal realm. A wave of your wand and you could bring your project schedule back from oblivion. A few incantations and a new product would reach the market twice as fast. You could work a bit of magic and expand your firm's capacity to handle new, revenue-generating projects. Gross margins would fall under your spell, so that your actual labor hours would always be *less* than your original estimates. Needless to say, with powers such as these, your firm would achieve unheard of competitiveness (and you would have more job security than the CEO).

Well, the methods of *lean project management* can enable you to accomplish the above prestidigitation, without the need to become a master of the dark arts. The techniques presented in this book constitute a flexible toolbox for slashing the waste from project execution. Whether your business involves contract work (in industries such as aerospace, engineering, information systems or construction) or the development of new products, you will find practical ideas *that can be implemented tomorrow* to improve the productivity and schedule performance of your project teams.

The intended audience for this book includes anyone who wishes to become more time-efficient. Project managers are at the front of the line, along with team leaders, functional managers, and improvement champions. Individual workers can also benefit from these methods, either to enhance their careers, or to relieve schedule pressures so that they can spend more time with their families. Virtually anyone in business will find value in these waste-slashing ideas.

To accommodate such a broad target audience, I've chosen a light writing style that I hope will engage you, and (dare I say) actually *entertain* you. This reflects my belief that interest is a prerequisite for learning. To hold your precious interest, I've enlisted a number of literary ploys, including case examples, fictional vignettes, question-and-answer sessions, step-by-step instructions, and even a bit of irreverent humor. Please don't take these attempts to conquer your attention span the wrong way. There is nothing trivial or lightweight about the concepts in this book, as the extensive footnotes and references will attest.

Every method presented herein has been successfully employed in dozens of firms spanning multiple industries. Many of the ideas have been distilled from practitioners just like yourself, who have attended my professional workshops over the past five years. Practical, understandable, deployable . . . what a concept!

Consider this your official welcome to the world of lean project management. I hope you enjoy the conversation we're about to have (even though I'll be doing most of the talking). My wish for you is to gain back time, and in so doing be able to enhance both your work performance and the quality of your life. So prepare to open your mind, engage your neurons, and enjoy the intellectual ride.

*Ronald Mascitelli*
December 2001

# PART 1

## Principles that Drive Project Efficiency

# The Five
# Principles of
# Lean Thinking  1

You've probably seen those little meters that runners strap to their ankles to tell them how far they've traveled (they're called "pedometers" for the pedantic among you). Suppose that a similar meter was available that could measure the work efficiency of project teams. This clever device records how much time a team member spends doing work *that their project's customer would willingly pay for*. Now imagine that you and your project team strap on these little gems and go through your typical workday. How much of your eight (or nine, or ten) hour day would register as value-added from the customer's perspective? Four hours? You're being an optimist. Two hours? Now you're getting a bit warmer. In many firms, project teams spend *less than one hour per workday performing work that is actually paid for by an external customer.*[1]

Before you shake your head in disbelief, let's consider a day in the life of a "typical" project team member. Jane is a software engineer working on a large network integration project. Her task is to write a system test routine that will be used to conduct final acceptance testing of a new network. She is sitting at her desk, head in hands, pondering her timecard.

"Forty hours this week, and at least another thirty next week, to complete this test routine," she mumbles under her breath, "the project manager is going to *kill* me! Where does the time go?"

Frustrated by her glacially slow progress, Jane decides to conduct a little experiment. Over the subsequent week, she keeps a log of her daily work activities, as shown in Figure 1.1. On a typical day, she arrives at work at about seven a.m., which gives her just enough time before her first meeting to get a caffeine fix and plow though the fifty irrelevant e-mails stuffing her mailbox. Status meetings at eight and nine, a customer call at ten, a command performance before the general manager at eleven, which will slip to one p.m., since no executive meeting ever sticks to an agenda. Pretty grim so far.

| Activity | Start | End | Value | Waste |
|---|---|---|---|---|
| Coffee, e-mails, voice mail, etc. | 7:00 | 8:00 | 0 | 1 hr. |
| Project status meeting (yuck!) | 8:00 | 9:00 | 5 min. | 55 min. |
| Resource planning meeting | 9:00 | 10:00 | 5 min. | 55 min. |
| Customer call (nightmare!) | 10:00 | 10:45 | 10 min. | 35 min. |
| GM dog and pony show | 10:45 | 1:15 | 0! | 2.5 hr. |
| Trip report, calls, etc. | 1:15 | 2:00 | 10 min. | 35 min. |
| Get node list from Bob | 2:00 | 3:00 | 0! | 1 hr |
| Revise SW test routine per node list | 3:00 | 4:00 | 1 hr. | 0 |
| DARN! This is an OLD list! Fix errors... | 4:00 | 5:00 | 0! | 1 hr |
| CAN YOU BELIEVE THIS??!! → | | | 1.5 hr. | 8.5 hr |

**Figure 1.1** – A log sheet showing one of Jane's typical workdays. Note that despite being extremely busy, Jane has virtually no time available to work on value-creating activities.

The afternoon offers a ray of hope; some time that is not consumed by meetings. Unfortunately, there is the expense report that must be submitted by five p.m. "or else," and several visits from "friends" looking to kill time. Finally at around two o'clock, Jane manages to start work on her software task . . . and hits an immediate snag. She needs a node list from the system design engineer to proceed with her work. An hour of hunting for the node list, followed by an hour of work, followed by another hour of making corrections when she finds out that she was given an obsolete document. Quitting time comes and goes, and Jane remains, still trying to create value in the face of insurmountable odds.

It is difficult to define "value" precisely, particularly in the context of creative or innovative work. It is far easier, however, to identify what is *not* value-creating. How much of Jane's typical workday actually generated revenue for her company? How much of your own? The purpose of this book is to teach you how to strip the waste out of your project team's daily activities, while achieving the highest possible quality and value. You will learn how to use dozens of practical and proven "lean" techniques *that you can apply tomorrow* to increase speed and boost profits. Before you can reap these rewards, however, we must first establish a foundation. In the next several chapters, I will present some concepts that will help you learn how to "see" project waste. With this groundwork in place, you will be prepared to apply the practical toolbox of waste-slashing methods described in Part 2.

## Three Kinds of Time

The first step toward identifying waste in projects is to define three "kinds" of time, as shown in Figure 1.2. The first we will call the *calendar time*. This is the familiar "start-date-to-end-date" task duration upon which project schedules are based. Now a naïve project manager might assume that calendar time for an activity has at least a vague connection to how many hours it actually takes to perform a task. Those of us with a few layers of scar tissue from bad estimates and late milestones know better.

The calendar time of a task is, in fact, driven by resource availability. If appropriate resources are sitting around waiting to execute a task, the calendar time for that task will be equal to what we will call the *work time*. This is the time it would take a full-time, dedicated individual to perform the required work (for now, we'll assume a one-person task). Why should these times

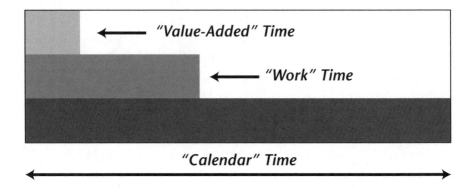

+ **CALENDAR TIME** - The actual duration of a task from start to finish.

+ **WORK TIME** - The percentage of the calender time that resources are available.

+ **VALUE-ADDED TIME** - The amount of the work time that is actually value-added . . . the rest is waste!

**Figure 1.2** – There are three kinds of time associated with any project task. The difference between calendar time and work time reflects the availability of resources. The gap between work time and value-added time is caused by non-value-added waste embedded in our traditional work methods.

be different? The reasons are all too familiar: multi-tasking of team members, waiting in queues, changing priorities, lack of needed information or materials, firefighting, and a host of other maladies. Unless an organization has a good handle on resource availability throughout the life of a project, calendar-time estimates will amount to little more than wishful thinking.

Clearly, if we can better align the calendar time with the work time for project tasks, we could achieve a more predictable schedule while reducing the overall duration of our projects. The easy way to accomplish this would be to dedicate team members to only one project at a time. Unfortunately, dedicated teams are a virtual impossibility in many firms, so we must find a way to ensure accurate estimates and minimal task durations even in a multi-tasking environment. Several of the lean methods described in this book are designed to accomplish exactly that.[2]

We can go further, however, in improving time efficiency.

Beyond the work time for a given task is something we will call the *value-added time*. This is the time required by a qualified individual working full-time on a task, *if all non-value-added waste were eliminated from their activities.* In other words, it is not enough to simply apply resources; we must also consider whether those resources are efficiently creating value.

Admittedly, value-added time is an ideal; a theoretical concept rather than a directly measurable reality. It does, however, serve to highlight our second opportunity to apply lean methods. Although your firm's project teams may never reach one-hundred-percent value-added efficiency, even a ten-percent movement in that direction is enormously valuable; ten-percent more projects, completed ten-percent faster, with ten-percent more profits. The remaining lean methods presented in this book focus on giving you and your teams that ten percent, and potentially much more.

## What is Lean Thinking?

The problem with eliminating waste from projects is that it is hard to separate the waste from the value. What part of the eight hours that a designer spends sitting at a CAD terminal, for example, is value-added time? If he stares at the screen for seven hours "thinking," and then works feverishly for one hour to complete a drawing, did that represent eight productive hours or only one?

Fortunately, we can avoid delving into the metaphysics of creative thought while still assuring an increase in project-team efficiency. It is far easier to identify what is *not* value-added than to specify what *is* value-added. Sitting in unnecessary, poorly run meetings is not value-added, nor is chasing after needed information. Avoidable mistakes and rework are unambiguously wasteful, as are unnecessary expediting and approvals. The first step in slashing project waste will be to "learn to see" waste.[3] We can then apply countermeasures, in the form of lean work methods, to eliminate it.

Luckily, some clever folks have blazed a trail for us. In the book, *The Machine that Changed the World* [4] the authors describe the Just-in-Time (JIT) production system developed by Taiichi Ohno and others at Toyota Motor Company. Unlike the many "observational" reports of Japan's breakthroughs over the past few decades, however, this book provides a deeper insight. The authors assert that underlying the almost childlike simplicity of Toyota's efficient operations are five fundamental principles. These principles have become the foundation for a highly successful improvement philosophy known as "lean thinking."[5]

Before we delve into this lean stuff, however, there are two important points that should be made. First, my use of the word "lean" in this book does not, in any way, imply downsizing. If I may distort a cliché, becoming lean does not require being mean. It is my intent to free up value-creating capacity, not to provide an excuse for upper management to swing the ax.

Secondly, I want to emphasize that lean thinking is not a religion (nor is any other "buzzword" improvement philosophy, for that matter). Most of us are sick to the point of tears with slogans, banners, and hollow vision statements, along with the ineffectual, knee-jerk changes they precipitate. Lean thinking, Total Quality Management (TQM), six-sigma, theory of constraints, balanced scorecard, core competencies, and the like, are just improvement tools. As the sociologist, Abraham Maslow, once said, "people who become proficient at using a hammer begin to see everything around them as a nail."[6] Tools should be used when they are *appropriate*, and then put away, not worshiped.

### The First Lean Principle

The five principles of lean thinking are not rocket science, as can be seen in Figure 1.3. They represent essential conditions to achieve both market acceptance *and* operational excellence. Despite their unassuming appearance, however, there is great power in these simple words.

The first principle states that we must "precisely specify the value of each project." That can't be too hard, right? Think again. What we are looking for here is not the opinion of your team, but rather the value that the *customer* (either internal or

---

**PRINCIPLE 1** - Precisely specify the **value** of each project

**PRINCIPLE 2** - Identify the **value stream** for each project

**PRINCIPLE 3** - Allow value to **flow** without interruptions

**PRINCIPLE 4** - Let the customer **pull** value from the project team

**PRINCIPLE 5** - Continuously pursue **perfection**

---

**Figure 1.3** – The five principles of lean thinking.[7] These simple principles define an ideal value-creating enterprise, and provide a high-level roadmap for waste-reduction efforts.

external) places on the deliverables of a project. Value is a nebulous thing: Without a clear picture of what value actually is, this seemingly simple condition can be amazingly difficult to achieve. We must therefore agree on a working definition for value. I propose the following:

### *Value is anything that a customer will gladly pay for.*

Now that is what I call a practical definition. Do you agree with it? Later in this book we will consider other, more strategic interpretations of value. For the time being, however, this rather mercenary perspective will serve us well. Incidentally, if your project has an internal customer (as is typically the case for process improvement projects, for example), just substitute "benefit" or "utility" for price in the discussions that follow.

With this definition in mind, how might we determine which tasks or activities on a project are value-creating and which are non-value-added? If we accept for the moment this rather strict "customer pays" concept, then it follows that any activity that does not directly drive the *price* a customer is willing to pay must only add *cost* to the project. Some of these costs are essential to delivering value, and must be retained. Other activities, we will soon see, are non-value-added, and can be eliminated without loss of price, quality, or customer satisfaction. In fact, I propose the following corollary:

*An activity on a project is value-added if it* **transforms the deliverables** *of the project in such a way that the customer* **recognizes** *the transformation and is* **willing to pay for it**.

What I mean by "transforms the deliverables" is that a customer must be able to detect the effects of an activity after the outputs have been delivered. Under these conditions, does the act of inspecting a project output, for example, add value? Assuming that the same quality could be achieved in a different way, would a customer know whether a project deliverable has been inspected or not?

Based on the above definition, inspection is non-value-added. Rather it should be thought of as an insurance policy to assure that value is received by your customer (much like a proactive warrantee). Since none of us would intentionally pay more for our car insurance, for example, it seems reasonable that anything we can do to reduce the need for inspection would result in eliminating waste.

What about those endless project status meetings? Is your customer willing to pay you for those (assuming that they are not required as part of your contract)? At first you might say, "surely our customers appreciate that we have good internal coordination." Think of it this way: If you were to run an advertisement in *The Wall Street Journal* that proclaimed, "Our firm has more status meetings than any of our competitors," would you gain any new customers?

You may have noticed that I have included the condition that "the customer recognizes the transformation" into the above definition. Although this might seem unnecessary, there is a large class of activities that fall into the category of "hidden value." Hidden value is anything that might increase the price of a project, if only the customer knew it was there. Increasing the reliability and robustness of a project output might be an example, provided that your firm doesn't communicate this improvement to the customer. A second example became clear in a recent conversation. A sales representative for a major system integration firm was complaining to me about the loss of a critical customer.

"I can't believe it," he moaned, "it just doesn't make sense. Our firm has, for years, offered what amounts to a lifetime warrantee on our projects. If anything goes wrong, we just show up and fix the problem. Last month, one of our competitors began offering a five-year unconditional guarantee, and we lost a key client because of it. How could those fools choose a five-year warrantee over a lifetime of free support?"

The answer to his question was simple. Although his firm had always fixed their customer's problems, they never actually documented this policy. From the customer's perspective, a five-year guarantee *that they recognized* was preferable to what appeared to be no formal guarantee at all.

For our definition of value to be useful, we will group project activities into three categories. In the first category we place pure value-added tasks, based on the above definition. We will call these activities simply "Value." The second category, which we will call "Type 1 Waste" is at least partially non-value-added, but is currently necessary to get the job done (I usually think of these tasks as "necessary but evil.") Type 1 tasks add cost to a project without directly affecting price. Finally, we can define "Type 2 Waste" as activities that are pure non-value-added; they are the "low-hanging fruit" in our quest for waste elimination. You might think of "Value" tasks as being like filet mignon, Type 1 activities as resembling round steak with the fat left on, and Type 2 as being just big globs of fat. Our objective going forward will be to immediately slash the Type 2 stuff, and subsequently attack the wasteful aspects of Type 1 tasks.

By applying these three categories of project activities, you can begin developing your waste-detecting vision. In fact, let's put your intuition to the test. Consider the table shown in Figure 1.4. The activities listed are typical of many projects (although you may have to extrapolate a bit to fit your specific situation). Grab a pencil, and before reading further, mark which category you feel best matches your experience with each activity.

How did you grade team coordination meetings? If you are like the thousands of students I've taught this material to over the past several years, you rated those nasty, overlong meetings as a "Type 1 minus."[8] Although team coordination is a necessity, there must be a better alternative to sitting through endless bickering over technical details and mind-numbing repetition of the same dull status charts.

| Activity | Value | WASTE | |
|---|---|---|---|
| | | Type 1 | Type 2 |
| Conducting a weekly team coordination meeting. | | | |
| Hunting for needed information. | | | |
| Presenting project status to upper management. | | | |
| Creating formal project documents (not funded by customer). | | | |
| Gaining multiple approvals for a project document. | | | |
| Waiting in queues for available resources. | | | |
| Gaining regulatory approval for a project deliverable. | | | |
| Spending extra design time to enable design reuse. | | | |

**Figure 1.4** – Several typical activities that take place during the execution of a project. How would you rank them in terms of value and waste, based on your personal experience?

We can go further with the next activity; hunting for information is clearly non-value-added. It is, however, a painful reality. Likewise, my students have voted almost unanimously that reporting status to upper management is Type 2, under our strict definition. The only caveats seem to be "management needs to be informed to guide the company," and "it is career limiting to not show up for status meetings." Both of these concerns are legitimate, but neither justifies the associated waste. Take heart – as with all of the above activities, there is a better way.

What about formal documents? It is amazing to me how many overlong, boilerplate-laden[9] documents are created as part of project execution. What is even less comprehensible is that the customer never sees most of these documents. Internal documents are not opportunities for creative expression; they are tools to transact information. Unless a document will be delivered to the final customer, it serves only one purpose; to enable the team to succeed. Internal documents are almost universally Type 1 (meaning that they are necessary, but could use some improvement), with a large subset that could drop off the face of the earth without anyone noticing.

Gaining approvals can't be value-added, right? The more approvals, the more waste. The same applies to waiting time in queues. These two "activities" are examples of the kind of organizational pathology that can turn an excellent firm into an uncompetitive sloth. A project-driven enterprise cannot tolerate the kind of "policing action" that multiple approvals represent, nor can queues be permitted to drive project schedules. These and other seemingly intractable organizational issues are addressed in Part 4.

The final two activities listed in my little quiz represent special cases. The first, gaining regulatory approval, should probably fall into a separate category altogether (perhaps a "Type 1B"). Externally imposed regulations or certifications, such as construction permits, UL approval, Federal agency approval, or even ISO 9000 registration, typically represent the "table stakes" of an industry. All competitors must have them to play the game, yet no one generally gains a price advantage by achieving them. External approvals may not add to your price, but they are absolutely essential; hence they should be accomplished in a least-waste-way.

The last activity in our exercise is troublesome. Design reuse is so tempting – so clearly good and right. Yet my professional students show an almost universal skepticism regarding its value (along with other forward-looking activities such as "lessons-learned" meetings). The reason is not hard to fathom; such reusable information requires time to prepare and archive, and unless it is used in the future, the invested effort is pure waste. Design reuse libraries, lessons-learned documents, project notebooks, etc. are either pure Value or Type 2 Waste, *depending upon whether anyone uses them*, and thereby unearths their hidden value.

### Identifying the Value Stream

The nature of the value created by project teams varies enormously from industry to industry. There are, however, two common elements. Every project creates *deliverables* that embody value, and every project has a *customer* who receives that value.[10] The customer for a construction project, for example, might be a major land developer. The deliverables in this case would include the physical structures "left standing" after the project is complete, along with plans, permits, and other essential documentation. For a new product development project, the product itself is the most obvious deliverable, with the end user being the associated customer. The needs of the production facility that will manufacture the product, however, must also be addressed. The deliverables in this case include all documentation, tooling, prototypes, and test procedures required to launch the design to production.

In each case, a project team is tasked with creating the required deliverables and successfully transferring them to their customer. Whether these project outputs come in *hard form* (physical objects or materials) or *soft form* (documents and information of all types), they represent the reason for a project team's existence. *Every task within a project should, therefore, be directed toward creating deliverables.* All other activities should be suspect.

The second principle of lean thinking states that we should identify the specific set of actions that create a project's deliverables. This sequence of activities is called the *value stream.* Although its description might sound similar to the typical project schedule, there is a critical difference. The value stream is a theoretical ideal; a sequence of exclusively value-added tasks. An example of the value stream for a generic system integration project is shown in Figure 1.5.

The concept of the value stream is useful as a visualization aid for waste detection and elimination. Many firms have embarked on "value-stream mapping" exercises to help them illuminate the waste in their project flow. (A practical overview of value-stream mapping techniques is provided in Chapter 9). At first glance, value-stream mapping might appear to be a warmed-over version of those tedious "business process re-engineering" exercises that kept consultants employed for several years.[11] For the time being, I will ask the reader to suspend disbelief and trust that the value stream is an extremely useful concept.

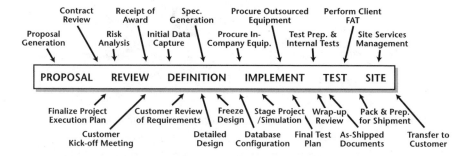

**Figure 1.5** – Graphical representation of a top-level value stream for a system integration project. A detailed mapping of your project's value stream can help highlight non-value-added waste, and guide you toward productivity-enhancing improvements (see Chapter 9).

## Removing Obstacles to the Flow of Value

The third lean principle is the one with the most meat (or should I say fat). In my experience, the majority of waste associated with project execution falls into the category of "obstacles to the flow of value." These obstacles come in many flavors, as shown in Figure 1.6. Functional departments, for example, can constrict the flow of value in several ways. In strong functional organizations, project execution often takes the form of a series of "hurry up and wait" exercises. The output of each major task is thrown "over the wall" to the next functional group, there to languish in a queue. Since each functional fiefdom (or silo, depending on your taste) has its own internal set of priorities, resources are applied inconsistently. Projects slowly drift through this type of organization without hope of prompt, predictable delivery.

Executive gate meetings and approval cycles are representative of an important category of obstacle, the *time batch*. A time batch occurs whenever a downstream "customer" for project

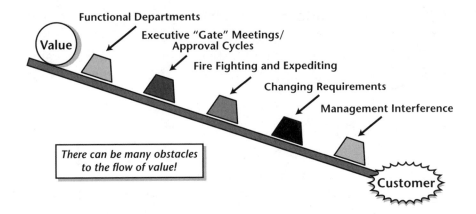

**Figure 1.6** – Several of the many potential obstacles to the flow of value during project execution. Note that the above barriers are all symptomatic of organizational problems; none has a place in a truly optimized project-driven enterprise.

information or materials must wait unnecessarily for delivery. A specification or bill of materials that can only be acted on after it has been formally released is an example of a time batch. Likewise, damming up project-team activities behind authoritarian "gate reviews" can be an enormous time waster. The elimination of time batches to achieve "just-in-time" information flow on projects is the subject of Chapter 2.

Continuing down our list of obstacles, firefighting has become so much a way of life in some firms that they have established permanent "tiger teams" to handle unanticipated catastrophes. This is analogous to a ski resort that has so many injuries due to poorly maintained slopes that it decides to "solve the problem" by building a hospital on the premises. Firefighting and expediting are symptoms of a broken execution process. To accept them as something that "goes with the territory" is to relegate your organization to endless turbulence and inefficiency.

Likewise, constantly changing requirements are typically accepted as a necessary evil, particularly when the changes are imposed by an external customer. In my experience, at least eighty percent of so-called "unanticipated change" could have been both anticipated and accommodated. Techniques such as staged-freeze specifications (see Method 6) enable project teams to communicate the impact of change clearly to their customers, and significantly reduce costly delays and overruns.

Management interference is a final example of an obstacle to the flow of value. This category encompasses the full spectrum of negative behavior, from chronic micromanagement to "punishing the messenger." In the absence of a well-defined execution process and clear roles for all involved parties, managers have a choice between excessive paternalism and benign neglect. Both of these extremes are damaging to employee morale, and neither satisfactorily achieves the desired goal; a successful project outcome.

In many firms, the *reason d'existence* for obstacles to the flow of value has been lost to time and employee turnover. Barriers tend to be imposed as stopgaps to prevent recurrence of a painful experience. Over the years, these band aids are applied layer after layer, until the value stream is choked down to nary a trickle. Since the original logic behind imposing these obstacles has been long forgotten, organizations fear removing them. Recall the familiar story of the daughter who cuts off the legs of her Thanksgiving turkey before roasting because, "that's how Mom always did it." It turns out that the reason why mom mutilated her turkeys was not to make them taste better; it was to fit them into her very small oven. When we come across legacy practices that seem incongruous, we must question them. We must ask "why" repeatedly until we find the root cause of waste.[12]

## Pulling Value and Keeping It Flowing

Let us pause for a moment to catch our breath. When considered collectively, the first three principles of lean thinking describe a highly efficient engine for value creation. Value is clearly specified, a waste-free flow of tasks required to create that value is identified, and all obstacles are removed to allow value to be delivered successfully. The final two lean principles help us to harness this value-creating engine and keep it running smoothly.

The fourth lean principle states that project teams should allow their customer to "pull value." The best way to illustrate this idea of customer pull is with a story. Long ago (in Internet years) a very creative firm developed a product called the Apple Newton. This hand-held computing product embodied break-through technologies that enabled handwriting recognition (sort of), task scheduling, and a host of other features. So original was the concept that a brand new product category was invented; the Personal Digital Assistant (PDA). With roughly a billion dollars in R&D invested, and some of the brightest minds on the planet involved, the Apple Newton could hardly miss . . . right?

Unfortunately, there was one minor problem; customers didn't understand how they would benefit from the product. It looked intriguing. It appeared to be powerful. But what problem did it solve? How was the customer better off after buying one? Ultimately, at a price of over seven hundred dollars and with a weight and size approaching that of a large brick, the Newton was a market disaster. What went wrong?

This story illustrates how even the best value-creating engines can sputter and seize. Today, customers demand clear benefit in return for their investment. Delivering technology for its own sake is not value-added. Only when new methods or ideas solve a well-defined problem for the customer does value burst forth. The Newton was a classic example of "technology push;" a product designed by engineers for engineers (or in other words, a solution in search of a problem). Ironically, after some paring of features and enhancement of performance, the Palm Pilot and other PDAs have achieved market success. Too late for Apple, but a boon for firms such as 3Com that responded to the pull of market need rather than the push of unbridled creativity.

We can apply this "pull" concept to the non-recurring world of projects, and not just for the final "paying" customer. Every task on a project has some type of deliverable, right? (If this were not the case, we certainly would have an excellent candidate for the waste bin). The deliverable might take the form of a document, a prototype, or even a decision (i.e., "we'll go with Plan A versus Plan B"). In any case, it follows that each task on a project must have a customer to receive its deliverable. As you will soon see, virtually every task can be made more efficient by establishing pull-type linkages with its downstream customer (see Chapter 3 and Method #2). Using a "customer pull" approach to linking key tasks on a project is such a simple way to eliminate tons of waste, yet it is rarely done, even in the finest project-driven firms.

## Never an End to the Search for Waste

With four principles down and one to go we have described a value-creating machine that is now tuned to respond to customer pull. All that remains is to establish a means to maintain and improve that machine's performance over time. The fifth lean principle implies that the work of waste elimination is never done; we must continue endlessly searching for waste. This makes lean thinking sound like a *Sisyphean* task.[13] Is it not sufficient to "lean out" a project, and then sit back and enjoy the fruits of your labor?

Unfortunately, the answer is an emphatic "no." Waste is the natural by-product of human endeavor. Without constant diligence, waste will creep back into every aspect of your work. The term *entropy* is used by physicists to describe this general behavior. The "law of entropy" states that things in our world always tend to become more random and chaotic over time. As an example, even the pyramids are looking a bit run down these days. Another few eons and they will be nothing but random piles of dust. Likewise (although the connection may have escaped you until now) you can clean your desk at work on Monday, but by Friday it will likely be a disaster area. As any good physicist knows, it takes *a continuous input of energy* to keep a highly ordered system functioning smoothly. A lean project is a highly ordered project; it requires constant vigilance to maintain and improve its performance. In short, it takes *team discipline and an ongoing intolerance of waste.*

Admittedly, the five lean principles described in this chapter are so high-level in nature that their practical application to your daily work may seem a distant possibility. Let me reassure you that, as with the next several "concept" chapters, I am simply laying groundwork here. The principles of lean thinking underlie all of the work that follows, lending credibility to the truly practical waste-reducing methods that represent the heart of this book.

## Learning Points for this Chapter

- There can be an enormous amount of waste in project work. Up to eighty percent of a typical workday can be consumed by non-value-added activities. Our goal will be to apply "lean countermeasures" to the sources of this waste, and thereby enable project teams to be far more efficient and productive.

- The Five Principles of Lean Thinking provide a framework for our waste-reducing efforts. They describe how an optimized enterprise should function.

- There is a difference between "strategic value" and "project value." Strategic value benefits shareholders, owners, and the long-term goals of the firm. Project value is what generates revenues and profits in the near term.

- We identified a working definition for project value. This definition can be used to help discriminate between waste and value in the nebulous world of project management and product development.

# Time Batches and JIT Information  2

*"From time waste there can be no salvage.
It is the easiest of all waste and the hardest to
correct because it does not litter the floor."*
*—Henry Ford*

Information is the lifeblood of any project. Whether the goal is to erect a building, design a product, or solve an intractable problem, it is information that drives value creation. It seems reasonable, therefore, to continue our search for waste by considering how information flows, or fails to flow, during project execution.

Consider the following scenario. Bob is a member of a project team tasked with installing underground cable for a local public utility. As part of his responsibilities, he must take soil samples every hundred feet to ensure that no environmental hazard finds its way into the region's water supply. At the end of each week, he boxes up his samples and ships them off to a nearby independent testing laboratory. There the samples sit in a queue for a few weeks, are routinely tested, and a report is sent back to Bob noting any significant risks in each batch.

Due to a very tight schedule, the project manager decides to proceed with laying cable and filling trenches, rather than waiting for the soil test results. This decision is justified by the fact that no negative findings have been reported in the region on past projects. As these things usually go, however, this proves to be a bad idea. Just a few weeks before the project deadline, Bob receives a very scary test report. Unfortunately, more than a month of work and several miles of cable have been completed before this information becomes available. Even worse, there is still a month of samples in the queue: will there be more bad news in the weeks ahead?

This example demonstrates one of the most common obstacles to the flow of value on projects; the "time batch." A time batch acts like a dam in the flow of information. Whenever time-critical data is delayed from arriving at the point where it is needed, a time batch has occurred. In the above example, several time batches are stacked together. The first is Bob's penchant for gathering up a week's worth of samples before submitting them for test. The second is his somewhat lazy decision to ship the samples rather than hand delivering them. The third is the laboratory's first-in-first-out (FIFO) queue, and the fourth is their decision to report findings for the entire week's samples, rather than reporting each result as it becomes available.

You might be thinking that this is just another example of a project risk that went sour. Sometimes these things just happen, right? In this case, the risk to schedule could have been virtually eliminated by breaking up time batches and enabling a "Just-In-Time" (JIT) flow of information. Even though the risk was considered to be relatively low going into the project, the potential consequences of a bad sample were devastating. A few simple steps could have avoided catastrophe. Samples could have been shipped daily by overnight delivery, or hand carried. The laboratory could have been incentivized to give priority to the samples. An "exception rule" could have been imposed that required the laboratory to immediately report negative findings rather than waiting to complete a full batch of samples. Even better, a daily on-site screen test might have been devised to detect significant concentrations of known environmental hazards. Any and all of these ideas would have reduced information delays, and possibly saved the project.

An assortment of common project time batches are listed in Figure 2.1. In each case, information that could enable efficient, low-risk project execution is withheld unnecessarily. Although these obstacles may seem benign when considered individually, in concert they typify a work culture that emphasizes command, control, and risk aversion over speed and efficiency.

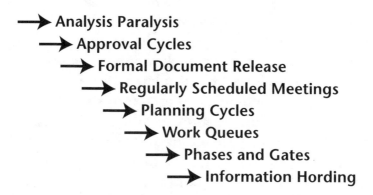

**Figure 2.1**: Several common examples of time batches that can occur during project execution. In each case, needed information is withheld from downstream activities, resulting in potentially avoidable delays.

### Analysis Paralysis

We humans do love to dither over our decisions. After all, making choices could be dangerous. If you make a choice, you might turn out to be wrong, and that would be the worst thing imaginable, right? Sorry – not making timely decisions is far worse. A wrong decision can often be corrected, whereas a "non-decision" cannot be corrected and yet *cannot succeed*. Unfortunately, fear of exposure to criticism can drive decision makers into an endless loop of analyzing, testing, studying, reanalyzing, and so on. This type of time batch is most common in projects where there is a high degree of uncertainty and risk. Another parable will vividly illustrate this problem.

One bright spring day, Sue arrives at work with an extra bounce in her step. While in the shower earlier that morning, a truly excellent idea popped into her head for a new product concept. Although she has only been with her firm a few weeks, she is convinced that her boss, the Director of Marketing, will turn cartwheels when she hears this gem. A merit bonus can't be far behind.

After several meetings with various director-level types, it becomes apparent that Sue's idea is not being viewed as the beauty queen she had hoped. Her boss is only lukewarm toward it, and no one else in the firm seems willing to take the ball and run with it. Moreover, Sue hears whispers in the hall that it is generally a bad idea to push too hard on new product ideas because "failed projects here are career-limiting."

Not a quitter, Sue decides to take on the role of the "product champion." She bounces from window office to window office, looking for executive support. At each turn she is told, "we just don't have enough information to move on this right now." Undaunted, she tries several means to overcome this barrier.[1] She holds brainstorming meetings, but they only reinforce the current "group think" dogma within the company. She purchases market research reports, but according to Mahogany Row they are biased, incomplete, and "never accurate." Finally, by way of appeasement for her relentless efforts, the executive team agrees to fund a "study project," with an inadequate budget and zero priority. Sue slinks back to her cubicle, and another "new broom" has gotten its bristles shredded by grinding indecision.

Decision theory tells us that it is impossible for an individual to possess all the information that can impact a decision. Even if a comprehensive information search were feasible, some of the earliest information gathered would become out-of-date before the last of it was harvested. Our only realistic alternative is to make "boundedly rational" decisions[2] in which we gather the highest value information we can find as fast as possible, evaluate it, and move forward. Unless you are betting your project (or your firm) on a given choice, analysis should be limited in time and cost. Being a project manager or team leader is all about making timely decisions; it separates the greats from the wanna-bes.[3]

## Approval Cycles

Dilbert timidly enters the office of his firm's Chief Financial Officer. He slides a bound report he's carrying under a towering pile of virtually identical reports. "I'll just wedge my business case in under all this stuff so next week when I ask about your approval, you can say you never saw it."[4]

If I have a personal pet peeve regarding business operations it is the cosmically silly way firms handle approvals. It is not uncommon for an important document to require six to ten signatures, most of which are Type 2 waste. There are only two reasons why a firm would require internal documents to go through multiple approvals: either, 1) the purpose is to gather feedback and gain concurrence, or 2) there is no trust in the organization and signatures are the only way to protect against blame and finger-pointing later. If the first case is true, I will give you a leaner solution. If the second case is true, your firm is choosing a "policing" culture over one that encourages personal integrity and responsibility. Here's a "lean rule" regarding formal approval cycles; if the signatures are not mandated by some governmental agency or are not essential for internal fiscal control, get rid of them. Sanctioning organizational mistrust and politics is criminally wasteful. Take away the signature lines, and ban both blame and excuses from your project work culture. A disciplined organization has no time for such things.

Now if the need for approvals stems from a legitimate desire for feedback and concurrence, we can achieve the same end while minimizing wasted time. The problem with document review cycles is that they are typically executed in serial, as shown in Figure 2.2. The "Milk Run" approach to routing a document can result in weeks of delays. One reviewer is out of town, so the document languishes in his "in" basket. Another reviewer disagrees with an earlier one, and makes changes or recommendations that are contradictory. You find this out at the end of the first review cycle, and are forced to reconcile changes and start the process all over again.

Here's a practical method for gaining rapid feedback and concurrence on a project document. Following the "Star" model shown in Figure 2.2, distribute a copy of the document to all reviewers simultaneously. The reviewers are given a 48-hour window to provide comments (the time period is arbitrary, but should be as short as is realistically possible). If no comments are received within the two-day window, the reviewer is assumed to have concurred and the document is released. If a reviewer is out of town, it is incumbent upon him or her to assign an alternate to review any incoming documents. If the reviewer cannot find the time to give the document adequate attention, he or she can notify the sender and leave it up to them to decide whether to

### "Milk-Run" Model for Document Approval

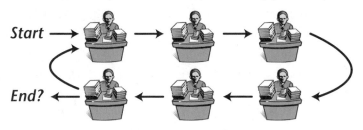

### "Star" Model for Document Approval

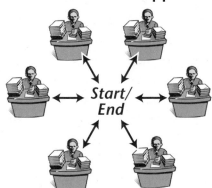

**Figure 2.2**: Two models for executing a document approval process. The "Milk-Run" model suffers from serial approvals, and can degenerate into endless iterations to reconcile changes. The more proactive "Star" model enables parallel review and approval, with time limits placed on reviewers before their approval is assumed.

delay release. Finally, if comments or changes are received within the approval window, it is the sender's responsibility to reconcile the changes, negotiate with the individuals involved, and send the revised document out for a final review cycle. In the worst case, the total duration of this process should be no more than a week, with two days being the most likely outcome.

Whenever approval delays drive the schedule for projects, it is appropriate to ask "why" several times. A word of warning, however. Some of the situations you will encounter are so ridiculous that it is almost embarrassing. Take, for example, the policy adopted by one of my client firms that mandates several levels of approval (typically a two-day delay) for the use of an *overnight courier service*. Talk about an organizational oxymoron!

## Formal Document Release

Whenever a time batch appears to be necessary, you should test your assumptions. This is particularly true for one of the most prevalent types of unnecessary delay to the flow of project information. It is very common for downstream tasks to have scheduled start dates that are driven by the formal release of a controlling document. The reason appears obvious; last minute changes to the document could impact downstream work. An earlier start could potentially result in wasted time and resources.

The justification for this type of time batch, however, is based on two less-than-robust assumptions. The first is that the formal release of a document precludes disruptive change in the future. Test this assumption against your own experience. Does it hold true? While it may be a bit harder to implement a change once a document is under release control, it is certainly only a minor inhibitor. If the possibility of change were a legitimate justification for delaying downstream actions, most projects would be on permanent hold.

The second assumption (related to the first) is that preliminary information is simply bad information. I disagree. If preliminary information can be released in a systematic and logical way, with the risk of change minimized, then an enormous time advantage can be gained. This concept is referred to as the "staged freezing" of a document (see Method #6). Rather than thinking of a document as a monolithic entity, it can be thought of as having layers of information. The first layer consists of information that is "etched in stone" right from the start. This portion of the document can be stage-released to downstream users. A second layer could then be defined which becomes firm a bit later in the document's development, and so on, as shown in Figure 2.3. As long as there is a clear understanding between the document creator and the downstream user regarding the risk of change, this system will work as well as a formal release of the entire document. Recipients of JIT information, however, must also develop a sense of how far they can go with preliminary feeds without creating potential waste downstream.[5]

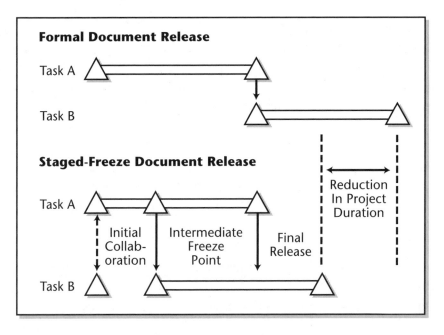

**Figure 2.3**: One of the most effective ways to break up formal time batches is through the use of "staged freezing" of documents. Points of freeze are agreed upon up front, and any preliminary information that is released is treated as though final approval has been received.

This approach has been successfully implemented in many industry sectors. The Boeing Company, for example, used a seven-level staged-freeze process for controlling documents during the development of the 777 commercial aircraft.[6] Without this process, the development time for such an enormously complex new product might be measured in decades. With clear and systematic layering and freezing of requirements, the actual development cycle was the fastest and smoothest that Boeing had ever achieved.

## Regularly Scheduled Meetings

Regularly scheduled meetings represent an insidious form of time batch. We have all been brought up in a work culture that assumes the need for such things. We clog our calendars with weekly team meetings, staff meetings, resource meetings, coordination meetings, status meetings, and even regularly scheduled emergency meetings. All these meetings occur whether or not everyone required for closure is present, whether or not there is a pressing reason, and whether or not there is an agenda, an action list, or a useful outcome.

What makes this situation problematic is that despite the smell of waste hanging thick in the air, it seems that we have no viable alternative. Without regularly scheduled meetings (weekly, monthly, quarterly, etc.) how could we get everyone's calendar to line up? I suppose we should feel justified, therefore, in decimating the weekly calendar of virtually every employee in our company, right? Let us not be so hasty. Perhaps if we test our assumptions we might find a better way.

The topic of how to optimize meetings will be covered in considerable detail under Method #3. Let me give you a bit of a preview, however. Is it true that there is no viable alternative to regularly scheduled meetings? If we strip away our preconceptions, it's easy to recognize that meetings should be event and urgency driven.[7] Coordination meetings, for example, should be more frequent when activity levels and information flows are high, and relatively infrequent during lull periods. Technical meetings should be held when the need arises, rather than waiting until the next weekly forum. Most other types of meetings should be triggered by exceptions to normal business execution. When things are running smoothly, why interrupt the flow of value?

If aligning employee's calendars is a concern, common blocks of time throughout the week can be "reserved" for meetings. At the beginning of each week, an event-driven calendar of necessary meetings can then be circulated, and all unused blocks of time can be released to perform actual work. There is a great deal more we can do to banish the waste of routine meetings, so stay tuned.

## Planning Cycles

If a business opportunity looks good in February, should it languish without funding or approval until August so that it can be included in your firm's next "Annual Operating Plan" (AOP)? The AOP represents the last bastion of corporate planning naiveté, now that the irrelevance of the "Five-Year Strategic Plan" has become generally accepted. Given the pace of change and intensity of competition in most industries, however, waiting for a once-per-year window to make resource commitments is clearly unacceptable. Any business opportunity that is subject to the "market clock"[8] cannot be allowed to dwindle in value while awaiting some arbitrary planning date.

To address this issue, many firms have implemented ad-hoc executive screening meetings to review new opportunities. Unfortunately, screening committees typically meet infrequently, and employ high-level members with intractable schedules. Moreover, most firms do not have a defined process and established criteria for a "go forward" decision. It is surprising that so much emphasis these days is placed on "project cycle-time" and "time-to-market," while the decision to actually start work is often significantly delayed.

Countermeasures to this type of time batch depend greatly on the industry and the nature of project opportunities. As a general rule, however, firms in time-sensitive industries should implement an early, well-defined, and highly efficient "pre-screening" process. The goal of this process is to weed out low-value opportunities quickly, and to place an "expiration date" on the more promising ones. Each opportunity that crosses this pre-screening threshold is then assigned a priority number and a "champion," and scheduled for timely review. This approach to screening and prioritization of new opportunities is discussed in Chapter 7 for the special case of product development, and in Chapter 9 for more general project work.

## Work Queues

A time-sensitive job arrives at the door of the drafting department. The deliverer begs for priority.

"This task is on the critical path of our most profitable project. Can't you fit it into this week's schedule?" he asks, in the pleading manner one reserves for evading traffic tickets.

"Look, I'd like to help you," responds the keeper of the in-box, "but rules are rules. Everybody waits in the queue; first in, first out. What could be fairer than that? If we had enough drafts people, this backlog wouldn't be necessary. Talk to human resources about hiring, don't complain to me about delays."

This scenario is so wrong-headed, I almost don't know where to begin. First, the use of the term "fair" when referring to internal task priorities is totally inappropriate. There is nothing democratic about project prioritization; it should be dictated by sound business judgment. Imposing a FIFO bottleneck into the critical path of a firm's projects is like throwing sand into the engine of value creation. Always, always, always, the next uncommitted resource must go to the highest priority task, based on a business-unit-wide prioritization. To do anything less is to reduce the productivity of not only the constraining department, but the entire value stream.

The second misconception in the above scenario is that adding more people is the answer to a bloated backlog. The amount of resources needed by each functional area to support a firm's value stream must be balanced with all other groups. The goal is to achieve an optimized throughput of projects. Hiring more people, without appropriate prioritization, is no guarantee of a shorter queue. After all, what is to stop low priority work from flooding in to consume any newly added capacity? In general, a backlog serves as a buffer against variability in the arrival of work. Resource centers such as drafting departments, for example, often maintain a few days of back-log to ensure efficient utilization of resources. Provided that these delays are considered "acceptable" by the center's "customers" (the project teams), this approach makes good sense. The "mini-buffer" has a morale benefit as well; employees of resource centers tend to get a bit nervous if they see an empty in-basket.

This is no justification, however, for allowing excessive lead times to develop. Once the acceptable lead time has been exceeded, the lowest priority tasks must be sidelined until the group gets back on track. Moreover, this mandate for short lead times avoids the darker side of the employee morale issue. High piles of backlogged work can be discouraging to workers and can make them feel that striving to meet project schedule commitments is futile.[9]

## Phases and Gates

I will have a great deal to say about phases and gates in Part 3 of this book, so I will only offer you an *hors d'oeuvre* for now. The idea of phases and gates was born in the days of governmental mega-projects. With dozens of prime and sub-contractors and extremely high levels of technical risk, post-WWII development efforts such as the Polaris Missile System spawned the need for a strong, risk-mitigating execution process. The resulting methodology utilizes predefined project phases and approval gates to control financial and technical risk, as shown in Figure 2.4. The process seemed so logical that by the mid-1980s many management consultancies began promulgating the phase / gate process as a "best practice" across virtually every industry.

There is some good news regarding phases and gates. If your firm: a) has never had a concurrent engineering process, b) does not understand cross-functional teams, and c) is generally in the dark ages, the phase / gate process is a step in the right direction. As you become more sensitive to the flow of value, however, you will recognize that "gates" can easily become big, wasteful time

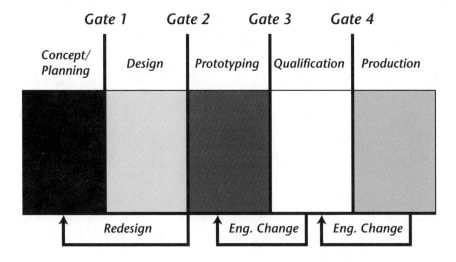

**Figure 2.4:** A typical phase / gate process for project execution. After each phase, a formal "gate review" is held before the project can proceed to the next phase. Useful for high-risk, multiple-contractor efforts, it can be a serious time-waster when applied to internal, quick-turn projects.

batches. Depending on phases and gates is like depending on training wheels; it's a great intermediary step, but definitely not the least-waste way.[10]

## Information Hording

Hail to the hero; that intrepid, clever soul that somehow overcomes organizational barriers and achieves breakthrough success. How we admire (or should I say resent?) those individuals who seem to rise above mediocrity to achieve legendary status in their firm. They break all the rules and work around the system, but all is forgiven when they save management's bacon. Ironically, such "heroes" are often cited as icons for "how the job should be done," despite the obvious hypocrisy of such a statement (clearly if everyone behaved as badly as heroes, there would be chaos).

A close relative of the hero is the guru. The guru is that sage individual who has spent their entire career becoming very good at one narrow specialty. As their expertise and reputation grows, the expectation for a guru to do actual work diminishes. They develop iron-clad job security based on their unique abilities and have no intention of losing that edge by freely sharing their knowledge with others.

Why include a discussion of heroes and gurus in a chapter on time batches, you might ask? The reason is to make one critical point; a culture that supports such creatures has institutionalized one of the worst forms of time batch. Big obvious delays such as approval cycles are easy to detect and mitigate. But what about a time batch that takes the form of a thick, viscous sludge, causing every information transaction on a project to be less efficient, less complete, and less timely? This is the illness suffered by firms with embedded hero worship; there is no incentive for the brightest in such firms to share their knowledge with others. In such an environment, information is power. If you have it and others don't, that makes you more powerful.[11] Each time a choice must be made between early sharing of information and withholding that information for personal reasons (like appearing indispensable to the team), a nasty little time batch will occur. The aggregate effect is like trying to run a race in thick mud.

Encouraging an entrepreneurial spirit is important, but condoning a culture that worships heroes and gurus is diametrically contradictory to achieving a low-waste enterprise. Recognition of individual achievement must be balanced with strong incentives to optimize the capability of the firm as a whole. For now, keep in mind that employees invariably behave in a manner consistent with management recognition and tangible reward. If your culture celebrates heroes, don't expect employees to place team interests above their own.

## The Ideal: Just-in-Time Information

Imagine a project team in which information flows are unobstructed by mistrust, knowledge hording, and territorialism. Each member of the team has a clearly defined role and a specific list of responsibilities and deliverables. No overlap and no "white space" is tolerated by this project team. When risk of change becomes acceptably low, information is frozen and immediately shared with all interested parties. When risk of change is high, preliminary information is "fed forward"[12] to harvest early feedback and avoid major issues downstream. Meetings are ad hoc and brief, collaboration is continuous, and all efforts are focused on making the project's deliverables a timely reality.

Now imagine an organization that deserves to own such a prized team. That organization respects the ability of the team, and understands the waste caused by imposing external command and control. Critical project metrics are defined and acceptable ranges are specified by management. If the team stays within those ranges, they are free to create value without interference. If one or more of the ranges is exceeded (e.g., schedule variance reaches some predefined threshold) then an "exception" is noted, and a review process is triggered to help determine corrective action. Information flowing into and out of the team is given the highest possible priority, with the typical "needs and feeds" being well defined in advance. Management plays the role of "infrastructure"; remaining in the background unless needed by the team to solve a problem beyond their authority or cognizance.

In such an ideal organization, we can begin to approach the JIT model for information flows. In so doing we will have taken a breakthrough step toward achieving competitive advantage in project execution.[13] Of all the time wasters on projects, the time batch should be given the greatest attention. Time is the one project constraint that cannot be either inventoried or bought back. Whenever we allow time to be batched or information to be delayed, it represents an unrecoverable loss. The continuous flow of needed information may be an ideal, but the alternative of endless delays and bottlenecks cannot be tolerated in a project-driven enterprise.

## Things to Keep in Mind

- A "time batch" occurs anytime that project information is withheld from those who need it. To eliminate time batches, however, we must pay careful attention to the risks associated with early information release.

- One of the most common forms of time batch is indecision. Unless you are betting the project on a given decision, it is generally better to make a prompt, well-informed choice and then make corrections as necessary going forward.

- Approvals, regularly scheduled meetings, planning cycles, and FIFO queues are all examples of traditional methods of operation that must be reevaluated in the context of speed and efficiency. There are better, higher value ways to accomplish the same activities. Just stay tuned . . .

# Minimizing Transaction Costs  3

*"The goal of communication is not to be understood, it
is to make it impossible to be misunderstood."*
—Quintus Tullius Cicero

Does the act of transferring information from one individual to another add value? We can answer this question easily, using our formal definition of value-added activities. Would an external customer know whether the information was transferred or not? In other words, does the act of transferring information (or materials for that matter) *transform* that information in some noticeable way? The answer is clearly no, yet the transaction of information and materials is a vital part of any project. It can be said that transactions are *enabling, yet non-value-added*; an excellent example of Type 1 Waste.

Minimizing the wasted time and cost associated with transactions represents an enormous opportunity to improve project efficiency. In surveys that I have conducted spanning several industries, over eighty percent of the easily identifiable waste in projects can be attributed to transaction costs. Another vignette will help illustrate just how ubiquitous this source of waste really is.

Dagny, the heroine of our story, has just one week to pull off a miracle. Three weeks earlier she was given the "opportunity" to serve as proposal manager for a critical new project. The customer had set a deadline of thirty days from receipt of their request for proposal (RFP), and now that deadline is looming large. The good news is that all five sections of the proposal are nearly complete. The bad news is that none of the sections are actually in her hands.

Section One is being written by an experienced veteran at an out-of-state division, who unfortunately seems to be addicted to e-mail. Several times over the past few weeks, Dagny has become trapped in a seemingly endless chain-letter e-mail discussion. Back and forth the messages go: response, forward, see attachment, return response, misunderstandings, more cycles, and still no resolution. Three times she has called this individual to set up a telecon, and three times she has received her "return call" in the form of yet another e-mail.

A relatively junior member of the marketing department is responsible for Section Two. With just two years of industry experience, this marketer still sounds like she is writing her master's thesis. Every sentence is weighted down with jargon and buzz words . . . and there are *a lot* of sentences. Page after page of scholarly dribble, with hardly a mention of product features or customer benefits. Lots of words, but essentially zero value.

The story is no better for the final three sections. Engineering is trying to release the technical specification that forms the heart of Section Three, but is being hamstrung by the Quality Assurance Manager, who has earned the hallway title of "Chief of Police." The test planning inputs to Section Four that were cobbled together by a couple of test technicians seem to make no sense to the engineers whose hardware will be tested. A meeting between both groups, facilitated by Dagny, sounded like a United Nations session, with test techs talking ATEs and "shake and bake," while designers discussed finite-element modeling and Monte-Carlo simulations.

Section Five is trapped in a time-warp. A representative from each of the firm's international offices was supposed to provide an input on capabilities and global reach. Unfortunately, it took two weeks just to organize a video conference with all parties to agree on format. Now she will have to suffer through a couple of all-nighters on the phone, harvesting inputs in every time zone from Bangalore to Buenos Aires. At this point, Dagny is wondering why she didn't just ghost write the entire proposal herself, and ask for forgiveness later.

In the above example, Dagny is faced with a frustrating paradox. All the information she needs is available in the heads of her proposal team, but "transaction inefficiencies," such as those listed in Figure 3.1, make that information unavailable in a timely manner. Section One is held up by a poor choice of media for communication. Section Two is rendered useless by excessive formality, jargon, and sheer information overload. Section Three is trapped by the illogic of internal policing. Section Four cannot converge without a shared language between designers and test engineers, while Section Five suffers from too many contributors over too much distance. Given another month or two, she surely could work it all out. Unfortunately, in a month or two her firm's competitor will be well underway with their winning project.

**Figure 3.1**: Several common causes of high transaction costs during project execution.

## Poor Choice of Media

It used to be so easy in the good old days. Pick up a phone or write a letter, not a difficult choice, right? Letters of the past represented formal documents, slow to arrive, but high in impact. If more immediacy and interaction was needed, you would ring up your party and have a conversation. In the days of yore, it wasn't difficult to select the proper media. Delays in written correspondence precluded any chance of urgent two-way exchange, whereas phone calls left no documentation and carried far less clout.

Enough nostalgia. Today we live in complex times. We have choices with respect to the media we use for communication. Facsimile, overnight delivery, two-day priority delivery, e-mail, groupware, EDI, voicemail, pagers, websites, cell phones, video-conferencing, multimedia presentations, and the list is expanding even as we speak. Unfortunately, the bright people who invented these powerful technologies failed to provide one vital element . . . *application instructions.*

Most of the above options have come on the scene in just the past decade or so, leaving us little time to gain experience in which technology to use where. As a result, transaction costs in many companies have actually increased as a result of poor choices of communication media. Just think of the mess we've made of e-mail. We clearly can't live without it, but the time wasted on sorting and deleting junk mail has become a sour joke in most companies. If a firm had the courage to quantify the time spent on such things, they would find that five to ten percent of a typical workday is consumed by e-mail machinations.[1] The expression "you've got mail" should be updated to "you've got waste."

For us to develop lean guidelines for the use of communication medium, we must first understand how these technologies differ. The first and most important distinction is whether a given medium is one-way or two-way.[2] One-way media, such as letters and e-mails, enable the sending of messages without the need for the receiver to be present. As the name implies, however, they are not well suited to two-way interaction. Hence, a big waste flag should go up whenever you see a chain-letter e-mail (more than one or two cycles between sender and receiver); this is clearly a misuse of a one-way technology. Two-way media allow for real-time interaction, and are best suited for transactions that require negotiation, explanation, or feedback. The problem with two-way media is timing; you need to have both parties simultaneously engaged to make the media work.

Precious days can be wasted trying to set up agreeable times for conference calls or video conferences.

Another distinction among communications media is related to the number of senders and receivers.[3] The most common category is the one-to-one interaction between a sender and a receiver. When an individual communicates with another, however, it is rarely a one-way monolog. Hence, one-to-one communication is frequently also two-way. What would you think is the most effective medium for such a conversation? As you no doubt guessed, a face-to-face encounter is by far the most effective way to complete a transaction between individuals.[4] The ability to read each other's facial expressions, respond immediately to questions, and discuss fine points until a conclusion is reached, is vital to any complex exchange of information.

As the complexity and ambiguity of the information to be transferred decreases, alternatives to face-to-face communication become more viable. This highlights a final attribute of communications technology – *bandwidth*.[5] The greater the information-carrying capability of the media, the greater the bandwidth. Hence, as the need for explanation and feedback decreases, the need for high bandwidth decreases. Face-to-face interaction has the highest possible bandwidth, whereas a phone call is adequate if the information to be transferred is relatively routine, and comprehension by the receiver is likely. If the understanding of information is certain, the communication need not be two-way at all. A one-way message is sufficient, by whatever media is most timely.

So it goes for one-to-many transactions, and so on. As the complexity of the information to be transferred increases, the need for high bandwidth and two-way interchange increases. Let's try a few examples. Can you think of a one-to-many transaction that is both one-way and low bandwidth? If the communication is one-way, we must assume that there is no need for real-time interaction. If it is low bandwidth, we can conclude that the comprehension of the receiver is likely. Distribution of a meeting notice or an announcement of some kind would be a good example. This type of transaction is the real forte of e-mail;

the one-to-many distribution of one-way information. A website is equally well suited, since many individuals can visit a website and extract information that was posted by a single individual.

Can you come up with an example of a one-to-many transaction that should be both two-way and high bandwidth? If the communication must be two-way, we know that some form of feedback or discussion is essential. If high bandwidth is required, the information to be transferred must be complex. Any ideas? An example of this type of interaction would be a presentation by a teacher or technical expert. If the topic of the lecture is nuclear physics or the state of the global economy, a face-to-face presentation and Q & A is mandatory. Less arcane topics, such as how to sell real estate, could be handled by video conferencing technology, or even multimedia distance-learning methods.

The choice of appropriate media is generally not black or white. Often several approaches will work perfectly well. It is more important to avoid totally inappropriate communication channels than to dither among good choices. Some guidelines for media selection are provided in Figure 3.2. As you go through these suggestions, try to imagine what the *worst* choice would be in each case. Does it make sense, for example, to use a fax to transfer a detailed drawing? What about attempting to carry on a conversation by playing voice-mail tag, or using videoconferencing for routine status or coordination meetings?

Before we move on, there are two types of communication media that deserve special attention; the first for its potential benefits, the other for its obvious waste. One of the most challenging problems in a project environment is to find ways to improve the efficiency of collaboration and knowledge sharing. This is particularly true when team members are scattered hither and yon. The introduction of Lotus Notes several years ago spawned a new classification of communications software known as "groupware." These tools allow for real-time collaboration, revision tracking of documents, systematic incorporation of multiple inputs, and much more. More will be said about this powerful new technology under Method #4.

Finally, we cannot leave the topic of media optimization without finding a remedy for e-mail waste. The good news is that a few simple rules, such as those suggested in Figure 3.3, can put a major dent in this inexcusable productivity drain.[6] Work rules of this type can be easily implemented, and will pay immediate dividends. Again, we are not going to waste our time on minor

| Project Transaction | Type of Communication | Bandwidth Required | Least Waste Option | Second Choice |
|---|---|---|---|---|
| Coordination Meetings | Few-to-Few, Two-Way | Moderate | Face-to-Face, "Stand-up" | Brief Telephone Conference |
| Collaboration Meetings | Few-to-Few, Two-Way | High | Face-to-Face, Event Driven | Video Conference, Event Driven |
| Distribution of Documents | One-to-Many, One-Way | Low | Post on Project Intranet Page | E-mail Attachment |
| Review/Approval of Documents | One-to-Many, Two-Way | Moderate | E-mail "Star" Distribution | Hardcopy "Star" Distribution |
| Routine Memos | One-to-One, One-Way | Low | E-mail | Fax/Overnight |
| Transfer of Detailed Information | One-to-One, Two-Way | Moderate | Hardcopy Plus Face-to-Face | E-mail/Fax Plus Telecon |
| Negotiations | One-to-One, Two-Way | High | Face-to-Face | Video Conference or Telecon |
| Formal Requests | One-to-One, One-Way | Low | Formal Letter | Faxed Letter |
| Team Training | One-to-Many, Two-Way | High | Face-to-Face | Real-Time Video |

**Figure 3.2**: Several forms of communications media and their applicability to various types of information transfer.[7] Choosing the appropriate media can significantly reduce the waste associated with transactions. Note that these are suggestions that should be adapted to your specific situation.

tweaks; it's the big silly stuff that we should attack first. One of my client firms imposed an organizational rule that no e-mail can have more than three "CCs." This simple policy has reduced their volume of e-mail traffic by *sixty percent*. Sometimes the best weapon against seemingly intractable waste is just a little common sense.

## Lack of a Shared Language

Once we have selected an appropriate medium for a transaction, we must decide what *language* will be used to communicate. A language is simply a set of symbols (words, numbers, data bits, etc.) that have an agreed-upon meaning. Transaction costs are strongly dependent on the degree to which all parties in a given transaction share a common language. In its most trivial sense, this should be pretty obvious. An executive at the global engineering firm, Asea Brown Bovari (ABB), for example, once joked that the official language of their company was "broken English."[8] Spoken language, however, is only a minor subset of

---

### "WORK RULES" FOR REDUCING E-MAIL WASTE

**Rule 1.** No more than three "CCs" per e-mail.

**Rule 2.** No more than two "cycles" back and forth between correspondents.

**Rule 3.** No unnecessary forwarding of attachments.

**Rule 4.** No unsolicited e-mails to management more than one level above sender.

**Rule 5.** No e-mail more than 20 lines in length (use network filter to block any that are longer).

**Rule 6.** Exclamation Mark (!) beside title is reserved for e-mails requiring **immediate** action.

**Rule 7.** No joke, frivolous, or unnecessary e-mails (employees can use personal e-mail for this).

**Rule 8.** Use "naming conventions" in e-mail titles to identify the type and timeliness of content:

PROJECT X – Designates which project the e-mail pertains to.

CUSTOMER Y – Designates which customer the e-mail pertains to.

PRIORITY Z – Designates timeliness of response.

. . . and so on.

---

**Figure 3.3**: Some possible organizational "rules" for reducing waste due to excessive e-mail traffic. Note that these are just suggestions; you can use one or all, and should feel free to adapt them in anyway that makes sense for your firm.[9]

the possible symbols used for communication. Data formats, drawing conventions, quantitative metrics, mathematical expressions, even acronyms and jargon, must have a shared meaning. A truly efficient transactional language must be understood by the receiver in *exactly* the same sense that the sender intends.[10]

Languages can often be discipline-specific. Software engineers in the US, for example, speak a "dialect" of English that is often unintelligible to hardware designers. Although the differences may be subtle, one misunderstood word or symbol can cause a satellite to crash into Mars, for example.[11] A bit closer to home, even the differences in terminology between plant sites in the same company can cause project teams to go off on wasteful tangents.[12]

A step-by-step process for reducing transaction costs caused by the lack of a shared language is provided in Figure 3.4. The first step is to establish among all parties the form of communication (e.g., words, pictures, etc.) to be used. We must then determine whether there are any boundaries between parties. A boundary is any natural difference between senders and receivers that could cause a communication disconnect. Some easily identifiable boundaries include functional discipline, geographic location, nationality, position within a company, type of industry served, type of product produced, etc. Once boundaries have been identified, we can apply appropriate countermeasures to break them down. The final step is to test the communication channel for fidelity.

Imagine for a moment the scene at a typical project kick-off meeting. Nice wood-paneled conference room. Samples of products scattered across the conference table. Lots of pens, t-shirts, and desk clocks with company logos emblazoned on them lying about. You get the picture. The project manager calls the meeting to order, and attendees are asked to introduce themselves. The gentleman to the right of the PM is the "paying" customer; the VP of Operations for a major retail chain. His firm has contracted with the hosts of this meeting for the installation of a new security system. He is a salesman by training and manner, with zero understanding of technology. Next seat down is Jean Taggart, the lead engineer on the project. She is a system specialist who understands security hardware like nobody else.

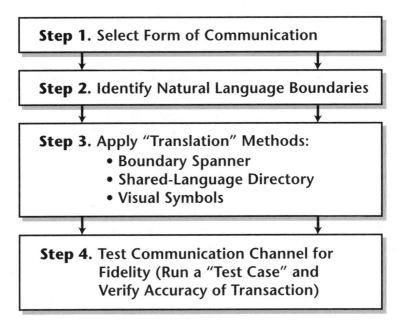

**Step 1.** Select Form of Communication

**Step 2.** Identify Natural Language Boundaries

**Step 3.** Apply "Translation" Methods:
- Boundary Spanner
- Shared-Language Directory
- Visual Symbols

**Step 4.** Test Communication Channel for Fidelity (Run a "Test Case" and Verify Accuracy of Transaction)

**Figure 3.4**: A step-by-step process for reducing transaction costs due to the lack of a shared language among communicators.

With years in the business, she can't be matched for design expertise, but hasn't stayed up on new digital technologies. The rest of the chairs are filled with technical types from every required discipline. Each is a specialist, most with advanced degrees, and all with a complete lack of business savvy.

What kinds of shared language boundaries might exist in the kickoff meeting described above? The customer will communicate in terms of loss prevention and customer safety, with no concept of how these goals might be achieved. That gap will have to be bridged for the customer's expectations to be understood by the project team. A second gap exists between Ms. Taggart and her designers regarding the use of the latest technologies. Finally, the technical types will need help to translate budget and time constraints at the contract level into design trade-offs and risk management at the technical level.

As you might expect, in any multilingual situation the best way to overcome communication barriers is through the use of translators. Individuals who understand the language on both sides of a boundary are vital to achieving successful transactions. These "boundary spanners" can act as mediators, and provide a means for establishing common symbols and agreed-upon terms.[13] An engineer with an MBA is potentially a boundary spanner (provided that the MBA includes at least *some* practical knowledge). A designer with experience in two or more technical specialties can be invaluable during performance trade-off discussions. A team leader with broad, system-wide technical knowledge can help ensure that no disconnects exist in the design of deliverables.

Participants in the value stream of a project must share enough common language to ensure high-fidelity communication. At Microsoft, for example, significant effort is made to establish project-wide standards for all terminology, from written language to software design protocols.[14] In addition, larger projects are partitioned into smaller chunks that are executed by teams with overlapping specialties.[15] Whatever the approach, as long as we humans are dependant on symbolic communication (i.e. we have not yet mastered the Vulcan mind-meld), the integrity of any transaction will vitally depend on establishing a shared language.

## Excessive Formality

Dirk needs to make eight copies of his marketing presentation before the big customer meeting at 3:00 p.m. Just before lunch, he drops by the copy center to submit his job. Unfortunately, he discovers that since his package exceeds one hundred pages, the job will require management approval. The attendant at the copy center hands Dirk a page-long reproduction request form, which must be signed by a director-level manager. In addition, the form requires a business justification for the copies, and suggests that the requester "consider other options to reproduction."

The above vignette typifies the kind of banal, bureaucratic formality that seems to infect every aspect of modern business. In the name of "cost control" many firms have allowed a thousand little barriers to the flow of value to build up over years of inattention. Instead of turning the above copy center into a roadblock, for example, why not just impose a few organizational rules regarding reproduction and trust your disciplined team to obey them? After all, you are more likely to sink the company over wasted time than over wasted copies.

The same kind of organizational formality can become a barrier to change and improvement. If every good idea must pass through a gauntlet of payback calculations, resource justifications, and screening gates, you might as well get comfortable with the status quo. Among the many apocryphal tales about the legendary industrialist, Henry Ford, there is one dealing with improvements to his innovative assembly line. When he ordered a significant redesign of the line, at considerable expense, his financial officer demanded to see payback calculations. Ford's response was that "the cost savings are so obvious that it isn't worth the money to calculate them."

The message should be clear; we must make intelligent trade-offs between formal organizational controls and the free flow of value. Both sides of the equation must be considered – the benefits of imposing a control process and the waste associated with its presence. Without such a balance, your firm can easily choke on its own excessive bureaucracy.


## Looping

The expression "two steps forward, one step back" must have first been muttered by a frustrated project manager. It is a commonplace for projects to suffer through one or more "loops" in the flow of value. Any decision point at which project deliverables may be sent backwards for revision and reevaluation represents a loop. Sometimes these loops execute several times before a resolution is reached. I can recall one example in which a project deliverable for a major aerospace contract was trapped in a Quality Assurance signoff loop for *six months*. Each time the document was submitted for signoff, the QA "team member" would identify one (and only one) change that was required. The revision would be made, the document resubmitted, and again it would be rejected with another trivial admonition. Iterative cycles of this type can become the value-stream equivalent of a black hole, yet they can almost always be eliminated through a few simple steps.

Loops are caused by a time batch that separates a deliverable-creating activity from the feedback necessary to validate that deliverable. The greater the separation in time between creation and feedback, the more waste will occur when a revision or iteration must take place.[16] Fortunately, loops of this type can be banished through one of the two methods shown in Figure 3.5.

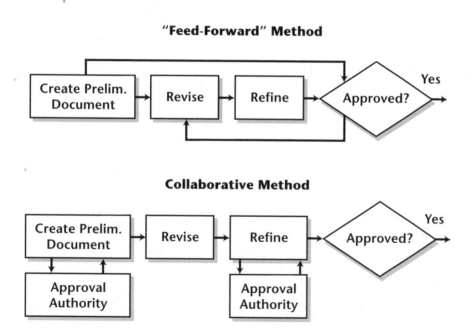

**"Feed-Forward" Method**

**Collaborative Method**

**Figure 3.5**: Graphical representation of the "feed-forward" and collaborative methods for elimination of time-wasting process loops. The feed-forward technique is appropriate when the required feedback is routine and easily understood. The collaborative model is more suitable when a great deal of discussion or negotiation is required.

In the first approach, a "feed forward" of preliminary information is provided to the individual whose feedback is required. This early feed allows for incorporation of comments and changes before the final deliverable reaches the individual's desk for approval. The feed-forward method works particularly well when the desired feedback is routine and easily understood. The checking of a drawing for errors or the review of a document for completeness are good examples of a feed-forward opportunity.

If the loop is caused by the need for trade-offs or knowledge sharing between the sender and receiver, a more aggressive approach is required. When subtle or complex issues are trapped in a loop, the solution is to tighten the loop until the process looks like a continuous collaboration (in a sense, we are including the loop-back process as part of the task itself). Shipping information back and forth in one-way, delayed communication must be abandoned in favor of using two-way, high-bandwidth interaction. Any time it appears that information is being "thrown over the wall" to another group, *break down the wall*. Otherwise, your project will grind to a halt while a game of information ping-pong drains the productivity of your team.

## Information Overshoot / Undershoot

The opening line of a very long letter sent by Julius Caesar to Pompay included an apology: "I regret that I didn't have time to be brief." Indeed, overlong, unfocused documents often result from not enough time being spent defining format and content. The "stream-of-consciousness" writing style may have worked for James Joyce, but in project communications, *brevity* is king. Any words beyond those needed to ensure a high-fidelity transaction are waste. Moreover, those extra words can actually obscure essential information and increase the chances of errors or misunderstandings. Project communication must be tight, focused, and transparently clear.

The danger of brevity, of course, is the possibility of "throwing the baby out with the bathwater." If you trim a communication too much, you may slice off some essential bits along with the waste. Information overshoot and undershoot are on opposite sides of the ideal center, as shown in Figure 3.6. A waste-free transaction provides the receiver with precisely the content required, in an optimal format, at the time needed for value to flow. I will have much more to say about optimizing the format and content of transactions under Method #2. Until then, take a look at a few of your most recent e-mails. How much time could you have saved the receiver while still delivering the same message? Now consider the Golden Rule.[17]

## Distance

With reports from the field being effusive in their praise, it is easy to assume that co-location solves everything. Just cram that dysfunctional project team into a common bullpen and magically all the barriers to communication simply dissolve. If only it were that easy. Co-location of a project team certainly reduces the pain of physical distance, but effective coordination

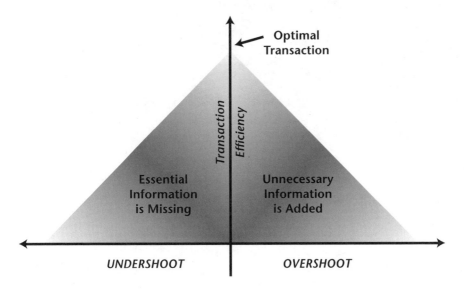

**Figure 3.6**: A balance must be maintained between ensuring a complete transaction of information and providing unnecessary information. The ideal is a brief, focused, and scrupulously complete communication.

and collaboration are definitely not guaranteed. If you were a military leader, for example, you would certainly prefer to have all of your troops co-located on the battlefield. How effective they are in battle, however, depends on strategy and tactics, not just proximity.

Some famous data on the probability of communication versus physical distance is shown in Figure 3.7. Evidently, the probability of communication decreases exponentially as the distance between individuals increases. Shrink the distance and transaction costs will surely decline. The advantages of close proximity among team members include accelerated sharing of

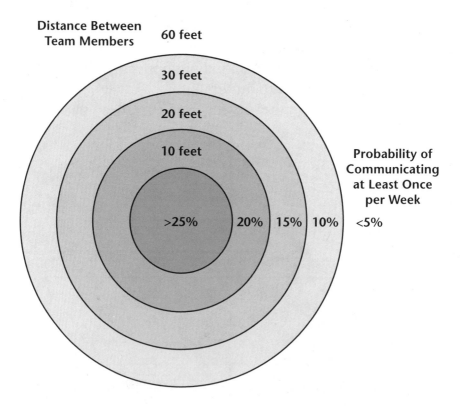

**Figure 3.7**: Probability of team members communicating at least once per week (without mandatory meetings) versus distance. Co-location is clearly advantageous as a means of encouraging intra-team communication. It is not, however, a substitute for an efficient communications strategy for collaboration and coordination.[19]

information, increased frequency of ad hoc discussions, sheltering of the team from outside intrusions, etc. Despite these obvious advantages, however, I have worked with co-located teams that have behaved like a disorganized mob, wandering aimlessly from one technical distraction to another. In this case, it seemed that the opportunities to yak about the project were so tempting that real work appeared mundane by comparison. Moreover, even the "rapid decision" potential of co-located teams can become a negative. Team members can easily feel disenfranchised if a decision is made in real time and out of earshot.[18]

The bottom line is that physical proximity is no substitute for an effective communications strategy.[20] The transaction costs of a co-located team will certainly be lower than that of a sprawling network, but to reap the full potential of proximity, appropriate work methods are needed. Coordination of the entire team, for example, should occur simultaneously, with clearly identified actions, deliverables, and due dates. Likewise, technical discussions can degenerate into endless, pointless meetings if technical collaboration is not structured into value-creating packets with measurable outcomes. Work methods such as those described in Methods #3 and #5 can turn "a room full of people" into a problem-solving powerhouse. All it takes is a little organization and discipline.

What if you're stuck with a team that is distance-challenged? Here are a few rules that can reduce the impact of team separation on project transaction costs. First, never divide responsibility for a complex deliverable among distant groups (depending on the nature of the deliverable, "distant" may be as little as 100 feet). Always divide responsibilities across clear and simple interfaces, with independent partitioning of requirements. Second, avoid any natural barriers that create cliques within the team. I once led a team that was divided into two groups by a single flight of stairs. Within a week, I heard comments like, "the upstairs guys don't think the downstairs people can handle such-and-such." Huddling in protective groups is embedded in our DNA. At the first opportunity, a segment of your team will establish its own identity and begin to look down on "outsiders." Give this type of behavior a very short leash, else your team will bicker like school children.

Finally, remember that the vast majority of value-creating work is accomplished within the heads of team members, not in meetings. All this free communication is wonderful, but too many transactions can be just as wasteful as too few. Ultimately, customers pay for outcomes, not discussions. A balance must be established between opportunities to interact and time dedicated to performing undisturbed individual work. The leader of a co-located team must define appropriate levels of coordination and collaboration, and monitor for excesses and deficiencies. Having your troops assembled on the battlefield is not enough; it is up to you to give them their marching orders.

### Poor Handoff

When is a task complete? Is it when the task owner says it's complete? No, that can't be right. Is it when the "deliverable" is complete for the task? Now you're getting warmer. How about when that deliverable has been received by the "customer" for that task? You're burning up . . . but still not all the way there. A task is complete *when the customer for that task agrees that it is complete*. In other words, when the customer acknowledges that all needed information has been received and understood.

The idea of forming linkages between tasks in a project is analogous to running a relay race. The first relay runner is responsible for completing a fast initial leg, but also for making a successful handoff to the next runner. If the baton falls, it doesn't matter how fleet of foot the runners are. Hence, relay runners will match speed with each other for several yards to ensure that a firm handoff is achieved. Likewise, it is the responsibility of the creator of a deliverable to "match speed" with the receiver of that information to ensure that the transaction is successful.

The above discussion foreshadows one of the most powerful lean methods described in this book; the use of customer-defined deliverables (see Method #2). This approach, which works for both external and internal customers, involves gaining early feedback on the desired content and format of delivered information. Furthermore, this method demands that the customer determine when a transaction is complete. If an earned-value system is in place, for example, a value milestone could only be credited when the customer for that task's deliverable agrees. Imagine the possibilities. No gaps, no white space, only tight linkages that bond together every major transaction in a project.

## Linked Flow: A Remedy for Transactional Waste

With visions of linked tasks and shared language dancing in our heads, we come to the conclusion of this chapter. Picture for a moment a project in which all transaction costs have been minimized. At the beginning of such a project, the team would agree on a set of rules for the use of communications media (e-mail in particular). In addition, a "dictionary" of project-specific language would be created that includes conventions for data transfer, drawing format, and all other symbolic communication. Natural language barriers would be highlighted and a "boundary spanner" identified to help bridge each gap when necessary.

As the project progresses, review and approval cycles that are internal to the company (not just to the team) are minimized. Project reviews, meetings, and all other forms of routine communication are stripped of formality, and focused on the transfer of essential information. Memos and e-mails are brief and precise, and key deliverables are scrupulously complete but devoid of unnecessary words, discussion, tangents, and nonessential boilerplate. Important transactions are linked in content and format, with the customer holding sway over completeness.

For projects that involve well-defined objectives and a clear execution process, the ideal described above can be realistically approached. As the degree of project risk and uncertainty rises, however, the ability to execute transactions with efficiency decreases. Perhaps in the extreme case of highly innovative projects, the correct model is not a relay race, but rather a jazz band. As a jazz ensemble performs, one musician will create a unique musical entity and then "pass it over" to the next musician to improvise and enhance. Ideas and notes blend together in a balance of creative freedom and mathematical precision. Music and creativity may seem to flow effortlessly, but make no mistake. The execution of a jazz performance requires high levels of transactional efficiency and discipline. Whether the notes are written on a page, or are the result of improvisation and creativity, it is linkage, synchronization, and shared language that enable a team to make beautiful music.

## Stuff You Should Remember

- Transaction costs – the time and cost of moving information or materials from one individual to another – are all Type 1 waste. If you could execute transactions with zero time and cost, your customer would be just as happy, and your profits would dramatically improve.

- Proper choice and use of communications media – especially e-mail – can save a great deal of time and money, and requires little effort.

- There must be a shared language across all critical transactions in a project. The customer (internal or external) must understand delivered information in *exactly* the same way as the deliverer intended.

- Loops in a value stream (due to approvals, mistakes, omissions, etc.) are unnecessary. They can be reduced or eliminated through a feed-forward of information or through continuous collaboration with downstream customers.

- "Dropping the baton" during the hand-off of critical deliverables can cause delays and loop-backs. It is critical that tasks be linked so that the customer (internal or external) holds sway on whether a transaction has been successfully completed.

# Defining Standard Work  4

It may seem like a contradiction in terms to talk about "standard project work." After all, a project is, by definition, a non-recurring activity to accomplish a unique goal. How can you standardize something that is unique? Yet despite appearances, much waste can be eliminated through standardizing some of the dreary, repetitive work of project teams. Examples include the release of drawings, the processing of engineering changes, creation of bills of material, the reporting of project status, etc. In each case, time can be saved and errors reduced by establishing a common approach to the work involved.

Imagine for a moment that you are a relatively new employee of a company and have been tasked with pulling together a technical specification. How would you know what format should be used? In the absence of a documented standard, you might: a) use the same format as in your previous job, b) find an example of a spec within your new firm, c) ask seasoned veterans what they would recommend, or d) just make up something that seems reasonable. No matter which choice you make, however, you are clearly reinventing the wheel. Wouldn't it be great if someone had created a technical specification *template* that could be tailored to your needs?

The advantages of such a template go far beyond saving a few hours of redundant effort. If all specifications within a firm have a common format, including paragraph numbering, units and measures, level of detail, and so on, all employees will know exactly where to look for needed information. Transaction costs, therefore, will be significantly reduced. Moreover, with a common format it is unlikely that critical information will be omitted, saving downstream revisions and costly errors. The repetitive use of standard formats or templates also enables *learning curve*[1] benefits to be gained (reduction in the time required to accomplish a task due to experience gained). Finally, suppliers, customers, and outside contractors will see a consistent and professional document, regardless of whether it was created by a veteran or a whelp.

The benefits described above are often referred to as capturing *economies of scope*. Most of us are familiar with the concept of *economies of scale*; the more frequently we do the same thing, the more efficient we tend to become. Economies of scope offer the same advantages, but depend on "factoring out" common elements among disparate activities. Hence, the more projects a firm executes, the more benefit can be derived from establishing a standardized approach to recurring project activities. To capture these gains, however, standards must be flexible enough to adapt to any reasonable situation. If we fail in this, our standardization effort will soon be relegated to the waste bin.

## The Four Levels of Standard Work

In the sections that follow, I will provide a brief overview of the four levels of standard work. A more detailed discussion of how to apply standardization to real-life projects is covered under Method #8.

One of the most prevalent mistakes that firms make when attempting to implement project standards is not recognizing the importance of employing varying levels of rigidity. If a standard imposes an unacceptable degree of constraint on an activity, either the activity will lose value, or employees will just ignore it. The four levels presented in Figure 4.1 range from detailed and restrictive to high-level and flexible. Selecting the proper level enables a much greater range of activities to benefit from standardization. Let's consider an example.

You have just been hired by a consulting firm that specializes in improving project efficiency. On your very first day, you are assigned to a client that has a major productivity problem. Virtually every project in the company is suffering from a complete lack of document control. There are no formal processes in place, so project team members do as they please. Nothing is consistent: formats, content, drawing sizes, dimensioning, part numbering, version control, even the meaning of critical symbols and terms. Certainly this is a company that can benefit from establishing standards for document creation and control. There are, however, a few challenges to be overcome.

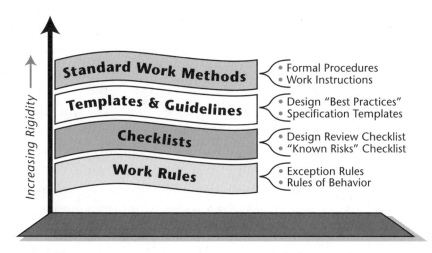

**Figure 4.1**: Four levels of standard work, ranging from the least flexible – Standard Work Methods, to the most flexible – Work Rules. Selecting the optimum level of constraint is critical to gaining benefits from standardization without sacrificing value.

First, not all of the above activities can accept the same level of standardization. In some cases, such as the formal release process for controlled documents, a very restrictive and detailed work instruction would be ideal. There is little to be gained by allowing flexibility in a release process, in fact the less variability the better. This rigid type of work standard would be unacceptable, however, for defining the *content* of controlled documents. In this case, creative thinking and customization are critical to success, so a very flexible guideline or template would be more suitable. Finally, some of the problems encountered by your client firm are discipline and culture related. For these cases, a set of "rules of behavior" must be established and enforced that guide the culture toward acceptable conformity.

Now that you have been clever enough to recognize the need for several levels of rigidity in your standardization effort, you might think your client is home free. Not quite. As you explore the requirements of several business units within the company, it becomes apparent that one standard cannot fit all. It appears that you will have to make a difficult choice: implement several very detailed standards to capture the maximum local benefit, or deploy a watered-down version that would enable reasonable conformity across the company. The good news is that this choice need not be made.

As can be seen in Figure 4.2, any given standard can be implemented as a series of tiered "umbrellas." At the lowest and most project-specific tier, the standard can be relatively specific and detailed. As one moves upward hierarchically (say to the business-unit level), a broader and less detailed standard should be established. At the highest tier, the same standard might appear as a very general guideline – almost a "strategic vision" for that particular activity across the company. In each case, however, it is critical that higher tiers of the same standard be *inclusive* rather than *exclusive*. In other words, all detailed standards must fit within the umbrella of the next higher tier.

Through creative use of the four levels of standardization and the umbrella concept for tiering the deployment of that standard, you will become a hero in your new role as efficiency consultant. Each project team will have at its disposal a grab bag filled with useful and appropriate templates, checklists, and work instructions that fit their particular needs. Management is happy as well, since all standards across the company are

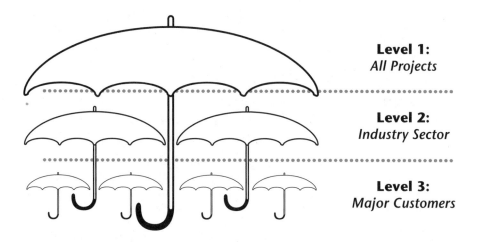

**Figure 4.2**: For standards to be effective throughout an organization, it is essential that they be tiered in their level of detail and specificity. As with the laws of our land, higher-level standards (analogous to state and federal laws) supersede lower-level standards (municipal laws). Higher-level standards must be general and inclusive, whereas lower-level standards may be specific to a given customer or project type.

deployed under a unifying corporate structure. Provide just enough guidance to optimize efficiency and strategic alignment, but nothing to inhibit the flow of creative juices where needed. Not a bad outcome for your first day in the consulting business.

### Level 1 – Standard Work Methods

The whole point of restricting variability in repetitive tasks is to reduce errors, omissions, and transactional waste. Naturally, the more that the variability of a task is constrained, the less opportunity there will be to customize that activity to specific needs. Hence, only the most routine tasks are candidates for a standard work instruction or method sheet, such as that shown in Figure 4.3. A highly structured work definition enables virtually anyone in a firm to execute an activity with speed and accuracy. Learning-curve advantages are maximized at this level of standardization, since the work is done in exactly the same way every time.

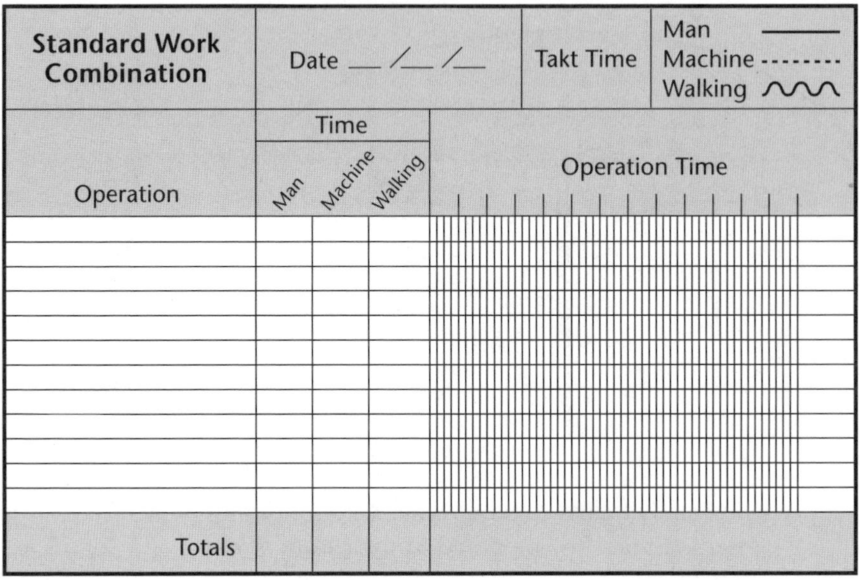

| Standard Work Combination | Date __ / __ / __ | | Takt Time | Man ———<br>Machine -------<br>Walking ∿∿∿ |
|---|---|---|---|---|
| | **Time** | | | |
| Operation | Man / Machine / Walking | | | Operation Time |
| | | | | |
| | | | | |
| | | | | |
| | | | | |
| | | | | |
| | | | | |
| | | | | |
| | | | | |
| | | | | |
| | | | | |
| | | | | |
| Totals | | | | |

**Figure 4.3:** Example of a standard work definition sheet that might be used for production or recurring process operations.

On the other hand, very few project activities are viable candidates for such Draconian standardization. On the factory floor we can conceive of many opportunities, but in project work the only realistic possibilities lie in the realm of administrative and operational tasks. Some examples are given in Figure 4.4. The good news is that it requires relatively little effort to establish a work instruction or procedure for these types of activities. There are a number of excellent books that can help guide this process, based on two decades of experience in the manufacturing arena.[2] Creating a standard work instruction is not difficult; the hard part is getting everyone in the company to follow it.

## Level 2 – Guidelines and Templates

A far more useful concept from the standpoint of project work is the idea of a tailorable guideline or template for recurring activities. At this level of standardization, only a super-structure is defined for team members. If a document is

**Figure 4.4**: Some opportunities to use standard work methods to reduce waste in recurring project activities.

involved, a skeleton outline might be provided, along with guidelines for how each topic and subtopic might be addressed. For quantitative tasks such as cost estimating, an automated template (e.g., a spreadsheet) could be developed that would guide the user through its application, and help ensure that calculations are consistent and correct.

An example of a deliverable-definition template is shown in Figure 4.5. By making the guideline or template tailorable to a wide range of applications, the maximum benefit can be achieved. Remember, however, that as with any tool employed by humans, useability is critical to broad acceptance. Avoid the "wall full of policy and procedures manuals" in favor of user friendly and approachable aids that are well within the comfort zone of the intended user. Besides, haven't you noticed the undisturbed layer of dust on all those policy manuals?

## Level 3 – Checklists

Have you ever heard of a pilot who does not religiously follow his or her pre-flight checklist before taking off? Checklists can enable economies of scope to be gained and critical errors to be avoided even in processes that require almost complete autonomy and originality. As I've already noted, it wouldn't make sense to define a "common innovation" or a "standard

## Project Deliverable Definition
### (Title of Deliverable Here)

**Purpose:**

**Triggering Event:** _____

**Dependencies:** _____

**Responsibility:** _____

**Internal / External Customer:** _____

**Approvals Required:** _____

| Content Checklist: | | |
|---|---|---|
| *Content Item* | *Format* | *Source* |
| | | |
| | | |
| | | |
| | | |
| | | |

**Figure 4.5:** Example of a deliverable-definition template that can be used to communicate customer requirements, linkages, timing, and contents for a project deliverable. Templates require a "fill-in-the-blank" activity on the part of the user.

brand-new product." We could, however, generate a checklist of important design considerations, such as known quality, reliability, or fabrication issues. The goal of such a list is not to constrain the user, but rather to remind him or her of critical issues that might easily be overlooked.

The opportunities for the application of checklists are endless, as can be seen from the small sampling presented in Figure 4.6. Here is the real kicker, however. *There is no more powerful tool for capturing lessons learned (or organizational learning in general) than a listing of items to be considered during future work.* As new problems are overcome, just an entry at the end of the appropriate checklist can prevent history from repeating itself.

A word of caution is needed here, lest you run off and express your wild enthusiasm for standardization in a wasteful way. There is a big difference between capturing important *reminders*

## Lean Design Checklist

| *Lean Design Guidelines* | *Impact (I)* | *Ease (E)* | *Priority (I x E)* |
|---|---|---|---|
| **I. Lean System Architecture** | | | |
| • Has every effort been made to reuse existing designs? | | | |
| • Is there a well-defined "platform" upon which all future enhancements / versions / derivatives will be based? | | | |
| • Is the percentage of total product cost attributable to this platform as high as possible? | | | |
| • Is the product designed to be as modular as possible? | | | |
| • Is the product designed to be scaleable to new versions? | | | |
| • Are interfaces between modules well defined and standardized wherever possible? | | | |
| • Has every effort been made to simplify the design? | | | |
| • Have all performance attributes been scrutinized for possible performance overshoot? | | | |
| • Have all features / options been tested for customer value? | | | |

**Figure 4.6**: An example of a design checklist used during project execution. Checklists provide an excellent means for capturing lessons learned from previous projects, without imposing unnecessary constraints or added work.

for project team members, and mandating that *superfluous work* be performed. A checklist is not the same as adding "belt and suspenders" tasks to every project in the company to avoid "another XYZ incident." One or two anecdotal problems are not sufficient justification for imposing additional work on all projects. Look for root causes first (i.e., ask "why" several times) before smothering projects under unnecessary band-aids.

## Level 4 – Work Rules

What if the inconsistencies among projects are a result of plain old human behavior? People are late to meetings, expense reports are not in on time, e-mail is being misused, task deadlines are being ignored, and so on. These are symptoms of an organization without appropriate work rules embedded in their culture. Although this may sound like the "soft-skill stuff" we all know and love, I am after far tougher game. The goal of work rules, at least in the context I invoke them, is to define clear boundaries of right and wrong for project-critical activities.

I've beaten the drum about organizational discipline several times thus far, but here is where we get serious. A rule, for example, that all contact with the customer by project team members must be promptly reported to the project leader can avoid dangerous communication loops and misunderstandings. A standard of behavior that mandates "customer" feedback on all internal task deliverables encourages accountability, linkage and flow. A work rule that prohibits abuses of e-mail can save everyone time. In each case, a simple, one-sentence rule is used to delineate acceptable and unacceptable behavior in unambiguous terms. Some additional examples of behavioral rules are given in Figure 4.7.

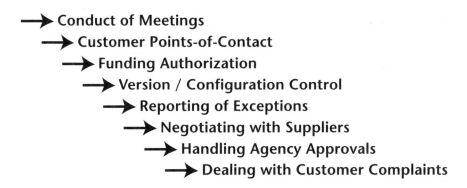

Conduct of Meetings
Customer Points-of-Contact
Funding Authorization
Version / Configuration Control
Reporting of Exceptions
Negotiating with Suppliers
Handling Agency Approvals
Dealing with Customer Complaints

**Figure 4.7**: Some opportunities to use work rules during project execution. Work rules establish a "black and white" criteria by which team member's activities can be measured. Rules create the superstructure within which exception management can operate.

Naturally, as with any discipline-inducing process, rules require enforcement. A high-performance, well-trained team can be trusted to report rule exceptions and maintain internal discipline. A novice team with "wild spirits" will require some gentle admonition when members stray. A repeat offender, whether due to ignorance or insolence, must be sent a clear message. Catering to stars is a sure way to unbalance your value-creating engine while fostering resentment among the less-than-stellar performers.

The use of work rules is fundamental to successful deployment of lean project management methods. A firm does not change its culture overnight. We must use rules to move the firm's culture toward a deeply embedded intolerance of waste. Much like putting braces on your teeth, consistent application of the pressure of rules can gradually migrate a company's culture toward new levels of efficiency and productivity.

## Knowledge Reuse that Actually Works

The above discussion hints at an intriguing additional benefit of standardization. By defining a structure for the work performed in a firm, we have established a practical method for capturing lessons learned and reuseable knowledge. I believe that project postmortems and the like are generally a waste of time. Unless a method exists for embedding a lesson into the way a firm does its work, the best that can be hoped for are vague recollections and inconsistent applications. Adding a critical lesson to a checklist, or even better, building corrective or preventative action into a template or standard work method, will enable every team to benefit from vital learning. Again I will repeat; if an action doesn't change the way people work everyday, then it doesn't improve the company.

One final note to underscore the potential opportunity offered by capturing economies of scope. There are some dramatic examples of firms using standardization as a successful competitive strategy. The leading engineering firm, Black & Veatch, for example, has developed a proprietary project estimating and management tool that represents a monument to knowledge reuse.[3] The software package is built around a set of standard structures, methods, templates, and databases that embody the way the firm executes its business. By capturing economies of scope in a very big way, Black & Veatch has been able to gain the lead in their industry segment, despite being only a fraction of the size of their competitors. Is there an opportunity such as this lurking in your little corner of the marketplace?

## Don't forget these key points

- It is possible to save considerable time and money on projects through the clever use of standard methods, templates, guidelines, etc. It is also possible to standardize out creativity and individual initiative. As always, a trade-off must be made to optimize total value.

- I have suggested four levels of standardization. At the most restrictive end are standard work methods. A bit more flexibility is afforded by standard templates and guidelines. If empowerment is the best approach, try a checklist to remind team members of critical issues. Finally, simple black-and-white work rules can modify culture and deter specific behavior problems.

- Standards should be inclusive. This means that a corporate-wide standard must be broad and general in nature. Business-unit-level standards can be a bit more specific to the products and customers of that unit. Finally, at the level of the project, much detail is possible, but all "tiers" must align with the higher standards. Think of the umbrella figure to visualize how this process works.

# Lessons from Information Theory

5

*"The most valuable of all talents is that of never using two words when one will do."*
*—Thomas Jefferson*

What is the difference between "information" and a bunch of words on a page? Does information that is communicated with fewer words have the same, or possibly even greater, value? These questions stab at the heart of project waste. Words are merely the messengers of information, they do not have a value unto themselves (unless we are creating poetry rather than project deliverables). Yet it is not unusual, for example, for an overzealous project team member to expand a straightforward document or deliverable into a complex dissertation – extensive figures and graphs, an attractive cover page, and detailed explanations worthy of a scholar. Although this situation fairly reeks of waste, such overachievement is often rewarded. After all, what is more impressive to a typical boss, a memo or an opus?

In Chapter 1 we discussed the difference between "work time" and "value-added time." Recall that work time is the actual hours spent by a worker on a given task, whereas value-added time is the portion of the work time that a customer would willingly pay for. How much of the work time associated with creating the tome I described above would a customer consider valuable? The answer is simple; only that portion which directly contributes to solving their problem. Overlong formal documents, complex communications, extravagant detail, or even a sincere desire to be "thorough and complete" can result in significant wasted time and energy. Furthermore, it is not just the time spent by the sender that is of concern. The receiver of a wasteful communication must sort through the chaff to find the wheat – a compounding of non-value-added effort.

The goal of project communication (particularly internal, intra-team communication) should be to convey essential information in the most efficient and unambiguous manner possible. This is no trivial challenge, however. If our word processors had a feature that displayed valuable information in red and irrelevant or excessive content in green, we would just delete the green stuff (now there is a value-added feature for the next release of MS Word!). What we need is some metric of information value that can guide us to more efficient project communication.

Fortunately, considerable work has been done on this subject toward a very different purpose; to maximize the efficiency of telecommunications networks. This area of research, known as information theory, can provide us with some qualitative guidelines for waste reduction, along with several tricks for optimizing information-carrying deliverables. Let me warn you, however, that if you have a bent toward creative writing, you will just have to find another outlet. As you will soon learn, when it comes to project communication, brevity is king.

## Focusing on the Unknown and the Unexpected

How much of your daily drive to work do you remember? Imagine yourself leaving your house in the morning: you start your car's engine, pull out of the driveway, pop in a nice CD and . . . presto, you are sitting at your desk at work wishing you weren't there. What happened in the interim is often a blank; you were busy daydreaming about the weekend or fuming over a situation at work. Your mind literally fails to record the routine and recurring images of your drive. What you do remember, however, are the *exceptions*: someone cuts you off in traffic, the house on the corner is being painted Pepto-Bismol pink, you had to take a detour, etc. This hints at the first useful principle of information theory; *the value of information is determined not by sameness, but by difference.*[1]

The reason why your mind blanks out routine data is that, over years of evolution (or by clever design, depending on your preference), the human brain has become an excellent filter for high-priority information. The more important an experience is to your health and welfare, the more likely it is that you will retain a vivid memory. Less important experiences will be subordinated, and numbingly routine activities, such as the drive to work, will be entirely disregarded. Instead, your mind puts in its place generic memories of a typical drive to work, and recalls only the stuff that was different on any given day.

As bizarre as it sounds, this concept forms the basis for much of our current telecommunications infrastructure. Some of us, for example, have had the dubious pleasure of participating in a video conference. At least in the old "copper wire" days, video conferencing was limited by a lack of bandwidth. You could only shove a limited amount of information through phone lines, and video images involve *a lot* of information. Hence, designers of these systems came up with a clever solution: What if you didn't send the entire image of a meeting each time the video frame is updated? Why not, instead, send only the portions of the image that have changed from the previous frame, and simply repeat what was already sent for the rest of the picture? This idea worked great, it turned out, if just people's mouths were moving from frame to frame, since a lot less information needed to be transferred. Unfortunately, if someone got up and moved around the room, much of the scene changed, and therefore considerably more data needed to be sent for each new frame. When this occurred, the video image would fall out of sync with the audio, and the result was that irritating "bad KungFu movie" look that drove many of us back to the telephone.

The above approach to moving information is generally referred to as data compression, a concept that is now used in virtually every application of data transfer. Why send repetitive, known data, when only unexpected or different information has real value? This powerful principle can be applied to any project communication. Consider the reporting of project status to upper management. If your project is on track, is it really necessary to show up for a status briefing just to report that "the sky is still blue" or "there are still stars out at night?" In principle, at least, the only topics that should be of interest to senior management are the *exceptions*; those issues which fall outside of "normal" project execution, and hence may require corrective action.[2]

Every transaction of information on a project, from trivial e-mails to deliverable documents, can benefit from this filter for information value. The trick is to transfer new and unknown information in a manner that is free of redundant or irrelevant filler.[3] This can be a bit of a balancing act, as can be seen in Figure 5.1. On the one hand (right side of the figure), any overshoot of essential content in project communication is waste. On the other hand (left side of the figure), we can easily be too terse, and leave out critical background or supporting information. Hitting the optimum is generally not worth the effort. We can, however, slash considerable waste from information transactions just by avoiding the extremes. The applications of this principle provided later in this chapter will demonstrate how easy it can be to exploit this concept in everyday project activities.

## Maximize the "Signal" and Minimize the "Noise"

The benefits of precise, to-the-point information transactions go far beyond just trimming a little fat from around the meat. A second principle of information theory demonstrates that by transferring only essential content, we can actually reduce the errors in that transmission. The idea is simple; if a valuable message is buried under a mountain of low-value filler, it is far more likely that the critical data will either be misinterpreted, or lost entirely. Just pick up your cellular phone and you can perform a simple experiment to bring this point home.

Call a friend on your phone and establish a clear connection. Conversation is easy, right? Now turn on the television, radio, or a blender – something that makes a lot of noise. Speak with the

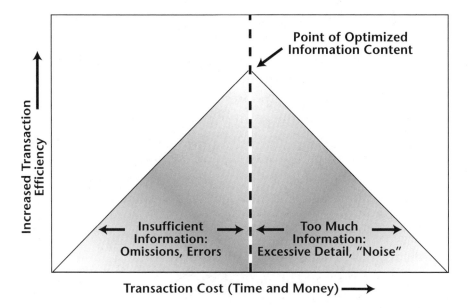

**Figure 5.1:** Conceptual diagram demonstrating that it is possible to either overshoot or undershoot the information required for a transaction. In either case, waste is created.

same volume to your friend and see what happens. Some words come through, while a few are either misunderstood or garbled. The more noise in the background, the worse it is for your friend, until eventually they will not understand a word you're saying. The lesson here is that noise can actually obscure the "signal" of valuable information.[4]

Excess words, data, or detail, beyond what is actually needed by the receiver, represent the "noise" in information transactions. One of my students recently offered a personal example. For several weeks Bob had tried in vain to get essential information from his project's customer. Each of the several e-mails he sent included a detailed explanation of why the information was needed, the impact that any delay would have on the project schedule, and a plea for assistance. Not a single response was received. After learning about the above concepts, he took a different approach. He pasted a "clip-art" drawing of a red stop sign onto his next e-mail message with the words "THIS IS THE STATUS OF YOUR PROJECT" written in boldface below. The response was immediate, and the information was forthcoming.

What is most interesting about this example is that after a conversation with the customer, my student learned that the reason he received no responses was that the customer completely misunderstood the point of his earlier messages. The customer thought that Bob was simply making excuses for why the project was going to slip schedule, and never realized that the problem was on his side. Somehow in that series of long-winded e-mails the purpose of the message was completely lost.

## Application #1 – The Power of Brevity

The quotation by Thomas Jefferson at the beginning of this chapter is representative of how many of the world's great thinkers have viewed the use of words. In the debates leading up to the creation of the Declaration of Independence, America's founding fathers showed themselves to be a mixed bunch indeed. Some were argumentative, several were stubborn, but all held in highest regard those orators who were able to sway opinion through the powerful use of words. Although he was not known as a spellbinding speaker, Jefferson was considered to be one of the most incisive minds present at the Second Continental Congress. His recognition of the power of brevity is not unique; indeed it is a common attribute of great leaders.

Near the end of World War II, Hitler's forces made a last-ditch attempt to push back what seemed to be an unstoppable march by the Allies toward Berlin. Through some clever maneuvering, Germany's panzer divisions managed to gain a dangerous advantage during what has been called "The Battle of the Bulge." In an obvious act of bravado, Hitler sent a message to American Major-General Anthony Mcauliffe, asking for his surrender. Mcauliffe's response has gone down in history as a monument to brevity. The message he sent back to Hitler consisted of a single word: "Nuts!"

Yet another example of a great leader possessing a way with few words was the first emperor of Rome, Gaius Julius Caesar.

Caesar was known to be both a great general and an excellent orator, and had little patience for long-winded debate and unnecessary babble. The great general provides us with a final example of high-value, unambiguous communication. During his campaigns in Asia Province, he was being badgered by Rome's impotent senate for updates on his progress. Finally he acquiesced and sent a message that may be the most famous in all of history. His words were *"veni, vidi, vici,"* which translates into English as "I came, I saw, I conquered." That pretty much says it all.[5]

## Application #2 – To Test or Not To Test

One of the great ironies of project management is that we spend the majority of our time trying to reduce risk and uncertainty, yet these are often the very attributes of a project that add value. Without uncertainty, our project team would be relegated to performing "turn the crank" tasks yielding commodity deliverables that solve trivial problems.[6] Indeed, risk is almost always proportional to reward, provided that the risk comes from the nature of the problem, and not our own ineptitude.

If risk is to be our constant companion, we must find a least-waste way to manage it. The traditional methods for reducing technical uncertainty in project outcomes are prototyping and testing. Prototyping (in this case, any early representation of a final project deliverable) provides us with opportunities to explore options and evaluate choices.[7] As we put our prototypes through their paces (i.e., as we test them), we learn how the final project deliverables might behave, and along the way we reduce our risk of not achieving a successful result. This process of test and discovery is key to adding value; in truth, it is what we are paid for.[8]

A brief example will illustrate this point. If we are contracted to build a standard tract house, little prototyping will be required, as shown in Figure 5.2. We can pretty much jump from approval of blueprints by the customer to final inspection, with only some routine progress sign-offs by inspectors along the way. In this case, the plan drawings represent our initial "proto-type" and the final inspection represents an acceptance "test," but there is little new learning going on. Of course, there is also relatively little profit being made.

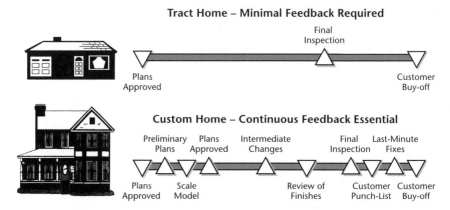

**Figure 5.2:** The creation of a well-defined and understood deliverable (such as the tract house shown above) requires only minimal communication between builder and customer. As the uncertainty in a project deliverable grows (such as would be the case for the customized home shown above), the amount of communication, feedback, prototyping, etc. must dramatically increase.

If, on the other hand, we are hired to design and construct a unique custom home, things will be different. We will want to explore choices and options with the customer, create some renderings and elevations, and perhaps even build a scale model to aid in visualization. Moreover, the discovery process will continue throughout construction. Frequent consultations with the customer, lots of "build it up and tear it down" changes, and much gnashing of teeth will take place as we approach the final project buy-off. In this case, "testing" will occur almost continuously, and our decisions about the final nature of the project deliverables will be significantly affected by the results. Greater uncertainty – greater reward.[9]

We can generalize the above situation to yield some simple rules regarding how and when to perform prototyping and testing during project execution. Rather than fearing uncertainty and avoiding risk, we should inoculate ourselves against failure through the appropriate use of these tools. As I noted earlier, success (and in particular, expected success) carries little valuable information. As painful as it may seem at the time, we learn far more from our failures. As the great innovator and founder of Polaroid, Ed Land, once asserted, "A failure is an event, the full benefits of which have not yet been turned to your advantage."[10]

Here are some rules to help minimize wasted time and money when the degree of technical uncertainty on a project is high.

## Rule 1 – Balance the Cost of Test with the Cost of Changes

Early testing is proactive, whereas downstream design changes are reactive. If early testing of prototypes can help avoid catastrophic schedule slips or unacceptable cost overruns caused by downstream change, then such tests are a virtual necessity. If downstream risk is tolerable, however, front-end testing should be thought of as an option, not a mandate. In some cases it may be more cost effective (and even more timely) to fix things downstream, particularly if the appropriate tests are difficult or expensive. For example, it is often easier to adjust the "human factors" of a project deliverable as it approaches completion rather than attempting to test every possibility in advance. Naturally, if this is your plan, sufficient flexibility should be designed into the deliverable to allow for some final tweaking. In general, *we should demand a positive return on any investment in early testing.*[11]

## Rule 2 – Avoid Big "Killer" Tests

Because customers pay for successful outcomes rather than intermediate testing, it may seem to be more cost effective to lump all testing or inspection into one "killer test" at the end of a project. As our home construction example illustrated, however, this can only work when the outcome of the test is essentially a known quantity. Routine projects can get by with a big "rubber stamp" quality test at the end. As the technical challenges of a project increase, however, waiting for the results of a killer test represents a dangerous time batch of vital information.[12] When a real possibility of failure exists, testing should be more frequent, target specific risk factors, and occur when the highest value will be gained by knowing the result (i.e., a JIT flow of pivotal information).

## Rule 3 – Design Tests that Bisect Possibilities

I have suffered through countless test data reviews that fail to yield any useful conclusions. The reason is always the same. Lots of tests were performed, but the right things were never tested in the right ways. As Sir Arthur Conan Doyle's Sherlock Holmes character is famous for saying, "when all other possibilities have been eliminated, whatever remains, no matter how unlikely, is the answer." This is a statement of deductive reasoning, and the lack of it in a project test plan renders that plan essentially useless.

First and foremost, tests must be controlled. This means that only one variable is measured at a time, with all other conditions being held constant (unless special methods such as design-of-experiment are used). Secondly, a test must be repeatable from one day to the next, from unit to unit, etc. Finally, a test should bisect the space of possibilities such that a large class of those possibilities can be eliminated through execution of the test, as shown in Figure 5.3. An ideal test plan, therefore, consists of a series of controlled, repeatable tests that successively bisect the set of possibilities. Such a plan is essentially guaranteed to yield a definitive outcome. Elementary, my dear Watson.

## Rule 4 – Make Sure Your Tests Affect Decisions

Testing for its own sake may provide excellent learning opportunities, but unless the customer is willing to pay for it, such extraneous testing should be handled under R&D funding, rather than as a tax on customer contracts. To determine where to draw the line in this regard, use a simple discriminator: Will

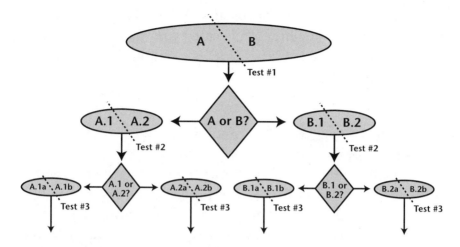

**Figure 5.3:** Testing must provide high-value information to justify its cost to a project. To ensure that this is the case, tests should be designed to bisect the space of possible outcomes, so that some class of possibilities can be firmly excluded from future investigation.

the result of the test directly affect a decision regarding how the project will proceed or how a deliverable will be created?[13] Unless a test impacts deliverables in a noticeable way, it violates our definition of value-added, and must be considered to be waste (at least from the standpoint of the project at hand).

## Rule 5 – Get the Customer Involved

One of the best ways to get the most from testing is to involve the customer in defining the test environment, the variables to be considered, and the way the results should be interpreted. Obviously, the applicability of this approach is project-specific, and may not make sense in some cases. However, when the conditions are right, a great deal of added information can be gained by having your customer become a partner in the discovery process. If nothing else, you will have several opportunities to condition your customer's perception of the project, and will gain their confidence through your openness to their involvement. Remember, an arm's length relationship on a project with high technical uncertainty is a recipe for disaster.

Better to bring your customers into your confidence than to force them to the sidelines. An isolated customer will have little sympathy when you are finally forced to admit that things have gone wrong.

## Application #3 – Exception Management / Team Empowerment

It is fitting that we end both this chapter and the first part of this book with the most vital and fundamental concept in lean project management. We have learned from information theory that there is no value in redundant or unchanging data. Therefore, if everyday we ask our team members, "are you on schedule," and everyday they answer "yes, so far, so good," we are wasting both our time and theirs. If each month we must stand up in front of management and report similar valueless data, more waste is created. There is something fundamentally wrong with the idea of command and control management; it requires repetitious sampling to derive its data, whether the data has value or not.

Consider an alternative. Suppose that a team commits to a series of schedule milestones. Now suppose that they are given a tight but reasonable "window" around those milestones, and told to report to management only if they will exceed those boundaries (i.e., they will be either unacceptably late or early). The rest of the time, the team members can go about their work with no need to report status, *because the status is already known by management*. In this ideal situation, management would assume on-schedule performance, unless an *exception* is reported.

Exception management is so powerful a concept, that it should be printed in boldface wherever it appears in this book. As long as an acceptable range can be defined for a given aspect of a project (e.g., cost, schedule, risk, performance, defects, and so on), you can employ management by exception.[14] Whenever a team member steps outside of these "control limits" an exception has occurred, and management must be notified, as shown in Figure 5.4.

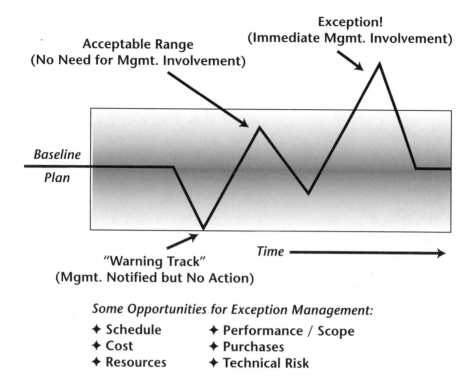

**Figure 5.4:** Boundaries can be established for team members that define an "empowered region" of activity. Inside this region, the team is allowed to innovate and create. If the boundary is violated, an exception has occurred, and management must be immediately notified to help mitigate the problem.

Those of you with a bit of factory experience might recognize that the above figure appears much like a Statistical Process Control (SPC) chart. On the factory floor, a machine or process step is tested to determine the range of performance that will yield a quality output (such as a part with no defects). This is called the "control range." When the machine is within these limits of performance, there is no need to test or inspect its work. If the machine drifts outside of the control range, an exception has occurred and the process will be taken off line for corrective action.[15]

Of course, projects are not assembly lines. For projects, we must define an envelope within which our team members can be empowered to work creatively. Inside the envelope, the team has considerable discretion. Outside the envelope, management must become involved to arbitrate and correct. To illustrate this idea, consider the property lines that surround your house (if you don't own a house, use your imagination). What would happen if one day a law was passed that eliminated all property lines? Chaos, right? Your neighbor would start building his or her swimming pool on your front lawn, and you might retaliate by letting your Rottweiler run amok in his or her flower beds. Property lines define a physical envelope in which homeowners are allowed considerable discretion, but also provide a clear boundary between acceptable and unacceptable behavior.

The equivalent of "property lines" can be established on a project by defining roles, responsibilities, and performance limits for each team member. Now you, the reader, may be thinking, "my team knows what they are supposed to do – they know where the lines are without me telling them." This assumption is almost certainly naive. True, team members typically have a general idea of what their job responsibilities are: a project schedule with defined tasks, a budget, etc. Are these not sufficient? Let me answer by extending my property-line analogy.

Suppose now that the government realizes that they went a bit too far by removing all property lines. They enact a revised law that reestablishes property lines, but allows for a ten-foot-wide "no-man's land" between each house. What would happen? Perhaps not quite chaos, but still a disaster. In some cases, both neighbors would vie to control and utilize this common margin, and in other cases, the unclaimed land would be neglected and become a weedy mess. This illustrates a more realistic situation for projects; some informal definition of roles and responsibilities exists, but there is also a lot of vague "white space." Sometimes this results in redundant work and toe-stepping, and other times things fall in the cracks. The bottom line; without sharp and clear boundaries, neither exception management nor team empowerment can work.

Indeed, exception management and team empowerment are really just opposite sides of the same coin.[16] Unfortunately, they are rarely implemented as such. Over the last decade, team empowerment has become the "emperor's new clothes" of management philosophy.[17] Everyone agrees it is the right thing to do, but somehow it never seems to live up to its great press. The reason should now be clear; without sharp performance limits and well-defined roles, a "self-managed work team" is really just an "unmanaged work team." You might recall the Dilbert cartoon in which the boss tells Dilbert, "After a few meetings of your self-managed team, you will distrust each other sufficiently that you will be begging me to micromanage you."[18] Talking about empowerment is easy; making it work requires *definition and discipline.*

Given the above mandate, opportunities to employ exception management on projects abound, as shown in Figure 5.5. Those readers familiar with "earned-value project management" will recognize that exception management is embedded in that proven methodology.[19] If a value milestone slips beyond specified limits in either cost or schedule, it is said to have an "unacceptable cost or schedule variance." This event triggers mitigating action by the project team and management.

Figure 5.5: Just a few of the opportunities to apply the waste-reducing technique of exception management to project work.

The utility of exception management can be extended far beyond the basic control of cost and schedule to encompass virtually every aspect of a project. During a design activity, weight, volume, and power budgets can be assigned to various components.[20] Within their budgets, team members can design to their heart's content. Outside of their budgets, some negotiating and reallocation is required. Allocation of human resources in a multitasking environment can also be managed by exception. A resource allocation plan for the next week or month can be established among all involved projects. As long as the allocated resources are sufficient, no further action is needed. Only when a project has an emergency need for additional resources must arbitration and redistribution occur.

The list of opportunities is endless, but reaping benefits from these opportunities depends on a critical factor: The empowered individuals or functions must possess the discipline to monitor their own defined limits, and immediately report exceptions. Teams will not develop this type of discipline overnight. Empowerment must be implemented gradually, in a manner similar to child rearing; the more responsibility displayed, the greater the freedoms that will be granted. So the next time your team screams for more empowerment, challenge them to prove that they are "mature" enough to deserve it.

---

It is now time to bring this final conceptual chapter to a close, lest I violate my own advice regarding brevity. Several of the practical methods presented later in this book build on the principles of information theory presented here; in particular the methods involving visual communication and customer-defined deliverables. Remember that over eighty percent of the easily recognizable waste in projects occurs during the transaction of information, so get out your carving knife and start trimming the fat. Enough said.

## Some Really Critical Points

- All information is not created equal. Information that is redundant, known, or in other ways "ho-hum" has little value. Information that is unknown, unexpected, new, and different has high value.

- Including low-value information along with the important stuff can cause mistakes and confusion in addition to wasted time. Any excess information beyond that which is needed is "noise," and can degrade the "signal" that the customer (or other users of the information) must receive.

- Opportunities to apply these concepts are everywhere, from project communications (where brevity is golden), to the testing of project deliverables.

- The most important outcome of these ideas is a mandate for the use of exception management to reduce waste in project execution. Repeated "sampling" of project status should be supplanted by the monitoring for exceptions to prearranged boundaries.

# PART II

## The Methods of Lean Project Management

# A Toolbox for Speed and Efficiency

**6**

*"If the only tool you have is a hammer, you tend to see every problem as a nail."*
*—Abraham Maslow*

Congratulations! Your mind is now expanded and your vision honed regarding value and waste. It is time that you receive your reward, in the form of twelve "lean methods" that can turn your project into a poster child for speed and efficiency. From now on we will be squarely in the realm of the practical. The intent of Part 2 of this book is to provide you with *techniques that you can use tomorrow* to eliminate non-value-added activities and wasted effort.

A "lean method" is simply a better way of doing project work. Each method addresses an important waste area for project teams, and includes both a broad discussion of the problem and several "countermeasures" that target specific situations. In other words, the methods are general techniques, while the countermeasures are specific solutions to specific problems. For example, a frequent traveler would benefit from a lean method entitled, "Packing a Suitcase." The countermeasures under this method might include: 1) How to avoid wrinkled shirts, 2) How to avoid forgetting things, and perhaps, 3) How to squeeze a week's worth of clothes into a carry-on bag without it getting jammed in the X-ray machine.

Before we explore how this toolbox actually works, I must

make an important distinction. Lean methods are *not* best practices, at least not in the traditional sense. A best practice is typically derived from benchmarking one or more successful companies. If you read a description that begins, "The XYZ company has become a leader in the so-and-so industry by doing such-and-such," it is surely a best practice that is being reported. What is wrong with best practices? Take your pick: 1) Your firm is not company XYZ, 2) You do not compete in the "so-and-so" industry, 3) The "such-and-such" practice depends on people that don't work for you, or 4) The description is so vague that a lot of risky extrapolation will be needed to implement it.

The methods and countermeasures described herein do not suffer from the dangerous limitations of best practices.[1] They do not depend on your firm being in a specific industry, or having a unique talent mix. Methods and countermeasures are *transferable, adaptable work skills* that can reduce waste in virtually any industry and with almost any project team. Moreover, sufficient practical detail and real-world examples are provided to allow everyone to take advantage of this toolbox. Rather than being based on the results of one or two companies, these methods have been successfully implemented in dozens of firms, spanning a broad range of industries. In short, they represent an instruction manual for efficient and productive project execution.

Before we dig in, here are a few guidelines for how to use the lean methods toolbox. As the analogy suggests, these tools can be used independently or in unison.[2] As you might expect, there are synergies between methods, so the benefits multiply rather than add as more of the techniques are used. This doesn't mean, however, that you shouldn't start by trying just one or two of the tools. There are no rules here, no dogma that must be followed. Choose the methods that make the most sense in your work environment, and save the rest for future use. My only request is that you commit to trying a few of these techniques immediately; the success you experience will give you confidence to dig in more deeply.

Although implementing a few lean methods can be accomplished with little effort, the greatest improvements will result from prioritizing opportunities based on their waste-reducing impact. To accomplish this, a step-by-step improvement process is described in Chapter 9. The process involves using a technique called "value-stream mapping" to create a visual representation of a specific task, process, or even an entire project. From this map, a set of prioritized opportunities are derived using a brain-storming technique known as a "value-stream blitz." Counter-measures are selected to attack the high-priority sources of waste, and a new "future-state" process map is created to document the improved state. This set of steps can be repeated as often as need-ed to drive waste from your projects. Please note, however, that this formal, step-by-step process takes both time and resources. If you can't justify the investment on your project, just pick a few appropriate lean countermeasures and get started.

One of the potential obstacles to immediate deployment of lean methods is the "monument" syndrome. A monument is any policy, process, or other officially sanctioned institution that appears to be an immovable object within a firm.[3] Sometimes the monument is a person; an intractable senior executive, for example. This is a tough situation, and must be handled deli-cately, else your improvement fervor may prove to be career lim-iting. The best approach that I have found is to work around the intransigent heavyweight by initially selecting lean methods that won't offend. Once there is ample evidence of improve-ment, try to make further initiatives appear to be the executive's idea. As transparent as this ploy sounds, it generally works (you can draw your own conclusions as to why).

A more insidious enemy to waste reduction measures is the operational monument; a deeply ingrained process that has become an accepted status quo in your firm. Perhaps the worst offenders here are the Draconian ISO 9000 mandates that many firms implemented under fear of being left behind in the quali-ty race. Let me be very clear about this: There is nothing in this book that cannot be successfully implemented under ISO 9000. Using a fat tome of (often irrelevant) processes as an excuse for not slashing waste is unacceptable. Push hard on this one if you experience it.

## Summary of Lean Countermeasures

| Method # | Lean Countermeasures | Method # | Lean Countermeasures |
|---|---|---|---|
| 1. Testing for Customer Value | • Performance Overshoot Test<br>• Excessive Complexity Test<br>• Least Discernible Difference Test<br>• One-Page Project Summary | 7. Visual Communication | • Visual Statusing of Exceptions<br>• Visual "Help Needed" Signal |
| 2. Customer Defined Deliverables | • Forming Task Linkages<br>• Strawmanning/Early Prototyping<br>• Feed-Forward of Information<br>• Eliminating Approval Delays | 8. Standard Work Methods | • Standard Work Methods<br>• Templates and Guidelines<br>• Checklists<br>• Work Rules |
| 3. Urgency-Driven Stand-Up Meetings | • Stand-up Coordination Meetings<br>• Lean Collaboration Meetings<br>• Three-Tier Schedule Management | 9. Risk Buffering & Critical Core | • Managing the "Critical Core"<br>• Core Value Milestones<br>• Risk Buffering |
| 4. Real/Virtual Project Room | • Physical Project Room<br>• Virtual Project Room | 10. Dedicated Time Staffing & Superteams | • Dedicated-Time Staffing<br>• Team "Filters"<br>• Resource Prioritization Methods<br>• Superteams |
| 5. The "Waste-Free" Design Review | • The "Waste-Free" Design Review | 11. The Reservation System | • Eliminating Queues and Wait Times<br>• Reserving Key Resources |
| 6. Staged-Freeze Specifications | • Staged-Freeze Specifications | 12. The Value-Added Scorecard | • The Value-Added Scorecard |

**Figure 6.1:** An "eye-chart" summary of the twelve lean methods described in this book, along with the lean countermeasures that are included under each method. Lean countermeasures are specific tips and techniques that can be applied immediately to slash wasted time and cost.

A summary of the twelve lean methods and their associated countermeasures is provided in Figure 6.1. The methods are presented in a roughly chronological order, from project negotiation and scope definition to execution techniques and metrics for success. Although each method can be used at almost any time, they will have their greatest impact at specific points in the project life cycle, as shown in Figure 6.2. At the end of each method section is a "method at a glance" table that helps the reader to identify which techniques are best suited to a given problem. Case examples, templates, and step-by-step implementation suggestions round out the documentation for each method.

A final message to the reader; *no excuses.* You may have been able to justify doing business as usual up until now, but this is no time to protect the status quo. Your future and the success of your firm depend on achieving excellence in project efficiency, and *you* are the vector of that achievement. So get fired up and see just how far and fast you and your team can go.

## Typical Project Life Cycle

| | Concept/Planning | Design | Prototyping | Validation | Delivery |
|---|---|---|---|---|---|
| Method #1 | ←————————————————————→ | | | | |
| Method #2 | | ←——————————————————————————→ | | | |
| Method #3 | ←——————————————————————————————————→ | | | | |
| Method #4 | ←——————————————————————————————————→ | | | | |
| Method #5 | | ←————————————————————————→ | | | |
| Method #6 | ←————————————————————————→ | | | | |
| Method #7 | ←——————————————————————————————————→ | | | | |
| Method #8 | ←——————————————————————————————————→ | | | | |
| Method #9 | ←——→ | | | | |
| Method #10 | ←——————————————————————————————————→ | | | | |
| Method #11 | ←——————————————————————————————————→ | | | | |
| Method #12 | ←——————————————————————————————————→ | | | | |

**Figure 6.2:** Although most of the lean methods can be applied at any point in a project's life cycle, there are periods during which the benefits are the greatest. The above graphic identifies these high-value points for a typical project schedule.

## Keep These Points in Mind

- Lean methods are straight-forward tools and techniques that can be immediately applied to project work.

- Although the methods are highly synergistic, you can select just one or two techniques and gain significant benefit. Choose the tools that offer you the greatest early advantages, and keep the rest in mind for future continuous improvement.

- Don't let "monuments," such as policy and procedures manuals or ISO 9000 documentation, stand in the way of improvement. Every method described in this book has been successfully implemented in ISO 9000 certified firms.

# *Testing for Customer Value*

> *"Nothing is cheap which is superfluous, for what
> one does not need, is dear at a penny."*
> —*Plutarch*

Does it make sense to squander time and resources doing work that your project's customer is not willing to pay for? Based on our definition of value from Chapter 1, any activity that does not ultimately draw dollars from your customer's wallet must be deemed non-value-added (again, we are not considering strategic investments here). Yet unpaid work is rampant on most projects, consuming precious resources and eroding profit margins. The worst part is that much of this wasteful activity is not performed in response to customer demands. In fact, just the opposite is true. Project teams inflict it on themselves due to ignorance of what their customer truly values.

Imagine that you are managing a proposal effort for a major aerospace company. Winning this contract could make the difference between a healthy year for your firm and painful layoffs. Unfortunately, the request for proposal from the government is written in typical military procurement jargon; lots of CDRLs (contract deliverables), mission envelopes, and Mil Standards, but little insight into what the customer *really* needs. The statement of work is vague and sometimes contradictory, and the technical requirements seem to violate the laws of physics. Worst of all, this is a fixed-price contract, so you have little room for error.

Under these circumstances, you are caught between a rock and a hard place, as shown in Figure M1.1. If your proposal undershoots the customer's expectations, you protect your firm's profits at the risk of losing the contract to a competitor. If you overshoot, you run headlong into a no man's land of technical uncertainty. The customer is no help in this either; on past contracts any solution your firm has proposed was enthusiastically embraced . . . at least for a while. Once the final deliverables were in their hands, you would begin to hear comments like, "you guys obviously didn't understand the problem," or "clearly this could never work in the field." Some of your deliverables have been criticized for being overly complex and unintelligible, while others were mocked as being naïve and trivial. Most of the profits on these past contracts had been drained away performing last minute fixes to placate an unhappy customer. Yet throughout the contract your government reps seemed to be on board.[1] What went wrong? Perhaps even more important; how

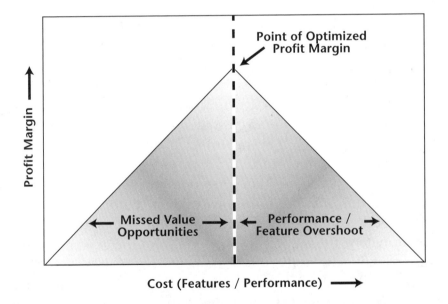

**Figure M1.1:** The now-familiar "optimization pyramid" applied to the deliverables of a project. As with most aspects of project execution, teams must try to avoid either undershoot or overshoot of requirements, because both conditions can erode profits.

can you avoid making the same costly mistakes again? In general, the less you know about your customer's needs, the more likely it is that you will either undershoot or overshoot an optimal solution. If you undershoot, you will be forced to discount your price or you will lose the contract to a competitor. If you overshoot, you must pay for the excess cost out of your profits. Either way, your profit margin is negatively impacted. If only your customers knew exactly what they wanted! On the other hand, if customers could precisely define their own solutions, why would they pay your firm the big bucks?[2]

Although undershoot of needs does occur, most firms today are sufficiently obsessed with customer satisfaction that overshoot is a far greater concern. In lieu of clear specifications and exact requirements, we tend to offer the moon and the stars. We propose the highest possible performance, or quality, or reliability, even if it exceeds the customer's needs (and sometimes our own capabilities). We suggest lots of features and options, although no direct connection to customer benefits can be identified. "Gold plated" solutions are selected, even when a simpler way could be found. All of this in the hope of hitting the customer's "hot button" and thereby winning the contract. Unfortunately, what may have initially looked like a profitable venture may end up being a low-margin albatross.

Typically we have little time to respond to requests for quotation; certainly not enough time to dither about exactly what the customer will and will not pay for. Hence, the most practical way to avoid profit erosion is not to seek an optimum, but rather to simply avoid gross overshoot. That is the purpose of this first lean method; to provide several tests for value that can quickly highlight potential unpaid work or excessive costs. After all, what better way to eliminate waste than to simply delete a chunk of unnecessary and unpaid effort before work has even begun?

## Countermeasure 1.1 – Testing for Performance Overshoot

In his recent and very popular book, *The Innovator's Dilemma*, Clayton Christenson describes a market behavior that is both simple and powerful: *performance overshoot*.[3] Christenson points out that many firms find themselves traveling along a "trajectory" of technical performance improvement. This trajectory reflects the driving specification or attribute that determines market acceptance and largely defines price. Reducing the size and weight of early cellular phones is a good example of a trajectory that dominated market acceptance. (Note to the reader: The countermeasures in this section are most easily explained using product examples, but apply equally well to any project deliverable). Increasing the speed of PC microprocessors or decreasing the weight of laptop computers are other examples. Just follow the yellow brick road of performance improvement with each new project and you're assured of a profitable hit. Well, that works for a while . . . .

Here's the rub. Eventually, the market gets enough of a particular performance attribute and begins to look elsewhere for value, as shown in Figure M1.2. Once cellular phones reached about the size and weight of a pack of cigarettes, more improvement along that trajectory got you zip.[4] Introduction of a faster microprocessor used to be a media event. Just the mention of higher speed was enough to justify shipping your like-new PC to your nephew in Buffalo and coughing up a hefty premium for the latest box. Not any more. Although the Pentium I microprocessor and those before it made great profits, the Pentium II was a disappointment. But the worst was yet to come. Lack of market interest drove Intel to introduce the much-touted Pentium III at a price so low that it cannibalized its own P2 market. Pentium IV's recent rollout has been a giant snore. What happened to the huge profits?

Intel overshot the market, and in the process may have wasted billions of precious R&D dollars. While their design teams were obsessing on processor speed, the marketplace grew tired of paying a premium for added performance that gave them little added benefit. Once the market saturates along a certain trajectory (e.g., microprocessors are fast enough, cell phones are small enough), some other attribute will begin to dominate market acceptance. For microprocessors the new trajectory (at

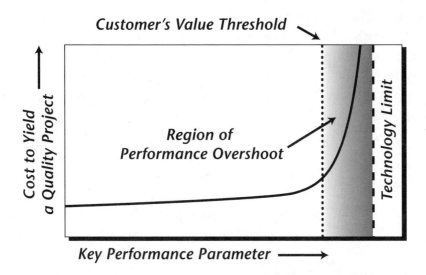

**Figure M1.2:** Improving performance along a well-established trajectory can increase both price and profits for a project . . . provided that the customer continues to value higher performance. Many projects overshoot the needs of the customer, resulting in increased project cost and risk without the compensation of higher price.

this writing) is lower price; general-use PCs have become a commodity item these days. For cell phones, size and weight have been overshadowed by improvements in clarity and service range, the addition of cheesy games, a color display, voice / data capability, you name it. Acceptable size is now a given, a "table stake" for playing in the game. Any firm spending a penny of R&D on further reduction in cell phone size, therefore, better double-check their market research.[5]

The above examples illustrate the first test for value in the deliverables of a project:

*If an incremental increase in a performance specification does not directly result in an incremental increase in price, then that attribute is potentially in the overshoot region (i.e., the waste region).*

This principle can easily be converted into a lean countermeasure by presenting it as a series of questions. If the answer to one or more of the following questions is "yes" there is a good chance that you are overshooting performance for a given deliverable of your project. Note that these questions can be asked at anytime in the life cycle of a project, from contract negotiations to final delivery. The goal is to avoid asking your team to hike up a steep and costly performance trajectory when "good enough" performance will do.

*Question #1* – Has one of the deliverable's specifications been under steady improvement for some time? If so, when was the last time the customer specifically asked for improvement of this attribute?

*Question #2* – Is the customer unaware of improvements in this specification? In other words, have you failed to "advertise" this improvement as a key advantage of your firm's technical approach?

*Question #3* – Has the cost of continued improvement along this specification's "trajectory" been increasing exponentially (i.e., very rapidly)? Is this cost driving the price of your overall project?

*Question #4* – If less time and money were spent on improving this specification, are there other performance improvements that could give the customer even greater value?

*Question #5* – Have any of your competitors recently executed projects that have focused on other performance specifications? How do your customers feel about this shift in emphasis?

*Question #6* – Is it difficult to demonstrate how added performance can measurably contribute to solving the customer's problem?

This countermeasure can be applied to something as big as the performance specs for a petroleum refinery, or as small as the amount of detail provided in project documentation. Once you suspect that overshoot may be lurking in the shadows, there is a simple method you can use to flush it out. Rather than offering your project customer a fixed target for the specification in question, offer them several levels of performance, along with an associated cost for each level (a rough estimate will do initially). If they bite at the high-priced option, you are safe from overshoot. On the other hand, if they take the low-priced alternative, you've just avoided some potential waste. By giving the customer a choice, you may learn that what has always been a fountain of profits has now run dry. Your challenge will be to identify a new set of performance improvements that your customer would be willing to pay a premium for.

## Countermeasure 1.2 – Testing for Excessive Complexity

Complexity is a breeding ground for waste in virtually every aspect of project execution. Excessive design complexity causes higher material costs, increased testing demands, and compromised reliability. Unnecessarily complex documents cause errors and misunderstandings. Even an overly detailed and intricate project plan may do more harm than good in coordinating team activities. Thus a second test for value in projects can be stated as follows:

*Provided that no value is lost (i.e. the same benefit can be achieved), the simplest way to execute a project task or deliverable is also the least-waste way.*

A few examples will vividly illustrate this point. Those readers who have suffered through the implementation of a new Enterprise Resource Planning (ERP) software package have experienced complexity in its extreme. Software suppliers would lead you to believe that to compete in today's world, every function and every desktop in your firm must be seamlessly automated.

Yet despite this dogma, I know of not a single firm that is satisfied with their enterprise solution, and most agree that only a tiny fraction of the capabilities of their ERP package is actually being used. The reason for this dissatisfaction is almost always rooted in excessive complexity. Even selecting a supplier requires wading through a mountain of arcane specifications and features. Tailoring the package demands that thousands of decisions be made by hundreds of job functions. And the implementation . . . oh, the pain of it! It seems that the only people who are happy with ERP are the consultants that feed on your firm for what seems like an eternity.

Unfortunately, a more highly evolved alternative to enterprise software solutions does not exist . . . at least not yet. It is worth noting, however, that when Toyota implemented their breakthrough lean production system, they tore out the computers and found a simpler way. The complexity of Manufacturing Resource Planning (MRP) software (a more humble cousin of ERP) was supplanted by the elegant simplicity of kanban cards, method sheets, and visual signals. Although automation of business operations is clearly essential, a revolution in simplicity is needed before ERP can attain its full potential.

In the world of products, complexity can actually be seen to *subtract* value. Firms attempting to make their products do everything for everyone often add feature after feature, until overall performance is significantly reduced.[6] The useability of consumer products, for example, is often compromised by too many controls, buttons, options, or features. Take a look at the remote control for your VCR. Do you have any idea what most of those buttons do? Wouldn't you pay *more* for a control that had just the stuff you really needed?

Likewise, several of the "improvements" made to MS Word over the past decade have been at the expense of convenience and useability.[7] I still haven't figured out how to stop the autocorrect feature from scrambling everything I type, and generally the "grammar suggestions" (annoying green underlines) make no sense at all. It is interesting that Microsoft claims that a new feature must be "twice as good as its replacement" to justify adding it to a new product.[8] Pardon my skepticism, but it seems likely that the designers themselves are making this determination, not typical users.

We can test for excessive complexity in project deliverables by asking the following questions. Again, if the answer to one or more of these questions is "yes," then a simpler way should be sought.

*Question #1* – Has the user friendliness (ergonomics) of the project deliverable been compromised during the design activity?

*Question #2* – Have performance levels been reduced to allow for the addition of new features or options?

*Question #3* – Is the reliability of the project deliverable a critical concern?

*Question #4* – Are there any attributes of the project deliverable that cannot be directly linked to a customer benefit, as viewed from the customer's perspective?

*Question #5* – Is the specification for the project deliverable a compilation of the needs of many different customers or segments?

*Question #6* – Could a "purpose built" solution (i.e., one that addresses a single need) provide greater value than a multi-purpose solution?

Although the above questions address contract deliverables, the same concerns about complexity apply to internal project documents, and in particular to project plans. Project managers must keep in mind that *project plans are non-value-added*; they only benefit the project if they save more time and cost than they consume.[9] A hundred-page project schedule with thousands of miniscule tasks and a spaghetti bowl of dependencies serves no purpose to either team or leader.[10] Remember that a plan is useful *only if it is used*, and the more complex you make it, the less it will serve as a living and working document.[11, 12]

So shut down MS Project, get up from your computer, and get out there with your team. Project management is not about Gantt charts; it's about being a catalyst for value creation.

### Countermeasure 1.3 – The "Least Discernable Difference" Test

I have suggested that project teams often add superfluous features or options to a project deliverable in an effort to exceed customer expectations (often referred to as "gold plating"). As admirable as this may seem, if the customer doesn't actually appreciate the feature in question, you have wasted your time and money. How might you determine if your customer is actually calculating the value of a given feature into their price equation?

In marketing theory this question is referred to as the "Test of the Least Discernable Difference." The idea is straightforward. Will your customer pay *a penny more* for a feature you are considering? Customers will generally take anything you offer them, as long as it doesn't affect the price. Extras may be nice, but price is calculated by hard-nosed consideration of benefits. Does the feature save time? Does it save money? Can it improve the quality of the customer's solution? If an added feature or option doesn't meet one of these criteria, the price stays the same . . . but your margin doesn't.

The least discernable difference will vary from customer to customer, as shown in Figure M1.3. If you do business with many customers, you will find that some will have more of a taste for extras than others. The majority of your market will home in on a middle-ground solution that does a good solid job. A smaller segment will look either toward a "quick and dirty" fix, or a "deluxe package." A very small percentage will aim for the extremes.

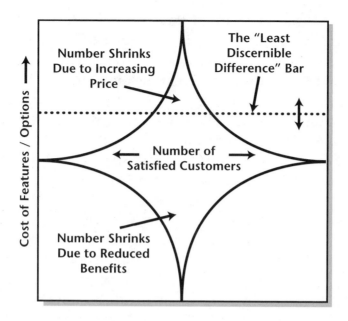

**Figure M1.3:** Conceptual diagram of the behavior of customers when faced with a range of features and options. The majority of customers will be satisfied with a "complete" set of features, but few extras. As the number and cost of features increases, fewer and fewer customers will appreciate these add-ons enough to pay for them. The reverse is also true: Cheaper deliverables with less than complete feature sets will be of interest to a decreasing number of "bargain hunters."

We can use this new insight to perform some useful trade-offs. Maximizing the size of your market, for example, is best accomplished by offering a solid, middle-ground solution. This is also likely to be the point of revenue optimization (since generally we can't raise the price fast enough on feature-laden project deliverables to offset the shrinkage in the market). The point of gross-profit maximization might be higher in the feature curve, however, depending on how much the added features cost to include (software features, for example, may have little or no recurring cost). Thus, depending on what your firm desires more, revenues or profits, you can aim for a target feature-set to accomplish your goal.

The problem is that we often don't know which features determine price, and which are just added niceties. In Europe, for example, there is a growing market for hand-held Internet appliances. The simplicity of these devices seems to appeal to Europeans, who have been reluctant of late to embrace ever-more-complex PCs.[13] Unfortunately, some of these products have taken simplicity to the point of compromising functionality.[14] Eventually, competition will sort this all out, but it often takes several years for a preferred feature-set to emerge from the confusion of such a new market.

Here are some questions that can help you identify your project customer's least discernable difference:

*Question #1* – If you were to offer your customer the option of purchasing a project deliverable with or without a given feature, would the feature be included? Could you raise the price of the deliverable by adding this feature?

*Question #2* – If your customer were to rank all of the features of your project's deliverables in order of importance, would the feature in question be near the bottom of the list?

*Question #3* – Does the customer need to be educated about the feature in question, or was it part of their initial requirements?

*Question #4* – How much would the size of your market shrink if you were to leave this feature out of future proposals? How much would it shrink if you included the feature and raised the price accordingly?

*Question #5* – Can you explicitly connect the feature in question to a benefit (from the customer's perspective, not your own):
    A) Does it save time?
    B) Does it save money?
    C) Does it improve quality or useability?

You and your project team should continuously reevaluate your assumptions regarding features, options, and performance limits to ensure that the customer really needs or wants them. Remember that a feature is just an attribute of your project deliverable; it may or may not provide a customer benefit. As a general rule, *benefits affect price, whereas features impact market size and acceptance.* Thus the inclusion of a new feature or option always represents a trade-off among price, profit, and breadth of market.

## Countermeasure 1.4 – The One-Page Project Summary

This final countermeasure provides an easy and fun way for your team to pinpoint the highest value aspects of your project (those that determine price and market acceptance). The idea for this exercise comes from a method used by several leading firms, including HP, Compaq, Sony, and Canon.[15] These firms use a one-page project summary to perform initial opportunity screening and approve funding. On that single page is typically a brief description of the project, a listing of the customer benefits it provides, and estimates of profitability, price, etc. Again, brevity is seen as an ideal; only the most critically important aspects of a proposed project can fit on a single page.

We can convert this powerful project screening tool into an activity that your team can perform early in your next project. A template is provided in Figure M1.4 for a "press release." Imagine that you are announcing the successful completion of your project to *The Wall Street Journal* (or whatever trade publication makes sense for your industry). Since print space is limited, your press release must clearly define your project and entice future customers with tantalizing benefits, all on a single page. The usefulness of this exercise as a waste reduction method lies in the following: If a feature or performance parameter doesn't warrant inclusion in this press release, it is probably below the customer's radar screen for value (i.e., your team should not waste time and money enhancing that attribute).

The press release incorporates three important items: 1) A positioning statement, 2) A list of key benefits, and 3) A list of key features. The positioning statement is simply a one or two sentence description of what the project output looks like and what problem it solves for the customer. This sounds simple, but some interesting debate may occur when you try to tie your team down to such a concise definition of the project. Work through any disagreements; the main benefit of performing this press-release exercise is to get the entire team to agree and focus. If the goals of a project cannot be stated in a sentence or two, there is something wrong with the value proposition for the project. [16]

---

### *Press Release*

*For immediate release . . .*
*Your Site Location, (Today's Date) —*
    *The XYZ Company announced today the successful completion of the _____ project. This project provides _____*
*_____. The customer for this project,*
*_____, indicated in a recent interview that they selected XYZ as their supplier due to the following key benefits:*
        *1) _____*
        *2) _____*
        *3) _____*

*The customer for this project also identified several features that they felt were particularly useful. These include:*
        *1) _____*
        *2) _____*
        *3) _____*

*XYZ President, Jane Schmoo, noted that the single most important benefit of their successful project was "_____*
*_____*
*_____."*

---

**Figure M1.4:** Template for a "press release" that focuses a project team on the most important benefits and features of a project's deliverables. This exercise can be performed at the kick-off of a project to establish a clear team mission, and should be employed as a touchstone throughout the project to test whether value has been optimized.

The listing of only a few key benefits forces your team to recognize that most customers will look no further when making their buying decision. Even in the most complex engineering or aerospace projects, there are typically only a handful of really critical benefits. A new power station customer, for example, would be most interested in low cost per megawatt-hour, low emissions, and high return on capital investment. The fact that the power plant will be equipped with a brand new automation and control technology will only be of interest if it enables or enhances one of the above benefits.

Finally, it is worthwhile to identify the highest priority features of your project deliverable. Although they may not directly impact the price of your project, offering several varieties of a deliverable may help draw in customers who have unique needs or constraints. When Apple introduced their first wave of IMac personal computers, for example, they offered five color choices, not because it allowed them to increase the price, but because it would enable greater market acceptance. Key features represent enticements that will draw in new customers and help retain current ones.

Once your team has agreed upon the positioning, features, and benefits that reflect your customer's driving interests, use this information as an ongoing touchstone for project efficiency. At each project design or status review, trot out these few items and test for value. In this way you can be assured that the majority of the team's efforts will be appreciated and rewarded by your customer.

## Step-by-Step Implementation

The leverage of the "test for value" countermeasures is greatest at the early stages of a project, and in particular during proposal development and negotiations. Anytime a specification or other requirements document is being refined, these qualitative tools can provide practical insight. Remember that you shouldn't try to hit a perfect "value bull's eye." Rather you should use these countermeasures to avoid gross undershoot or overshoot of performance, features, or options. They are decision tools, not measurement tools: Use them to guide your choices and trade-offs once all available information has been considered.

## What You Will Need

For a typical application of these countermeasures, such as during specification negotiations, even a small amount of pre-work can be very valuable. You should try to gather as much information as possible on the cost impact of added features or increased performance. You will also want to query your customer, if possible, as to their constraints, interests, and preconceptions. Naturally, this should only be done for those specifications that are potentially challenging or costly. Don't worry if you have limited time to hunt for data. The highest value information generally presents itself early in the search process.

## Who You Will Need

In an ideal world, your team and your customer would sit across the table from each other and have meaningful dialog about features and performance. If that scenario is possible, then go for it. If you are not so lucky, you can make do with far less. The critical ingredient is that both sides of the decision must be represented. If you have a contract customer, they should be present. If you have an undefined customer (such as for products), someone with the proper perspective must play the market's advocate. Even a one-on-one meeting to test for value can work great, provided that the individuals involved have sufficient clout to enforce whatever agreement is reached.

*Step 1* – Gather the information and the people together in one place (or by phone / videoconference). If the countermeasures will be used as part of a broader design or spec review, there is no need for other preparation. If you plan to have a meeting specifically to search for waste in your project's deliverables, provide a description of the four countermeasures to participants in advance. From this point forward, I will assume that you are holding such a focused meeting.

*Step 2 –* Begin your meeting by establishing the outcome that you desire. Is it a list of specifications accompanied by optimized values? Is it a set of action items to investigate waste candidates more thoroughly? Remember that if you don't know what outcome you are trying to achieve, your meeting will be less than efficient (see Method #3). Whatever form of outcome you choose, make sure that it will have a tangible impact on the scope of work for your project.

*Step 3 –* You must next determine the driving benefits your customer desires. If your meeting is informal, try using some adaptation of Countermeasure 1.4. If a more formal atmosphere exists, simply have the group brainstorm on critical benefits, and then rank them on a subjective scale (e.g., one through ten, with ten being the greatest benefit). For large projects, you may wish to use a value-focusing tool such as Quality Function Deployment (QFD)[17] to gather this information.

*Step 4 –* Now agree on a list of the features, options, or performance specifications that are driving price. You don't need to be precise here; include anything that may be relevant. Keep the list to a manageable size, and if necessary use a subjective ranking process to prioritize and trim.

*Step 5 –* Finally, apply the tests for value. Using a format similar to the template provided in Figure M1.5, address each cost-driving item individually. First apply Countermeasure 1.1 by asking the group if there is any potential for overshoot of performance. Since much of this activity is subjective, you are really looking for hot prospects. If the group agrees that there is overshoot potential, discuss what actions would be required to define and eliminate the waste. Limit the discussion to just a few minutes per test; use an action list or "parking lot" to capture where more work is needed.

## Testing-for-Value Worksheet

| Attribute or Design Element Under Consideration | Subjective Rating (1-5 Scale) | | |
|---|---|---|---|
| | Overshoot | Complexity | Excess Features |
| | | | |
| | | | |
| | | | |
| | | | |
| | | | |
| | | | |
| | | | |
| | | | |
| | | | |
| | | | |
| | | | |

**Figure M1.5:** Template for a "Testing for Value" brainstorming meeting. The goal of such a meeting is to identify gross overshoot or undershoot of performance, and excessive complexity of project deliverables, and to highlight unnecessary features and options.

Proceed to Countermeasure 1.2 by asking the group if complexity has compromised cost or performance. Finally, address feature creep by justifying each optional feature in terms of its impact on the critical customer benefits for your project. The discussion must always touch on those three or four benefits that you identified in Step 3. Is added performance providing added benefit? Has a deliverable become too complex to meet one or more of the project's driving goals? Are added features increasing cost without impacting price? The process of asking these questions will almost certainly uncover waste-slashing opportunities for your team.

## How to Measure Success

The most important metric of success in the application of Method #1 is customer satisfaction. If you have "optimized" your project's profitability at the expense of a delighted customer, you have failed. The whole point of testing for value is to ensure that the customer gains full benefit from your work. Reducing costs and boosting margin by trimming valued features or performance is like "throwing the baby out with the bathwater."

Other metrics of success include: 1) Projected profit margin before and after testing for value, 2) Time or resources saved by eliminating non-value-added features or performance, 3) Reduction in project risk due to simplification of deliverables, etc. The bottom line is this: The closer you come to hitting the bull's eye of customer value, the better all of these critical metrics will look for your project. How's that for leverage?

## Testing for Customer Value

**Overview** – Provides several tests for value that enable project teams to reduce overshoot and undershoot of performance, deliverable complexity, and unnecessary features / options.

### Waste-Slashing Benefits

1) Eliminates wasted time and cost of excessive performance and complexity.
2) Helps discriminate those features and options that add value from those that don't.
3) Provides several techniques for focusing a team on the key attributes of a project deliverable that provide customer benefit and determine price.

**When to Apply** – At any point in the execution of a project, but early application will help avoid waste later in the process.

**Who Can Use It** – Can be used at the highest levels as a tool during contract negotiations, and at the level of the individual team member to optimize the value of intra-team transactions.

### Typical Implementation Profile

|  | Low | Med. | High |
|---|---|---|---|
| Non-Recurring Cost | X | | |
| Recurring Cost | X | | |
| Time to Implement | X | | |
| Need for Mgmt. Champion | | X | |
| Short-Term Benefits | | X | |
| Long-Term Benefits | | | X |

# Linked Tasks and Customer-Defined Deliverables

*"There is nothing so useless as doing efficiently that which should not be done at all."*
*—Peter Drucker*

First question: Does every activity or task performed on a project have a "deliverable?" In standard project management parlance, project deliverables represent the end-items that a contract customer receives. If we expand this definition a little, however, to include internal as well as external customers (i.e., other members of the team, management, regulatory agencies, etc.), then the answer to the above question is affirmative.[1] Every meeting, every support task, every funded activity should, *indeed must*, have a tangible output. Even if the deliverable is simply a decision (e.g., "Let's go with Design A instead of Design B"), it is still a measurable outcome.

Second question: If the above is true, then do all of those tasks or activities have customers? This one should be obvious. If each task or activity has a tangible output, then someone must be using that output to move the project forward. If this were not the case, then that task would be pure waste. Therefore, we can conclude:

***Every project task or activity has both a deliverable and a customer (either internal or external).***

We could, therefore, treat individual tasks as "mini-projects;" each one must satisfy its associated customer for the overall project to proceed successfully. In traditional project management, this relationship would be called a "task dependence," as shown in Figure M2.1. The problem with this terminology is that it implies a passive, almost "throw it over the wall" relationship between tasks and customers. Without some kind of *linkage* between dependant tasks, there are sure to be gaps, correction loops, errors, and omissions. Instead, a lean project should be thought of as a series of linked activities, *in which the customer for each output collaborates with the creator of that output to define format, content, and successful delivery.*

I'll share a personal horror story that illustrates how vital this idea of customer-defined deliverables can be. During my days in

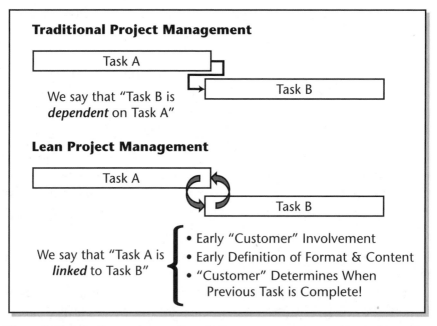

**Figure M2.1:** In the parlance of project management, we often refer to the connection between tasks as "dependencies." This can imply an "over-the-wall" connection between Task A and Task B. In Lean Project Management, we insist on tasks being "linked" such that the content and format of internal deliverables are developed collaboratively, and the Task B "customer" determines when Task A is officially complete.

aerospace, my team was responsible for developing an advanced computer that would become the "brain" for a military satellite. The computer consisted of a single, very dense circuit board that required a revolutionary fabrication technology. Only a sole supplier in all the world could perform this fabrication. Unfortunately, we didn't take the time to carefully define our interface with this fabricator. In particular, we failed to establish exactly how the design files must be formatted to interface with their automated fabrication line.

I'm sure you can guess the rest. After racing against time to complete the design, we found that the supplier's information system couldn't read our files. With the satellite's launch date only a few weeks away, we stumbled again and again, ultimately taking *three months* to complete the transfer of data. A critical launch date was missed, due to nothing more than a bad hand-off. If we had simply run a test file through the fabricator's system early in the project, we could have worked the bugs out in parallel and avoided a high-visibility failure. I hope the countermeasures that follow will help you avoid experiencing such a trauma first hand.

## Countermeasure 2.1 – Forming Task Linkages

The whole point of completing a task is to enable someone else to use the output you've created. Self-satisfaction is not a measure of success in project work; even for internal deliverables, it is *customer* satisfaction that counts. Fortunately, satisfying another member of your project team, or even your management, is considerably easier than putting a smile on the paying customer's face. After all, in principle at least, you are all on the same team.[2] Hence, there is really no excuse for "arm's length" relationships and "over-the-wall" hand-offs of internal deliverables.[3]

Consider a sports analogy. When athletes run a relay race, they must not only run their leg of the relay as fast as possible, they must also complete a successful hand-off to the next runner. All the speed in the world won't win the race if the baton is dropped. To avoid such a senseless loss, runners practice the hand-off repeatedly. As one leg of the relay is completed, the next runner begins to match pace with the first. They run side-by-side for a few steps to be sure they are in sync and then the baton is passed to the next runner, but not without a strong "tug" of assurance that the hand-off has been successfully completed.

This analogy perfectly illustrates the essential elements of a linked task:

- Early collaboration to define the exact needs of the task's customer (i.e., practicing the baton hand-off prior to a race).
- A brief period of collaboration upon task completion to ensure that the task team and their customer are in sync (i.e., matching pace with the next relay runner).
- A well-defined hand-off process (i.e., placing the baton firmly into the next runner's hand).
- Agreement by the customer that the transaction has been completed successfully (i.e., the strong tug by the next runner).

As with most of the countermeasures described in this book, any of the above elements will help reduce overshoot, undershoot, delays, and errors. If all these elements are in place, it will be virtually impossible for your team to drop the baton. The remaining countermeasures in this section will make it easy for you to link up your tasks and get value flowing smoothly on your project.

## Countermeasure 2.2 – Strawmanning & Early Prototyping

One of the most important elements in establishing linkages between tasks is to precisely define each task's deliverables in terms of the internal customer's needs. This can be a major pain, however, if the receiver of a task output has little idea of what an ideal deliverable should look like. We can resolve this dilemma through the use of strawman documents and early prototypes.

At the inception of a project task, the task leader could offer an example of what should be delivered to the task's customer. This might be a version of the same deliverable from a previous project, a rough generic outline, a quick-and-dirty model; anything that can serve as a starting point for refining the customer's needs. It is far easier to converge on a deliverable definition if you begin with something that is "close to the mark." This strawman (the term implies any document that is intended to be modified after feedback is received) or prototype might be iterated several times before agreement is reached, as shown in Figure M2.2. Although this requires a bit of up-front effort, the process is far less wasteful than the guesswork handoffs typical of many projects.

Projects that require regulatory approval can benefit from treating those agencies as customers from the very beginning of the project. Procter & Gamble, for example, is meticulous about

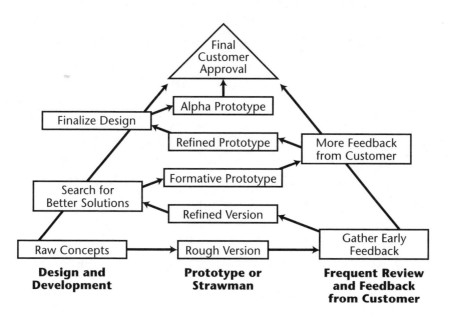

**Figure M2.2:** The best way to ensure that an internal or external deliverable satisfies its "customer" is to gather frequent iterative feedback. For straightforward transactions, little feedback is needed. For complex or uncertain deliverables, many feedback iterations should be used to avoid wasted effort and project delays.

defining all necessary approvals in advance of new product introduction, and treats regulatory forms and paperwork as important project deliverables. This has enabled P & G to accelerate their product launches by months and even years. In another example, by treating the Federal Aviation Administration (FAA) as a customer, Boeing has been able to incorporate regulatory requirements into their front-end design work. This approach resulted in elimination of a two-year test cycle during development of the 777 aircraft.[4]

Early prototyping and strawmanning of deliverables is particularly useful for complex activities such as software development.[5] Software teams can use "throw away" prototypes to gain early feedback on high-risk features or performance.[6] Prototyping the user interface is particularly important for establishing customer expectations and refining system requirements. In fact, early and frequent prototyping or strawmanning can draw even the most reluctant internal or external customers into more of a partnership relationship.[7] The enhanced feedback that such a partnership provides can enable a task team to move quickly and precisely toward meeting its value-creating objectives.

## Countermeasure 2.3 – Feed-Forward of Information

As the completion of a task approaches, there are steps that can be taken to dramatically accelerate a successful hand-off. For relatively complicated deliverables (ones that require significant time for the customer to review and approve) a feed-forward technique can be used, as shown previously in Figure 3.5. A nearly complete version of the deliverable can be provided to the task's customer a few weeks prior to "final" delivery. An early feed allows the customer to pre-review the deliverable in parallel with the last stages of task completion. This enables efficient incorporation of last minute fixes, and will significantly shorten the approval cycle once a final version is ready for review. Upon completion, you can simply provide the customer with an "errata" sheet of the differences between the document or item they reviewed and the final version.

A feed-forward approach should be used anytime a relatively formal approval is required before the project can move forward. A document subject to approval by quality assurance, for example, could be fed forward to the quality engineer in plenty of time for a careful review. Last minute tweaks could be addressed in a quick "sign-off" meeting at the end of the task. Other examples include providing management with an early feed of capital requirements so that approval of funding requests won't become an obstacle to the flow of value. Even the external customer (in appropriate cases) can be given near-complete project deliverables to review and provide "punch lists" of required changes. In all cases, bringing the customer early into the approval process minimizes wasted time and enables a clean, efficient hand-off.[8]

## Countermeasure 2.4 – Eliminating Approval Delays

The last countermeasure in this section attacks the final obstacle to lean closure of a task; gaining sign-off of the completed item. I'll be blunt about this one: Too many firms have allowed long approval cycles to become a substitute for effective management practices. If your firm's management is counting on approvals to ensure that work is being done properly, they are institutionalizing both a tremendous source of waste and a culture of mistrust. I believe that formal approvals (i.e., signatures by managers on approval lines) are required on only three types of project transactions:

- Contractual and legal commitments by the firm, as required by customers or regulatory agencies.
- Commitment of financial resources to fund activities outside of the firm (or in some cases, the funding of internal development or improvement projects).
- Any routine customer correspondence by project team members that impacts topics broader than the immediate project at hand.

In all other cases, a review and concurrence cycle (*sans* signatures) is sufficient to gather feedback and keep people informed. If you have a handful of signature lines on internal project documents, *get rid of them.* At most, the author of a document and the immediate internal customer should sign on the bottom line. All others are bystanders who can add the same value through more informal means.

Whether formal approval or informal feedback is required, we should always use the "star method" presented earlier in Figure 2.2.[9] The least-waste way for approvals goes something like this. The creator of a deliverable provides a copy (assuming it is reproducible) simultaneously to all individuals on the approval or review list. For documents, this can best be done by posting the file on an intranet page and having people "pull" the information. A fixed time period should be specified for return of comments and feedback; I like 48 hours, but use your own judgment here. After comments are received, a revised version is created along with a list of changes, and the deliverable is resubmitted for final review. If nothing is heard from reviewers within the specified period, their approval is assumed.

I know what you are thinking. Yes, this approach requires trust and discipline. Yes, it is a political challenge to implement. Yes, it precludes any shred of "cover your ＿＿＿" mentality. I won't deny it; attacking the approval process in your firm is like eating an elephant; you need to take small bites over a long time. That being said, any progress in this direction will reduce one of the most insidious root causes of waste in any firm: a culture of mistrust and the denial of responsibility. Progress along this path will pay handsome dividends along all others.

### Step-by-Step Implementation

The following steps will guide you toward establishing low-waste, high-fidelity linkages between project tasks. The first place to focus your efforts should be on major, critical-path tasks that drive your project's overall schedule: development of a specification, for example, or the creation of a bill-of-materials, drawing package, or construction plan. The best time to establish these linkages is during the early planning stages of a project, but anytime is the right time if your project is already underway. Pick two or three key hand-offs for the first implementation of this method. Gain some experience (and perhaps establish a template or two for future projects, see Method #8) and then use your success as a launching pad for deployment on every future project.

## What You Will Need

You can begin implementation with little or no advanced preparation, but the following items will help make the process move more efficiently. (Note that the discussion that follows focuses on establishing *internal* task linkages.)

- A "strawman" example of the deliverable in question, either from a past project or from your best understanding of the customer's requirements.
- An estimate of how long the creation of the deliverable will take, when it should be completed, and when might a preliminary feed forward of information be available.
- A determination of the format that would be most efficient for the delivery. This might entail discussions with your Information Technology (IT) department if CAD files or other proprietary data forms are involved.

## Who You Will Need

All that is typically needed to form a linkage are two face-to-face (or video conference) meetings between the task leader and the task customer. The first meeting takes place as early in the project as possible. The second meeting should occur when the deliverable is completed and ready for receipt and verification by the customer. Others who might contribute to this process might include the overall project leader, selected members of the task team, and an IT representative if appropriate.

***Step 1*** – Upon initiation of a task, the responsible person meets with those individuals who will use the task's output. At this meeting, an agreement is reached as to what the output should include, the format for that output, and how the transaction will take place. For example, a design engineer might meet with test engineers to define the items to be included in a test plan, the format for parameters and ranges, and the method for transferring this deliverable to the test group. Special care should be taken to ensure that a common language of units, acronyms, symbols, etc. is understood by both sides of the transaction. (Here a "strawmanning" process can be used, see Countermeasure 2.2)

***Step 2*** – If the linkage between tasks is one that will be repeated frequently, either on the current project or on future projects, then it may be worthwhile to create a *template or checklist* (see Method #8) that "standardizes" the deliverable. This will save time and reduce errors on all future transactions of this type. For example, a test plan template could be created that would give design and test engineers a starting point for defining a specific project's test needs.

***Step 3*** – Once the format and content have been agreed upon, the task progresses normally until a few weeks (depending on the length of the task) prior to completion. At this point, consider whether a feed forward of the nearly completed deliverable would reduce the review and approval time upon final delivery (See Countermeasure 2.3). If a feed forward is to be used, make it clear to reviewers which sections are essentially frozen and which are still under development.

***Step 4*** – Once the deliverable is complete, a meeting should be held between the task leader and the customer. At this meeting, the completeness of the deliverable should be verified and any questions answered. If a feed forward was used, provide the customer with an errata sheet of the changes that occurred between the preliminary and final deliverables.

*Step 5* – The customer approves the deliverable, and the task that created it is complete. If multiple approvals are required, use the star method mentioned in Countermeasure 2.4. *Note that a task is not considered to be complete until its customer(s) agree that it is complete.*

## How to Measure Success

There are several quantitative metrics that you can use to track your success in implementing task linkages and customer-defined deliverables. The first is the length of approval cycles. Put a time stamp on a typical capital request or other important document and see how long the approval cycle really takes. Then apply the above countermeasures and you'll be amazed at the time savings.

Another excellent metric is on-time completion of deliverable hand-offs. This one requires you to compare the "old way" of arm's length transactions to the "new way" of linked tasks and customer-approved deliveries. You could begin by measuring on-time completion of intermediate deliveries on projects with and without applying the countermeasures. You could also monitor the number of correction or omission loop-backs that occur prior to a successful hand-off.

One final comment. In terms of impact on the success of a project, we should not forget the most important linkage of all: a project charter agreement between management and team. A project charter defines the key constraints and critical targets that will determine a successful project.[10] Work this linkage early, continuously, and aggressively. Building a tight but flexible bond between management and the project team is pivotal to achieving short-term project efficiency and long-term growth and profitability.

## Method #2 at a Glance

# Linked Tasks and Customer-Defined Deliverables

**Overview** – By involving the "customer" for a task's deliverable (either internal or external) in the definition of that deliverable, we can eliminate wasted loop-backs, errors, overshoot of content, and incomplete hand-offs. Linked tasks enable smooth and efficient transactions and predictable schedules.

## Waste-Slashing Benefits
1) Elimination of error-correction loops.
2) Avoidance of overshoot or undershoot of contents.
3) Improved schedule control and predictability.

**When to Apply** – This method can be applied to every important transaction on your project. Anytime one task is dependant on another for a feed of information or materials, this technique can reduce the time and cost of that hand-off.

**Who Can Use It** – Task leaders are the most frequent users of this method, but anyone who creates deliverables for use by others should apply the countermeasures presented herein.

## Typical Implementation Profile

|  | Low | Med. | High |
|---|---|---|---|
| Non-Recurring Cost | X | | |
| Recurring Cost | X | | |
| Time to Implement | X | X | |
| Need for Mgmt. Champion | X | | |
| Short-Term Benefits | | X | |
| Long-Term Benefits | | | X |

# Urgency-Driven
# Stand-Up Meetings

*"Meetings are indispensable when*
*you don't want to do anything. "*
*—John Kenneth Galbraith*

D o meetings create value? In other words, is all that time you
spend bouncing from staff meeting to coordination meeting to customer meeting to status meeting really necessary?
Absolutely not. In fact, according to a recent survey by
researchers at 3M, the average executive spends one-and-a-half
days per week in meetings, and judges no more than half that
time to be productive.[1] The rest of the time is squandered waiting for people to show up, waiting for your topic of interest,
waiting for the endless tangential discussions to die down, etc.
And this assumes that there is a legitimate reason for the meeting in the first place.

Scott Adams, the author of *The Dilbert Principle*, received an e-
mail from one of his readers that went something like this: "A
guy at my work actually came into a meeting that had nothing
to do with his department. When asked what he was doing there
he said that he just didn't feel like he was 'working' unless he was
in a meeting, and this was the only one going on in the building
that day."[2] In some industries, this "meeting culture" is so perva-
sive that the only times available for real work are nights and
weekends. Unfortunately, we can't eliminate meetings entirely
(as much as this may seem tempting); group communication is

central to the successful execution of any project. On the other hand, are we *really* communicating in all those poorly run meetings?

The countermeasures described in this section attack this monumental cause of frustration and wasted time for project teams. Basically there are only two legitimate reasons for gathering people around a conference table: either to *coordinate* or to *collaborate*. Coordination is the process of connecting together the actions of a group so that they remain focused on a specific goal. In the case of a project team, coordination generally consists of determining what tasks people will be starting or completing in the near future, and what information or materials they will need from others to execute those activities. Technical issues should not be discussed in coordination meetings; their sole purpose is to facilitate execution of the project plan.

Collaboration meetings are very different animals. In collaborative meetings, knowledge is shared, trade-offs are made, decisions are arbitrated, and technical problems are solved. Collaboration requires in-depth discussion, whereas coordination demands only a top-level overview. Collaboration may only involve a few specific individuals, whereas coordination is most effective when all interested parties are involved. Collaboration meetings should be event-driven (meaning that they should be scheduled based on the occurrence of a specific problem or need), whereas coordination meetings should be urgency-driven (implying that their frequency should reflect the pressures of the project schedule). In short, coordination and collaboration meetings are different, *and therefore should be handled as separate project activities.*

Our first salvo in the battle to eliminate wasteful meetings has been fired. We are going to abandon the ossified institutions of "weekly project coordination meetings" and "regular technical meetings." Instead, we will treat meetings as the project tasks they are; scheduled based on urgency or need, focused on creating valuable deliverables, and executed in a lean and efficient way. No longer will meetings be the plague of your daily planner. Well . . . at least we can make them slightly more pleasant than a root canal.

## Countermeasure 3.1 – Stand-Up Coordination Meetings

Coordination meetings represent the "drum beat" of a project. A rapid, driving beat will impart energy and urgency onto a team,[3] whereas a leisurely (read here "weekly") beat signals that things can wait for a few days here and there. Yet the weekly coordination meeting is an institution in most firms, making it the most common form of time batch in project management. If you don't believe that a time batch of just one week can be wasteful, consider Figure M3.1. When is the work that is reported in a coordination meeting actually performed? Typically the

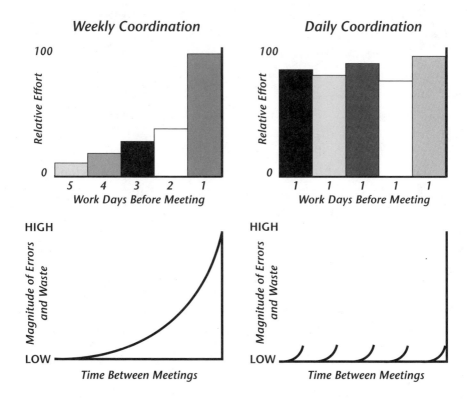

**Figure M3.1:** When is most of the work that is reported in a "weekly team meeting" actually performed? With frequent coordination, work is apportioned more evenly throughout the week, and a focus on creating real value can more easily be maintained. The lower portion of the figure demonstrates another key benefit of frequent coordination; a reduction in the impact of errors or changes on team efficiency.[4]

day before the meeting – or perhaps even ten minutes before. People skew their entire workweek based on when they must report progress . . . implying that the rest of their time is focused elsewhere, or perhaps not focused at all. Furthermore, if a mistake, error, or change occurs in the interim between meetings, there is a strong tendency for team members to hold that information until the next weekly forum. During that holding period, however, a lot of work is being performed by other team members. Much of that work might prove to be fruitless if the reported error affects their work.

The combination is insidious: A tendency to perform work in leisurely, weekly batches, combined with delays in reporting critical errors and changes. The best way to recognize this is to imagine that you are driving a car with an unusual steering problem. The steering wheel has a one-minute delay; turn the wheel, and a minute goes by before the car reacts. This dangerous delay allows you only two choices. Either you can drive very slowly to avoid having an airbag moment, or you can gun the engine and pray that things will work out. It would be so much easier, safer, and more efficient if the car's steering responded immediately to your needs. Is this not also true when "steering" the actions of your project team?

Frequent, even daily coordination of a project team can yield a multitude of benefits at essentially no cost. The trick is to jettison the old idea of an hour-plus formal meeting in favor of quick, intense stand-up meetings. I have seen this technique yield startling results in dozens of firms spanning virtually every industry. In fact, of all of the countermeasures presented in this book, I recommend that you try this one first. You will not be disappointed.

Here's how stand-up coordination meetings can be deployed on your project. First pick a point in your schedule that requires high levels of coordination (e.g., preparation for a design review, initial prototype testing, key customer delivery, etc.). It is important to remember that the benefits of frequent coordination are only realized if your project is entering a period of intense activity. Urgency should be the driver for the frequency of meetings.

During early planning and concept development stages, for example, a weekly or twice-weekly format might be more than adequate. As the intensity of interactivity increases, however, daily coordination becomes a mandate.

Use the pressure of an important upcoming milestone as an excuse for introducing a daily stand-up meeting with the entire team. The meeting should take place at a time that is convenient for the majority, but I suggest either at starting time (i.e., 8:00 a.m. sharp) or just before lunch (i.e., 11:45 a.m.). The location should also be convenient for the majority, and have sufficient space to accommodate all the members of your team. Finally, *the duration of your stand-up coordination meeting should be no more than ten minutes*, or alternatively, no more than one minute per attendee.

This last mandate is the key to making this countermeasure work. If these stand-up meetings are as wearisome as the weekly ones, we will be far worse off. Instead, the meetings should consist of a brief visit with each person to answer three simple questions:

- What value did they create yesterday?
- What are their plans for today?
- What do they need from the rest of the team (or others) to accomplish their value-creating objectives?

The point is not to engage in lengthy discussions, nor to micromanage. Only essential coordination information is shared. Any technical or other important issues should be captured in a "parking lot" (usually a white board or flip-chart easel) for future collaborative meetings. Literally, the facilitator (who could be any member of the team, not just the team leader) should demand that the team members, "present only things we don't already know." If team members are spread out geographically, a dial-in teleconference can be used (don't waste time and expense on video conferencing for a simple coordination meeting). Team members in other time zones can be contacted separately by the team leader and their inputs and needs shared with the main meeting each day.

Beyond the obvious benefit of imparting a sense of urgency to team communication, frequent stand-up meetings offer at least six additional benefits, as shown in Figure M3.2. These efficient meetings provide an invaluable opportunity for your project team to develop a shared language. Each discipline has a chance to hear what all other disciplines are doing, with a focus on the linkages and needs of each function. Moreover, if a language barrier is detected it can be rapidly rectified.

→ Creates a shared language among team members

→ Allows for real-time reallocation of resources

→ Enables a focus on value-creating activities

→ Establishes a clear work plan for each day

→ Provides a mechanism for cultural change

→ Builds team identity and emotional commitment

**Figure M3.2:** Six critical benefits of using frequent stand-up coordination meetings during periods of intense activity on your project.

The second powerful benefit is the ability to reallocate your resources almost instantly. This enables immediate adaptation to change, helps the team to absorb shocks, and provides a great way to handle fire fighting and sustaining engineering emergencies. The third benefit of urgency-driven stand-up meetings is that they provide a mechanism for focusing the team on value-creating work. It is easy for lots of waste to creep into a week's worth of project work. It's much harder for waste to accumulate if priorities and progress are reported daily. A designer that just can't let go of a drawing will experience continuous peer pressure to wrap it up. Those fire fighting requests from senior management can be addressed quickly, smoothly, and non-invasively. Finally, any missing information or lack of cooperation will be put in the spotlight every morning, ripe for resolution by the team.

The fourth benefit of frequent informal coordination is that each team member leaves the meeting with a clear work plan for the day. Working on the right things, at the right times, with all the information needed to proceed, is the essence of efficient project work. Frequent coordination forces team members to carve their tasks into smaller work packages, and report steady progress rather than batched milestones.[5] The improvement in team productivity due to just this single factor is amazing. Knowing what to work on and being allowed to do that work . . . what a concept![6]

The final two benefits support the "soft side" of team productivity. Daily stand-up meetings have become a central part of the work culture in many firms. These ten-minute quickies provide employees with frequent opportunities to see their boss, hear critical issues, close the loop with co-workers, take pride in their successes, and receive balm for their failures. The entire workday in some companies revolves around what happens in these meetings. Workers feel increased commitment to their teammates, since they are frequently reminded of the importance and interdependence of their work. They become emotionally committed to making their project a smashing success. After all, productivity starts with the commitment of the team, and daily meetings provide a fertile ground for gaining this emotional buy-in.

A few examples of daily coordination in action are warranted before I close this discussion. Most of you probably recall the opening to the old TV show, *Hill Street Blues*. The precinct sergeant would call roll and go through assignments, announcements, and major new crimes. This quick roll-call meeting represented a daily "stand-up meeting" for the officers; a vital necessity when conditions in a precinct can change overnight.

In manufacturing companies, daily coordination is often a morning ritual on the factory floor. A brief stand-up meeting before each shift change allows for last minute modifications to the production mix, along with disposition of repairs, maintenance, improvements, and assignment of other responsibilities. Finally, in the software industry many firms are following Microsoft's lead by using "daily build and synchronize" events to ensure that parallel code development is always well coordinated.[7,8] These daily build meetings are not an option; they have become a mandatory work rule at many software companies.[9]

### Countermeasure 3.2 – Three-Tier Project Planning

We can easily extend this concept of daily project coordination to encompass our entire approach to schedule and task management. All we need is a simple action-tracking sheet, like the one shown near the bottom of Figure M3.3. This action list is not intended to track the day-to-day minutia; it is a listing of the critical deliverables and milestones that a project team faces over the next two-week period. At the beginning of each week, the team leader updates the action list to include another week of schedule milestones, thereby providing a two-week "rolling window" of visibility for the team. During daily stand-up meetings, this action list can be used as a touchstone for progress on critical items. As milestones are achieved, they are removed from the list. If an important new event is identified, it can be added to the list for future tracking.

The beauty of this approach to progress monitoring is that you will need no other mechanism to manage your entire project schedule (and earned-value plan, for that matter, if one exists). The daily meetings and action-tracking sheet represent Tier 3 of a three-tier approach to lean schedule management. When milestones are reported as completed or delayed, this information can be folded upward into a three-month detailed project plan (Tier 2). As each month passes, the detailed schedule is expanded to include another month, always providing a three-month rolling window of in-depth planning.

The reason for performing detailed scheduling of tasks only a few months into the future should be obvious. On most projects, things will change so much in three months that any detailed planning beyond that point would be so much nonsense. Instead, simply maintain a Tier 1 "work package" plan that identifies key customer milestones and major tasks. Note

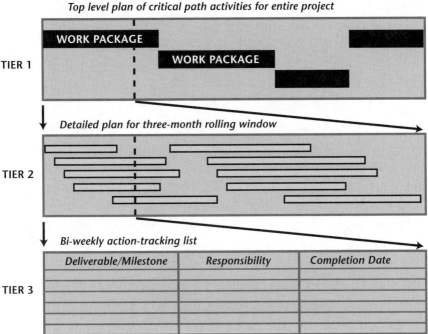

**Figure M3.3:** A three-tier approach to maintaining a project schedule. The first tier is an overview schedule that consists of just milestones and large work packages. The second tier expands the first into a detailed three-month rolling-window schedule. The third tier is simply an action-tracking sheet that is maintained and updated in your team's stand-up coordination meetings.

that you should select a length of rolling window for Tiers 2 and 3 that makes sense for your project. Quick turn projects might use only a one-week window for daily meetings and a one-month window for detailed planning. A reasonably stable, long-term construction job, on the other hand, might use a one-month window for stand-ups and a six-month window for Tier 3. However you adapt this countermeasure, it is sure to reduce planning and statusing time, while providing a solid connection between the master schedule for your project and what your team is actually doing each day.

## Countermeasure 3.3 – Lean Collaboration Meetings

Now that we have an effective method for handling project coordination, we must deal with meetings in which collaboration takes place. The approach that I propose for collaborative meetings has proven to be effective in many firms. It does, however, require a bit of culture change to be broadly accepted. Collaboration, just like any other funded project activity, must be deliverables-driven. A meeting is non-value-added unless some tangible deliverable (e.g., a decision, outcome, trade-off, action list, etc.) is generated that impacts the end results of the project.

In this countermeasure, I suggest a set of rules for collaborative meetings that can dramatically increase their value, as shown in Figure M3.4. These rules are rooted in common sense, but may clash at first with your firm's work environment. In many firms, there is an air of complacency about meetings that may make it hard to convince people that real discipline is needed. Fundamentally, people need to view meetings as *exceptions* rather than the rule. Regularly scheduled meetings with lots of invitees and an endless agenda are part of an outdated, operations-driven culture. Intense, ad hoc gatherings that are scheduled when the need arises are fundamental to a project-driven enterprise.[10] We should always keep in mind that meetings take people away from performing *real* work.

The first recommended rule for executing a lean collaborative meeting is to restrict its duration to no more than one hour (with the possible exception of design reviews or customer meetings). In one firm that I work with, administrators actually kick people out of conference rooms after their hour is up and lock the doors. I have found after twenty-something years of managing projects that there are very few issues that cannot be addressed in an hour. Without a time limit, meetings will grow to consume the space allowed and will often fail to generate a useful outcome.

To make a one hour time limit possible, I suggest a second rule: Address only a single topic (or a few closely related topics) in each meeting. I believe that multi-topic agendas covering widely ranging subjects are a breeding ground for waste. By focusing on a single topic, you will be able to select the right

**Rule #1.** Restrict meeting to no more than one hour.

**Rule #2.** Have only a *single*, or several closely related, agenda items.

**Rule #3.** Only invite those people who have a need to be there ON TIME . . . all others are NOT WELCOME.

**Rule #4.** Provide pre-work in advance.

**Rule #5.** Do not begin until everyone in the room agrees on the "deliverables" for the meeting.

**Rule #6.** Any tangential issues or comments are recorded in a "parking lot" for future discussion.

**Figure M3.4:** A few simple rules to follow when facilitating collaborative meetings. When used in concert, these rules will eliminate a great deal of wasted time.

people (and only the right people) to attend. Moreover, the entire meeting can be directed toward a clear goal, thereby reducing the number of tangential discussions. Finally, you can eliminate that most wasteful of all individuals; the meeting sitter. Rule three states that only people with value to contribute should attend a meeting. These individuals should show the courtesy of being on time, and should be admonished if they are late. Most important; meeting sitters are not welcome. Non-essential individuals can slow a meeting down, and can potentially add unnecessary cost to your project. Uninvited attendees should be asked to leave. After all, from a management perspective, an employee sitting in an inappropriate meeting is no different than that person taking a nap in their car for an hour.

Pre-work should be provided for meetings that will refer to a documented body of information. This can be attached to the e-mail notification for the meeting, or can take the form of a few hyperlinks or file names of documents to be reviewed prior to the meeting. Peer pressure should be brought to bear on any team member who fails to prepare properly. No meeting time should be spent on catching individuals up or reviewing known material.

The most important rule by far is rule five. *Every collaborative meeting must begin with a definition of what the outcome should be.* What tangible deliverable are we creating here? What form should it take? Who will document it? Who is the customer for it? How will it affect our project's success? This is not as time-consuming as it sounds. Just a one or two sentence informal statement is enough. For example:

- We are here to review technical data and decide on which option to move forward with. The deliverable is a brief statement documenting our decision, which will be provided to management and our contract customer.

- We are here to look over recent test data and decide on what actions need to be taken. The deliverable is a prioritized list of recommended actions, with names and dates assigned, which will be provided to the project manager.

- The purpose of our meeting is to assess the risk of changing suppliers for some critical materials. The deliverable is a brief risk assessment and recommendation statement, which will be provided to our procurement representative for the project.

The reason why the fifth rule is so important is that once such a statement is in place (naturally, you should only spend a couple of minutes on this), the remainder of your meeting can be laser-focused on creating that deliverable. Any tangential issues, important or otherwise, should be captured in a "parking lot" and addressed in subsequent meetings. Hence, the final rule enforces a strict "no sidetrack" mandate for the group. Make the required deliverable happen and get back to work; that should be the anthem of every project meeting.

## Step-by-Step Implementation

The good news is that implementation is easy; the hard part will be getting your team and your management to accept the change. Frequent stand-up meetings will take a little getting used to, but ultimately your team will love them. Lean collaborative meetings are harder to institutionalize, since organizations tend to backslide into less disciplined behaviors over time. Don't fret if you can't gain overnight acceptance. Even a few modest improvements to your firm's meeting culture can relieve schedule pressures and improve team morale and responsiveness.

## What You Will Need

For Countermeasures 3.1 and 3.2 you will need an action tracking list similar to the one shown at the bottom of Figure M3.3. You will also need to select an upcoming event or milestone that is sufficiently scary that your team will accept the need for daily coordination. Naturally, if you run your project like a dictatorship (not necessarily a bad thing), a motivating event will not be needed.

For Countermeasure 3.3, you could really benefit from some buy-in by executive management. A "policy statement" by a business-unit executive wouldn't hurt the credibility of your initiative. You will also need to perform some informal training. An in-firm video that shows an example of a lean collaboration meeting can be very effective.

## Who You Will Need

Who indeed? For lean coordination meetings you would like to have all interested parties present, either in person or by phone. If this is not possible, consider using several smaller groups that meet daily and exchange information every few days. In general, you shouldn't try to coordinate groups over about fifteen people. If your project team is larger than this number, divide the team into logical chunks and have subordinates run separate daily coordination meetings. You can then meet with the subordinates and cross-pollinate information.

For lean collaborative meetings, you should select invitees that can measurably contribute to creating the desired deliverable for that meeting. More important, you should be sure to invite a "critical mass" of individuals that are capable of reaching a valid conclusion. One problem with holding meetings on an as-needed basis is that people's schedules may not sync up. To avoid holding meetings with less than a quorum, try asking all team members to block out several common "meeting slots" in their weekly schedule. These slots can be reserved for meetings until the beginning of each week and then released if not needed.

The following steps apply to running a stand-up coordination meeting with your project team:

*Step 1* – All attendees are present at the designated place and time. By the way, people can sit down at a stand-up meeting, provided that they don't get too comfortable. (Keep the doughnuts and newspapers out of reach).

*Step 2* – The meeting is called to order. The meeting facilitator makes some brief announcements that are of general interest (one minute).

*Step 3* – The facilitator issues an action list for the week (assuming that this is a Monday meeting).

*Step 4* – The facilitator asks each team member, in turn, to report his or her status. This means that each person answers three questions: 1) What work did they complete yesterday? 2) What will they work on today? 3) What information, help, or materials do they need to proceed? Each person should also report the status of any near-term action items that they are responsible for (one minute per person).

*Step 5* – Other issues or topics are captured on a parking-lot board. After all coordination is complete, these items are quickly dispositioned. Those not interested in these issues can leave the meeting (two minutes). Note that if there is little or no new information being communicated in your stand-up meetings, you should ask the team whether the frequency should be reduced. Let the team own the meeting, but be sure that you increase the frequency again as the next critical milestone approaches.

## How to Measure Success

There are certainly ways to measure the time savings that can be gained from these countermeasures. I wouldn't bother if I were you. Remember my previous quote by Henry Ford. When he was asked by his financial executive to justify a huge new investment in production improvements, his response was, "The benefits are so obvious that it isn't worth the cost to quantify them." Try these countermeasures out for a month or two and you will be convinced of their effectiveness. If you still have a burning need to quantify something, you can use the time you save in meetings to measure more interesting stuff.

## Method #3 at a Glance

# Urgency-Driven Stand-Up Meetings

**Overview** – Meetings can be an enormous drain on project productivity. This method provides simple techniques and rules that enable highly efficient coordination meetings and effective and brief collaborative meetings.

**Waste-Slashing Benefits**
1) Reduction in wasted time due to poorly run meetings.
2) Improved project coordination and communication.
3) Acceleration of project work rate.
4) Ability to reallocate resources rapidly and precisely.

**When to Apply** – Every project meeting (including customer meetings) should follow the simple guidelines described here. The highest value application is during periods of intense collaborative work that require frequent and effective communication.

**Who Can Use It** – Anyone responsible for leading a project status review, coordination meeting, or other team gathering.

**Typical Implementation Profile**

|  | Low | Med. | High |
|---|---|---|---|
| **Non-Recurring Cost** | X | | |
| **Recurring Cost** | X | | |
| **Time to Implement** | X | | |
| **Need for Mgmt. Champion** | X | | |
| **Short-Term Benefits** | | X | |
| **Long-Term Benefits** | | X | |

# Real / Virtual
# Project Rooms

*"Almost all people are intelligent.*
*It is method that they lack."*
—F. W. Nichol

Sometimes a great idea is just lying there right under your nose. The method described here is just such a jewel. In many industries, particularly in aerospace, responding to requests for proposal (RFPs) is a way of life. Proposal teams are pulled together on a moment's notice, and are often given only a few weeks to respond. Under these demanding circumstances, proposal teams often set up a "war room" to improve efficiency and coordination. The proposal war room is a designated physical location (usually a confiscated conference room) in which all current materials associated with the effort are located. The most recent versions of proposal chapters might be hung on the walls in paper envelops. Drawings, mockups, pictures, customer correspondence – everything relevant to the proposal can be found at this one location. Needless to say, you can also find most of the proposal team in their war room, day or night.

I suggest a more politically correct name (let's call it a "project room") but the idea is the same. Each major project in your firm should have a central repository for documents and materials that is easily accessible to all team members. Perhaps more important; every document that is located in this project room is, *by definition*, the most current released version. Centralized information access combined with effective version control are a powerful duo. Think of all the wasted time you could eliminate hunting for information, sorting through multiple versions, or using obsolete documents.

Ah, but your hand is raised. "We don't have enough room at our facility to set up dedicated project rooms," you say. "We don't have enough office space to give everyone a desk, and our only conference room is booked day and night with (over-long, non-value-added) meetings." Well, technology has come to save the day. Yes, major projects should indeed have dedicated physical project rooms. *All projects*, however, should have a "virtual" project room. A project-specific web page on your firm's intranet (if you don't have an intranet, then substitute "a folder on your network server") is a great alternative to a physical venue, as discussed in Countermeasure 4.2.

Furthermore, with teams these days spread out over multiple cultures and time zones, the need for an electronic "shared space" has become compelling.[1] A virtual project room can become a catalyst for global team collaboration and information sharing, enabling both immediate access and effective version control of documents. If your stock price is up, your firm could consider deploying the latest "workgrouping" software packages that enable real-time collaboration. Even if your software budget is non-existent, however, a small-scale implementation can be achieved. If your firm has a website, you are already halfway there, so don't be intimidated. The countermeasures in this section are easy, valuable, and immediately effective . . . but then again, so are all the others.

## Countermeasure 4.1 – Physical Project Room

The idea of establishing a physical location to serve as the epicenter of project information sharing and collaboration is attractive. You can hear the echo of collocation in this first countermeasure, except that in this case, we are extending the concept to include centralized information as well as people. In fact, even when office logistics (or politics) makes collocation of a team impossible, a physical project room can provide many of the same benefits.

It is not necessary to allocate a big conference room or bullpen for this purpose. Depending on the size of your team, you may wish to try a more modest approach; for example, a roll-away cork board can do the trick for smaller projects.[2] All that is necessary is that a single location be identified for all project documents and information, and that a system of revision control by calendar date be instituted. Your "project room" could be just a file cabinet somewhere, an out-of-the-way corner of your building, or even a team member's office.

The general structure of a physical project room is shown in Figure M4.1 (this assumes a large project that is deserving of a dedicated space). Visual communication should be used wherever possible (see Method #7). In other words, try to use symbols, colors, graphics, or other visual means to make the project room easy to use and foolproof to update.[3] A table might be provided at the center, as long as it doesn't become the gathering point for a coffee clutch. White boards and cork boards line the walls, with designated slots, locations, or envelops for various types of information. A computer terminal should be provided to allow access to data files, and enable a link to your project's virtual

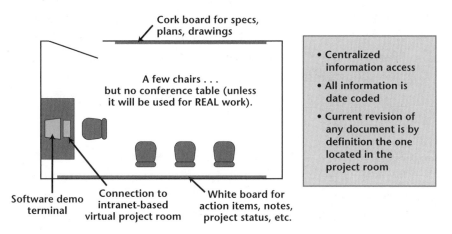

**Figure M4.1:** A suggested structure for a physical project room. The goal is to create a shared space that is a repository for critical documents, prototypes, and other commonly used information.

project room (see Countermeasure 4.2). Teleconferencing and possibly video conferencing capabilities should also be provided if the project involves external stakeholders.

Clearly this idea is not new; dozens of firms commonly use one version or another of this countermeasure. National Semiconductor and Polaroid, for example, have set up shared spaces for teams to use as collaboration areas.[4] A number of aerospace firms, including Boeing, Aerojet, Hughes, and Lockheed Martin use dedicated project rooms for major contracts. Companies in the engineering services industry (e.g., power plant construction, IT system integration, etc.) often use centralized "staging areas" at their own facilities to integrate, test, and validate systems prior to installation. At Invensys, a control system integrator, the system staging area has been supplemented with several roll-out boards that contain current information, action items, key milestones, etc. The message here is that you may already be using project rooms and don't even know it.

One final comment before we move on. As discussed in the next section, the emergence of our digital world has all but eliminated the need for a physical location for documents. Today, "virtual" project rooms are really the answer for document control and centralized information access. That being said, the idea of a physical locus for your project team still has merit. What better place to hold your stand-up coordination meetings, for example? I suggest that you consider the trade-offs. If space at your facility is as scarce as hen's teeth, go directly to Countermeasure 4.2. If your project warrants some extra square footage, however, the project room concept can enable you to use that space wisely.

## Countermeasure 4.2 – Virtual Project Room

There are many ways in which information technology can improve project team productivity, but none surpass the virtual project room for value and simplicity. Create a central data repository for all information, documents, drawings, schedules, etc., that is accessible to the entire team, anywhere in the world.[5] Now use this repository as a control point for current versions of the above items, and direct the team to "pull" information when needed (as opposed to distributing copies of everything to everyone). No space needed for a physical room, no problem connecting with team members from hither and yon. In fact, the only disadvantage of the virtual project room over a physical one is that there is no place for the coffee maker.

If your firm has not stepped up to Internet technology in a big way, you can implement the virtual project room as a nicely organized file directory on your network server. Groupware applications such as Lotus Notes are another avenue for applying this countermeasure. That being said, there is nothing more versatile and ubiquitous than the Internet, so I will assume from now on that we have selected that path to implementation.

Thus, we are going to set up a project-specific website on your firm's internal Internet (referred to as an *intranet*). The website should be access controlled, meaning that only people with a need to know are given password access (and only a *very* select group is permitted to modify the site's contents). Now everyone on the project team can have the latest version of almost anything at his or her fingertips, as shown in Figure M4.2. But there's more. The waste-saving benefits of the virtual

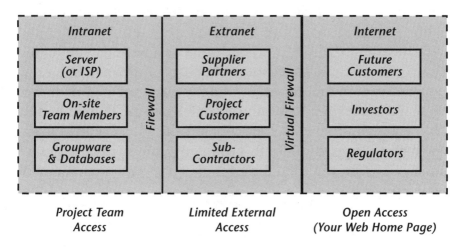

**Figure M4.2:** An example of how a "virtual project room" can provide centralized information access both to the members of a project team, and to external stakeholders within and outside of your firm.

project room can be extended to stakeholders outside of your firm as well. By using a "virtual firewall," password access can be extended with excellent security to outsiders (depending on the gifts of your IT department, of course). Now customers, suppliers, subcontractors, consultants, regulatory agencies, and others can have round-the-clock access to selected portions of your site.

Think of the possibilities! Designers and suppliers can collaborate on a common set of CAD drawings, and share responsibility for updating bills of materials. Customers no longer need to pester the project manager for routine data or status updates.[6] Subcontractors are brought under the same version control system as all other team members.[7] Even management can be kept at bay with an "exceptions" section of the project website dedicated to their needs. The opportunities to reduce transaction costs, increase speed, and eliminate errors are absolutely endless.[8] American faucet-maker Moen, Inc., for example, was able to reduce the cycle time for new product development projects from 24 months to 16 months by employing web-based collaborative design. The time saved using this method has enabled their design teams to work on three times as many projects during the same period.[9]

Moreover, the task of creating an *extranet* site (an intranet with external access) for your firm's projects is not complex and certainly not expensive.[10] If your firm has a website, you're well down the road. Don't let the technology scare you. This same approach is routinely used as a supply-chain management tool in hundreds of firms, large and small.[11] So let the IT folks handle the details while you work the contents. Just don't procrastinate. With all the opportunities this countermeasure provides to save time and effort, you should get going on this like you have a hot coal in your pocket.

### Step-by-Step Implementation

The following steps describe the process of setting up an intranet website to serve as a virtual project room for your team.

Once you have some experience with an internally accessible version, it is easy to extend your site to external customers, suppliers, etc.

## What You Will Need

You will need two things to get started: a few hours of project funding to cover the non-recurring cost of creating the website, and some content that is ready for loading. The recurring cost of adding and changing material will be minimal, since most software applications these days (word processors, spreadsheets, financial packages, etc.) have "direct write to web page" capabilities. Hence, you can assign various team members to handle the updating chores, and only use the IT guys and gals when you need major changes.

The content is entirely up to you and your team. Use Figure M4.3 as a starting point, but also try using a little imagination. Ask your team, "What information are we constantly using, looking for, exchanging, reporting, etc?" Don't get bogged down trying to be overly comprehensive; only put things on the website that will actually be accessed and used.

| **Internal Team Information** | **Supplier Information** |
|---|---|
| • *Specifications* | • *Requests for Quotation* |
| • *Drawings* | • *Purchase Orders* |
| • *Databases* | • *Bills of Materials* |
| • *Plans and Reports* | • *Quality Requirements* |
| • *Test Data* | • *Delivery Schedules* |
| • *Standards and Templates* | • *Procurement Forecasts* |
| **Management Status Reporting** | **Customer Status Reporting** |
| • *Status of Cost / Schedule* | • *Status of Cost / Schedule* |
| • *Customer-Related Issues* | • *Resolution of Customer Issues* |
| • *Minutes of Meetings* | • *Current Release of Key Documents* |
| • *"Exception" Reporting* | • *Status of Requested Changes* |

**Figure M4.3:** Some types of information that could be included in a virtual project room.

## Who You Will Need

Other than various members of the team to contribute and update content, the key player in all of this is your friendly IT professional. If your firm has an internal IT department, there will almost certainly be someone there who can set up a Spartan but friendly website; easy, provided that you already have a company website and Internet service provider (ISP). If your firm has no such capability, there are dozens of experts out there that would love to do the job for a pittance. In fact, most ISPs offer a rudimentary site-design and update service for a few dollars on top of their monthly fee.

*Step 1* – Gather your team together and determine what information you would like to include in your virtual project room. Start with high-value, major documents and drawings, not trivial memos. Better to err on the side of too little content at first, than to overshoot and waste effort.

*Step 2* – Find a trusty IT person to help you lay out your site. It is useful to select an example site that you like, or perhaps have the IT person suggest a few sites that you can visit. Keep it painfully terse and simple. Remember, *creating this site is non-value-added*; it must pay back its cost during the life of the project. So pass on the award-winning graphics in favor of good ergonomics.

*Step 3* – Have the IT person create a mock-up or prototype of the site for review by the team. Get some outsiders to look at it as well. Once you have agreed on an acceptable look and feel, turn the IT folks loose and get it ready for prime time.

*Step 4* – Bring up the website and assign responsibilities. You will need, at a minimum:

- Someone to be responsible for version control (assigning dates to new versions of content that supersede old ones).
- A person to update each piece of recurring content,

such as schedules, costs, bills of materials, etc. This is easy, since it can be the same person who is assigned to create those items.

- A sustained contact in the IT organization that can help you with future modifications.

*Step 5* – Gain a month or two of experience using the site. After this period, hold an improvement meeting with the team and brainstorm on possible enhancements. You might also provide an e-mail address on the site for suggestions. Revise the site and at the same time consider inviting some external stakeholders to join the party. Keep working to improve and enhance the site; there are new opportunities surfacing every day to exploit this exciting new technology.

## How to Measure Success

Lots of things you could measure, but again I don't think it's worth the effort. You could, for example, estimate how much time is currently spent handling one of your project's key controlling documents – a specification works well. Add up the following times for your old paper-pushing process:

- How long does it take to gather inputs for revisions?
- How much time is spent distributing hard copies of each revision?
- How much time is spent maintaining formal version control?
- How much time is wasted by team members who either must search for a current revision, or end up using an obsolete version?
- And so on . . .

Yes, you could probably quantify each benefit of a virtual project room, but here is an easier way to convince yourself. Can you think of a better way to organize your project's information and keep it current? If so, my e-mail address is techper@att.net. If not, get started.

## Method #4 at a Glance

# Real / Virtual Project Room

**Overview** – Creating a centralized information repository for all important project documents, data, drawings, etc., reduces search times and avoids team members using out-of-date versions. A physical project room can serve as a focal point for team collaboration, while a virtual project website or file directory can efficiently store and organize information.

### Waste-Slashing Benefits
1) Eliminates wasted time searching for information.
2) Enables team members to "pull" data, rather than distributing documents repeatedly throughout a project.
3) Reduces errors caused by out-of-date documents.
4) Can be made accessible to external customers or suppliers.

**When to Apply** – Every project, big or small, should employ at least the virtual project room concept. If you are in the middle of a project, you can still benefit from implementing this method for the remainder of your effort.

**Who Can Use It** – Any team leader or project manager.

### Typical Implementation Profile

|  | Low | Med. | High |
|---|---|---|---|
| Non-Recurring Cost |  | X |  |
| Recurring Cost | X |  |  |
| Time to Implement |  | X |  |
| Need for Mgmt. Champion | X |  |  |
| Short-Term Benefits |  | X |  |
| Long-Term Benefits |  | X |  |

# The "Waste-Free" Design Review

*"The trouble with most of us is that we would rather be ruined by praise than saved by criticism."*
—Norman Vincent Peale

With this method, we will take on the granddaddy of all meetings; the project design review. There is no activity on a project that has higher leverage; success or failure may depend on whether these risk-mitigating events are effective. It should not come as a surprise, however, that despite their vital importance, design reviews can become a barrel full of waste. Long hours are often spent bringing attendees up to speed, rehashing routine design decisions, indulging the same old pet peeves, and schmoozing the customer (or management, depending upon whose approval your project requires). In many firms, it seems that the whole point of design reviews has been lost. Rather than giving a design the intensive scrubbing it needs, too much effort is spent selling the status quo. In some cases, design reviews have become superficial "dog-and-pony shows" intended to pacify customers and "put on a good face."

Just so we're clear on this, design reviews serve two functions: 1) To ensure the functionality, performance, and producibility of the proposed deliverables, and 2) To allocate resources and priorities going forward.[1] If a design review yields nothing more than smiles and slaps on the back, *it has failed*. There is no value in a meeting that produces no new information. Blessings are fine for moving a project forward, but the great potential of design reviews lies in identifying problems, not receiving a rubber stamp. The following story will illustrate two different approaches to reviewing a design; you decide for yourself which approach has higher value.

With twenty-five years in the company, Dirk had seen it all. He had hired into ABI Engineering as employee number five – only the two founders and some administrative help had preceded him. Since that time, ABI had grown from a small garageshop operation into one of the premier civil engineering firms on the West Coast. Hundreds of employees, a dozen offices worldwide . . . and lately a bureaucracy to rival General Motors. Unfortunately, the founding partners had proven to be far better engineers than they were executives. As the company had grown, a command-and-control organization evolved in response to the fears and insecurities of the owners. Customers were given sanitized information, and design reviews such as the one Dirk was currently attending had become carefully choreographed love-fests. No disagreements, no dirty laundry, and consequently almost no value.

With only five years before retirement and a well-established reputation as a lovable curmudgeon, Dirk was in a unique position to change all that. He had grown frustrated with the defensive style of ABI's design teams; their designs were perfect, and don't let anyone dare contradict them. Although this "protect the status quo" attitude had been prevalent for some time, lately ABI's engineering group had grown openly arrogant and closed minded. Not surprisingly, in recent years the quality and timeliness of projects had begun to slip, and customer "punch lists" had grown long enough to require a table of contents.

Well, no more. Today Dirk would stir the pot. Since there were no customers in the room for this internal review (admittedly it is generally not a great idea to open the kimono too wide with customers present) there was no excuse for a wimpy, sugarcoated review. After the opening comments were finished, Dirk struck.

"Excuse me, Henry, but I have a crazy thought," he offered to the meeting leader, with a hint of sarcasm in his voice.

"Before we dig into the details, why don't we first agree on what the whole point of this design review is supposed to be? I have a sneaking suspicion that no one in this firm actually remembers." This spurred a flurry of defensive reactions, but Dirk pressed on.

"How many people here think that the point of a design review is to celebrate a great design effort by the team?" A few hands went up at first, but they slowly dropped as people became embarrassed by their pride. "OK," he continued, "Let's see who believes that design reviews are opportunities to defend our designs against all comers?" This time no hands were raised; the atmosphere in the room had become wary. Where was Dirk going with this?

"Let me give you a lesson from Engineering 101," he offered, in his best professorial tone. "Design reviews are about getting good designs right, making them work, and delivering them to the customer promptly and profitably.[2] Reviews should serve to predict and prevent errors, not just reinforce our preconceptions.[3] Hence, if we leave this room today without a long list of potential problems, issues, or corrections, *we have wasted our time.*" Despite some horrified looks, there was enough favorable murmuring in the conference room to encourage Dirk to go farther.

"Instead of spending the next eight hours listening to a repeat of what most of us already know, let's get serious and find some faults with this design. I suggest we spend our time brainstorming on what could possibly go wrong between now and project completion.[4] No suggestions are bad, and no arguments or defensiveness are allowed from the design team. Anything and everything goes. Once we have a list of possible problems and risks, we can discuss each item objectively and rank them as a group. I guarantee that we will discover a lot of hidden problems and hopefully save the company from another less-than-stellar delivery."

Unfortunately, just as a small cadre of support began to develop for Dirk's "revolutionary" idea, one of the founding partners rose and made a pronouncement.

"Now wait just a minute, Dirk. In this company, I want our

design teams to fix problems *before* they are discovered in a design review. I want to see clean, crisp reviews, with an absolute minimum of issues or problems." Some of the audience snickered, until they realized that the founder was serious. Dirk felt deflated. Yet another valiant attempt at improvement had crash landed due to executive obstinance. The good news was that there had been a surprising amount of support for his idea; evidently others had grown tired of having their legitimate concerns shot down by the design team. The bad news was that the founders were not likely to change their ways, and had recently threatened to stay at the helm into their dotage. As Dirk slumped back into his chair, it occurred to him that early retirement was looking more attractive every day.

## Countermeasure 5.1 – The Waste-Free Design Review

Information theory says that if we don't learn something new from a review, we have missed the whole point. This is not to say that your firm's current approach is wrong; in fact you may already be following a "best practice" for project design reviews.[5, 6, 7] The purpose of this countermeasure is to make *any* design review more efficient and considerably more valuable. You can choose to use my approach in total, or you can adapt the central ideas to fit with your established process. Either way, the value of your reviews will go up and the time required will go down.

To accomplish this we will borrow a page from the "Six-Sigma" process improvement philosophy. Specifically we will adapt a methodology known as Failure Modes and Effects Analysis (FMEA).[8] Those of you who have employed this format for reviewing designs (sometimes also referred to as Design – FMEA or D-FMEA) can attest to its effectiveness at pinpointing weaknesses and risks. In the simplest terms, FMEA utilizes a negative brainstorming process to identify risk issues and errors, and then provides a ranking scale for setting priorities. I have retained this essence, but have made a few modifications that generalize the methodology and adapt it to a typical project design review environment.[9] Note that this same method is also highly effective when applied to project status reviews, "gate reviews," go / no-go meetings, screening meetings, or any other critical decision meeting [10, 11]

A comparison of classic FMEA and what I glibly call the "waste-free design review" (WFDR – I admit to a bit of hyperbole in the title) is shown in Figure M5.1. As you can see, I've made only minor modifications to this established and proven method. Instead of focusing on failure modes alone, we expand our brainstorming process to interrogate in turn all important aspects of a deliverable's design. What can cause missed target costs? Are there any integration issues? What possible errors, omissions, incompatibilities, or defects might we encounter before (or after) delivery? Will we be able to meet all performance targets? Each of these questions is considered by performing a short (typically one-half to one hour) negative brainstorming exercise. The constraints you select are up to you, but at a minimum you should validate all performance and

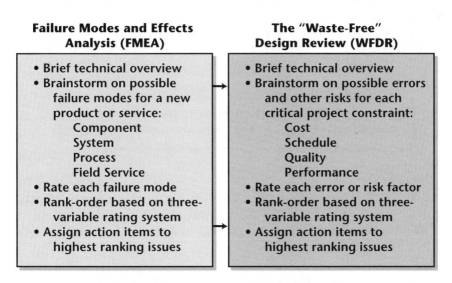

**Figure M5.1:** Comparison between a traditional Failure Modes and Effects Analysis (FMEA) meeting and the proposed "Waste-Free Design Review" format. The primary advantage of this format is the negative brainstorming process that intensively scrubs the design under review.

delivery / integration requirements. Other possibilities might include service, maintenance, interfaces, components, suppliers, subcontractors, reliability, ergonomics, and so on.

The only other significant change that I've made to the FMEA formalism is to adapt the "ratings and rankings" to a more generalized project format. After all brainstorming sessions have been completed (never start ranking and prioritizing before all constraints have been interrogated), a group ranking exercise is performed. Using subjective numerical scoring (usually a one-to-five scale, with five always being a "bad" thing), the group rates each suggested risk factor based on three criteria, as shown in Figure M5.2.[12] The three ratings are then multiplied together to yield what I call an "Action Priority Number (APN)." Risks with the highest APN should receive the highest priority for preventative or corrective action.

| IMPACT (I) | PROBABILITY (P) | ACTION REQUIRED? (A) |
|:---:|:---:|:---:|
| How much would the proposed error or risk jeopardize the success of the project? | What are the estimated chances of the error or risk occurring on this project? | Are safeguards already in place to detect and correct the possible risk or will a preventative action be required? |

**I X P X A = Action Priority Number**
**(An effective way to rank possible errors / risks.)**

Figure M5.2: Three criteria that can be used to rank order possible errors or risks in a design. Each criterion is evaluated using a subjective one-to-five scale, and the product of all three ratings is used to determine which items should receive prompt attention.

A step-by-step description of how a waste-free design review is executed is provided in the next section. You are free to adapt this general approach to fit within your existing design review process, or you may adopt the entire recipe as your baseline practice. You may even consider using the WFDR approach for an informal and internal team "pre-review" prior to the full-dress performance for the customer. Either way, there are a few rules that should be followed, as shown in Figure M5.3.

**Rule #1.** Restrict meeting to no more than ONE DAY. (Divide project into smaller chunks and review separately if necessary).

**Rule #2.** Provide pre-work in advance—no more than ONE HOUR should be spent on answering background questions.

**Rule #3.** Only invite those people who have insight into possible risks and errors in the design—quality more than quantity!

**Rule #4.** Perform "negative brainstorming" in which any error or risk is accepted as a possibility—ratings will sort it out.

**Rule #5.** Only one hour should be spent on each critical constraint of the project—all constraints must be covered equally.

**Rule #6.** Rate errors / risks based on their IMPACT, PROBABILITY, and ACTION REQUIRED. Assign action items.

**Figure M5.3:** Some simple rules that can dramatically improve the value and efficiency of project design reviews.

First, avoid multiple day events, or if you have no other choice, carefully partition the review to reach closure on a subset of topics at the end of each day. Ratings and priorities will not be consistent if they are dragged out over several days. Next, all attendees should be given pre-work so that very little time will be required on the day of the review to bring people up to speed. If you must tutor management or the customer, try doing this on a preceding day with a small subset of your team in attendance. Design reviews that are simply educational events may serve a marketing purpose, but they will fail to serve their *intended* purpose.

The third rule is to only invite people who can add value (or who determine the future of your career, of course). Go for quality of attendee rather than quantity. It is better to have a smaller, more intense and active group, than a large "theater audience" that mostly sits and observes rather than participates. Once you have such a group assembled, perform your negative brainstorming without judgment as to the value of any suggestion. This is really the key to this countermeasure being effective. Fundamentally, I am turning the "rubber stamp" approach to design reviews upside down; attack weaknesses rather than celebrate strengths. If you do nothing else to change how you do reviews, just substitute negative brainstorming for formal presentations and defensive dogma. You will see a noticeable difference in the quality and quantity of corrective actions that result.

### Step-by-Step Implementation

The waste-free design review uses a simple, step-by-step process in which each critical constraint of a deliverable's design is interrogated by a cross-functional team for potential weaknesses, errors, or waste.[13] If the review you are planning is itself a contract deliverable, discuss the possibility of using this approach with your management and customer. If the review is for internal consumption, don't waste your time getting permission. Let the attendees know in advance that they will *really* need to study their pre-work and be prepared for *this* meeting, and then go for it.

### What You Will Need

Each attendee should be provided with a design "overview" one week in advance of the meeting. If you want your review team to be prepared and effective, try helping them out a bit. There is nothing more intimidating than a huge pile of unsorted and undigested design documentation. Allocate some time in advance of your review to create an efficient, organized, and (if possible) brief overview package. Give reviewers at least a week of time with their package, and make yourself and your team available to answer questions. Remember, any time you can save by doing this advanced work will give you more time to squeeze value from your review.

For the review itself, all you will need is a flip-chart easel (for harvesting brainstorming ideas) and a bunch of rating and prioritization forms, similar to the one shown in Figure M5.4. Of course, it wouldn't be a design review without viewgraphs, so bring enough overheads to answer design questions if they come up. This type of review does not require a formal presentation, so your slides can be relatively informal and raw. Use them only if you reach an impasse with your group; otherwise try to avoid tutoring individuals at the expense of the entire audience.

## Design Review Worksheet

| Design Element Under Consideration | Potential Error or Risk to Project | Subjective Rating | | | Priority Ranking |
|---|---|---|---|---|---|
| | | (I) | (P) | (A) | |
| | | | | | |
| | | | | | |
| | | | | | |
| | | | | | |
| | | | | | |
| | | | | | |
| | | | | | |
| | | | | | |
| | | | | | |
| | | | | | |
| | | | | | |

**Figure M5.4:** Template for performing the ranking of issues during a Waste-Free Design Review.

## Who You Will Need

The design team leader typically facilitates a WFDR meeting, but the only real requirement is that the facilitator understands, at least at a high level, all aspects of the project. Participants should meet several criteria. First, they must have a realistic chance of contributing insightful suggestions. Second, they should be of an appropriate disposition, meaning that if a person is known to be argumentative or highly defensive, you should consider bypassing them. If this is not possible, try to pair up such individuals with someone from your team who can gently guide them away from disruptive behavior. Finally, choose people who have non-overlapping bodies of knowledge. A little redundancy in key areas is a good idea, but people with broad and unrelated experiences can bring a fresh perspective to your review.

Once the meeting convenes, you will proceed as follows:

*Step 1* – The "rules" and "deliverables" of the meeting are established right from the start (see Method #3). These will be dependant on the nature of the project, the degree of its completion, and the disciplines represented. Typically, the deliverable for the meeting is a prioritized list of action items, with responsible individuals assigned and due dates noted. These actions are corrective or preventative in nature, with the goal of eliminating future risk to the development and completion of the project.

*Step 2* – Each aspect of the design is considered and brainstormed upon by the group. The order of attack and the list of attributes to review is up to you and your team, but here is a typical list:
    1) Ability to meet customer requirements.
    2) Ability to meet target cost.
    3) Interface to use / application environment.
    4) Safety / serviceability / life-cycle cost.
    5) Any other important design constraints.

*Step 3* – Have the group spend roughly 30-60 minutes on each of these aspects. Use negative brainstorming (meaning that the audience's suggestions are all negative in nature) to identify any possible risk, error, or other potential problem. The goal here is to aggressively wring out issues prior to final delivery.

***Step 4*** – Once the brainstorming for all design requirements is complete, you will rank, as a group, the various risks or issues, using a format similar to that shown in Figure M5.4. The three ranking criteria are as follows:

**Impact (I)** – This is the impact that the potential problem would have on the successful completion of the project, on a subjective one-to-five scale, with five meaning very high negative impact (a project killer), and one meaning relatively low impact (a minor annoyance).

**Probability (P)** – This is the probability of occurrence of the proposed risk or problem, scored on a subjective one-to-five scale, with five meaning virtually certain, and one meaning very unlikely. For example, if you were concerned about losing a key employee, that risk might receive a "one" ranking if the person has just bought a house in the neighborhood, but might be ranked a "five" if they have already posted their resume on the Internet.

**Action Required? (A)** – This last ranking assesses the need for action beyond the measures already in place in your project plan (or covered under your firm's standard policies and procedures). A "five" rating here means that there is no way that the suggested risk will be corrected without a specific action being assigned. A "one" ranking implies that the risk would almost certainly be caught through normal procedures (such as routine testing, inspection, etc.). Again a "five" means ACTION WILL BE REQUIRED (bad) and "one" means NO ACTION NEEDED TO AVOID THE RISK (good).

***Step 5*** – After all potential risks have been scored, multiply the three metrics together for each risk to create an Action Priority Number (APN = I x P x A). The highest APNs represent those risks or errors that demand immediate attention. Assign action items to the highest APN numbers, along with names of individuals to execute them and dates for completion. Be sure that someone has been selected to monitor progress of these actions (typically the team leader, as part of their stand-up coordination meetings).

## How to Measure Success

There are several ways to measure the benefits of the waste-free design review countermeasure. For example, you could compare the number of action items assigned after a WFDR meeting to the typical number derived from previous reviews of equal complexity. You could also subjectively assess the value of the actions identified: How much time, money and embarrassment will be saved as compared to previous reviews?

It might also be interesting to ask the audience at the end of a WFDR review to rate the effectiveness of the meeting (on a subjective one-to-ten scale, just for variety). If the rating is low, it might be worthwhile to ask for improvement suggestions on the spot. Finally, you could estimate the preparation time and meeting time required for a WFDR in contrast to previous reviews of similar complexity.

Unfortunately, the one benefit that makes the WFDR really compelling is not easily measurable. How much is the one insightful suggestion that saves your project worth to you? Would that suggestion have been made without the safety and freedom of a negative brainstorming process, or would it have been stifled by defensiveness or arrogance?

## Method #5 at a Glance

# The "Waste-Free" Design Review

**Overview** – Design reviews that serve as a rubber stamp for project designs are all too common. At best, most reviews waste time and yield only a short list of improvements. This method decreases the time required for a review, and enables identification of many more opportunities for risk reduction and error correction.

### Waste-Slashing Benefits
1) Saves the valuable time of design-review attendees.
2) Identifies a greater number of design improvements, errors, and project risk factors, such as schedule or cost growth.
3) Reduces defensiveness that can block valuable suggestions.

**When to Apply** – This method can work for a small peer review of a component design, as well as for a major customer "dog-and-pony" show. It is best used when there is no need to protect the image of the team or the firm (open kimono).

**Who Can Use It** – Anyone responsible for facilitating a design or project review.

### Typical Implementation Profile

|                        | Low | Med. | High |
|------------------------|-----|------|------|
| **Non-Recurring Cost** | X   |      |      |
| **Recurring Cost**     | X   |      |      |
| **Time to Implement**  | X   |      |      |
| **Need for Mgmt. Champion** | X |    |      |
| **Short-Term Benefits** |    |      | X    |
| **Long-Term Benefits** |     |      | X    |

# Staged-Freeze Specifications

*"All of life is the management of risk, not its elimination"*
*—Walter Wriston*

Here's one for you to think about: Is there always a trade-off between speed and risk in project execution? Those of us who have worked "crash" programs know how difficult accelerating a project can be. The safety of serial task execution must be abandoned in favor of many parallel activities. Protection from changing requirements dissolves with each preliminary release of unstable information. Lots of scrambling as so-called "firm" specifications waver and design "decisions" are abandoned. Extra bodies are added to absorb the rework and backstop areas of high uncertainty. It makes my blood pressure rise just thinking about it. But all of this is unavoidable, right? Just the price you must pay for attempting a really aggressive schedule.

Ah, but perhaps there is a way to balance yin and yang – a secret bargain we can strike between risk and speed that will bring harmony (and success) to our project universe. Suppose that we found a way to "fool" our old nemesis, risk, into believing that our project has bowed to its demands. No "preliminary" releases of information . . . that would be risky. Instead, we simply divide our big, safe, formal releases into a few smaller ones. Then all that scary parallel activity doesn't look so scary, provided that each release of "frozen" information *stays* frozen.

Herein lies the secret of winning at the risk / speed game: Divide big controlling documents (aka, time batches) into subsets, with each subset being treated like its own, formally released entity.[1] A specification, for example, could be divided into three "parts." The first part would define those critical items that drive the top-level design of deliverables. The second might firm up factors that impact the detailed design of low-level elements. A final section could include information needed to begin procurement of long lead-time items. Each of these well-defined sections would then be treated like a separate, formal release, resulting in a staged-freeze process for specifications and other controlling documents, as shown in Figure M6.1.

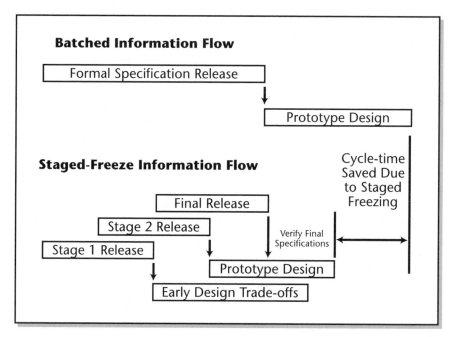

**Figure M6.1:** Graphical representation of a Staged-Freeze process for a specification or other controlling document of a project. The greatest benefit of Staged-Freezing is the ability to execute tasks in parallel with manageable risk.

Think of a specification as being a "soft" representation of the final "hard" deliverables of a project. In the early stages of a project, specs are often vague and amorphous, despite being defined "under contract." Customers change their minds, new discoveries cause rethinking of decisions, hidden constraints appear out of nowhere . . . you know the drill. As these soft requirements firm up, we are able to begin acting on them to create the hard form of our final deliverables. Unfortunately, it is difficult to separate the firm specs from the liquid ones, and often neither the project team nor the customer has the discipline to freeze requirements and make it stick.

The countermeasure described in this section won't make the risk / speed trade-off disappear, but it will tip the scales in your favor. By defining clear freeze points for subsets of information, we are drawing a line in the sand that says, "before this point, change is annoying . . . after this point, change is *painful*." Ten percent of the time, your customer will ignore this boundary and stick it to you. Ninety percent of the time, however, freeze points can provide the discipline needed to forestall unnecessary change. In some cases, you can even negotiate staged-freeze points into your contract. Change imposed after the agreed-upon freeze points triggers either an automatic slip in delivery schedule, an increase in budget, or both. The proposed approach is not perfect, but if even a fraction of unanticipated changes can be corralled into pre-freeze periods, much time and money will be saved. More important, it enables the project team to put the burden on the customer (or management, or other vacillating stakeholder) to acknowledge and take responsibility for disruptive change.

## Countermeasure 6.1 – Staged-Freeze Specifications

Take that skeptical look off your face. It is indeed possible to discipline your customer (and even your management, but don't tell them I said so). The reason is simple: Everyone benefits from adherence to a staged-freeze process. Rather than the antagonistic, trust-free relationships that often exist between team and stakeholders on quick-turn projects, this countermeasure provides a common-sense method for working cooperatively and sensibly. Embedding staged-freeze points into the development of guiding documents for a project allows all parties to work together to make the schedule happen.[2] Without these agreed-upon boundaries, every change, minor or otherwise, becomes a bone of contention, and even legitimate complaints about scope-creep sound like the team is crying wolf.

Before we dig into the details of this technique, let's consider a familiar example. Imagine that your company has transferred you from your Silicon Valley headquarters to a new facility in Kansas. Your family is uprooted and not happy about it. You have taken up residence in one of those chain motels that have a number in their name. Yet despite the inconvenience, you and your spouse are committed to having a custom home built for your family. After selling your two-bedroom cottage in Sunnyvale, you have enough capital gains to purchase a small county in the Corn Belt. A ranch-style palace can indeed be yours, but time and tempers are running short. How can you help your contractor accelerate his construction schedule without ending up with a catastrophe?

Discussions with your builder will yield immediate results. Just ask what things must be decided on by what dates to ensure that there will be no schedule delays. When must sinks and tiles be chosen? Can windows be moved after the foundation is set? Can we install an all-electric range after the electrician has completed work? At every point, the concept of staged-freezing is evident. Once the foundation is set, your chances of changing the floor plan of your future home are severely limited. Yet you are still free to change the color of the master bath fixtures from teal to raspberry. Running the plumbing for an extra set of showerheads is a minor change before drywall is in place – afterwards, it is a nightmare. You get the picture.

Imagine your options for making changes in your custom home as resembling a narrowing funnel, as shown in Figure M6.2.[3] At inception, you can have whatever you desire. Once concrete is set, you can have any elevation and floor plan you want . . . provided that it fits the freshly poured foundation. And so it goes. Options are limited as time progresses because prior decisions or commitments systematically preclude them. All we must do to avoid much pain and suffering is to stay within the funnel; recognize the pain threshold for each critical decision, and corral changes into the time before pain.

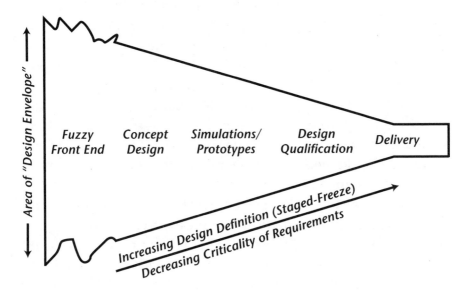

**Figure M6.2:** The design of a project deliverable should be thought of as following a "narrowing-funnel" model. At the onset of a project, all options are open to meet customer requirements. As the project progresses, decisions and commitments are made that begin the narrow the range of options available. It is important to remember, however, that within the funnel there are still opportunities to innovate.

A detailed description of how to implement a staged-freeze project specification is provided in the next section. There are, however, a few variations on this theme that are worth discussing. One of the most challenging aspects of building a project-driven enterprise is the transition of new technologies into routine project execution. This is clearly the case for high-technology product development, but can be equally difficult for engineering firms, IT system integrators, and other direct-contract industries. Why not try defining a "technology readiness point" in your R&D process that freezes the evolution of new ideas at a realistic level of maturity?[4] Prior to the freeze, a new approach would be considered unacceptably risky. After crossing the readiness point, the new technology would be considered acceptably safe for deployment.

Software development presents another excellent opportunity for the use of staged freezing. A complex software application could be partitioned into prioritized modules; those sections of code with the highest risk could be developed early in the project, verified, and then frozen.[5] The customer might even accept a staged buy-off of the code, provided that final integration can be achieved. By front-end loading the tricky stuff, you will have more time to react to trouble later on. Once frozen, these tough modules should become stable pussycats, enabling less risky modules to be integrated around them.[6]

Finally, consider using staged freezing of requirements and other controlling information as a means to accelerate regulatory approval of your project (if this is required). The Boeing Company, for example, was able to work with the Federal Aviation Administration during development of the 777 aircraft to implement a seven-stage design freeze process. This enabled them to weave required regulatory testing into their development schedule, and avoid a serial two-year certification process upon completion of their aircraft. Moreover, the transition to rate production was accelerated due to the increased confidence that manufacturing planners had in the stability of information.[7]

Just a final admonition for those firms with the antisocial habit of carrying two versions of a specification; one that the customer (or marketing, in the case of product development) agrees to, and one that actually guides the design team. I cannot say this more strongly: *Only one document should be called the specification in any project, and it should be the master controlling document for the entire effort* (along with, and reconciled to, the contract statement of work). If necessary, a joint committee between involved stakeholders and the project team should be convened to work out differences between contract or customer needs and engineering capabilities. Only a single requirements document should guide project work.[8]

## Step-by-Step Implementation

For the whole idea of staged freezing to work, some enabling factors must be present. First, the management of your firm must be willing to support, yea verily they must enforce, the discipline of requirements freezing. It is easy to talk about *external* customers being channeled into proper behavior, but it is a rare executive that willingly gives up his or her right to change their mind. A "contract" agreement between management and the project team should be established that explicitly spells out the responsibilities of both the project team and the executive team for enforcement of a staged freeze.[9]

Secondly, a configuration or document control process must exist to make the freeze points effective.[10] Prior to freezing a requirement, a change only requires the concurrence of the team. After this critical boundary is crossed, however, the requirement should be placed under informal (or even formal) configuration control, and an Engineering Change Order (ECO) (or like procedure) would be required to alter that specification. The ECO process provides an excellent forum for the design team to voice their concerns about schedule and cost impact, and to formally document who has initiated the change and why. Sometimes all it takes is a bright light to reign-in undisciplined behavior.

## What You Will Need

Although you can use staged freezing in any phase of a project, the ideal time to establish these boundaries is either during contract negotiations or at project kick-off.[11] Although little hard information may be available at this early point, here are some useful items to gather if they are easily obtained:

1) A proposed bill of materials, with any known long-lead items identified.

2) A set-back schedule for final delivery that identifies as many driving constraints as possible (this is basically a critical-path schedule, but focused on lead times for end-of-project tasks).

3) Some past history as to which items or requirements tend

to drive schedule, and which tend to be susceptible to change in mid-project.

4) A description of the proposed engineering change control process for your project.

Finally, dig up as much information as possible about the interface of your project deliverables to the customer's use environment. An interface freeze should come early and be carefully considered; massive rework can result if the interface to the use environment changes.[12]

## Who You Will Need

The "who" is probably more important than the "what" for this particular countermeasure. At project inception, a meeting should be called between the newly formed team and all relevant stakeholders (or separate meetings if stakeholders are many and varied). It is critical that *decision-makers* are present; without a definitive mandate to freeze specifications, all the talk and agreement in the world won't hold water. The following steps describe how this meeting might progress.

*Step 1* – As with all meetings, the first step, once all parties have gathered, is to define what the desired outcome of the meeting should be. In this case, you will want to reach an agreement on the following items:

1) How many freeze points will be established?

2) Who are the "customers" for the frozen information that will benefit from each staged release? (Note that there is no point in freezing requirements if there is no schedule advantage in doing so.)

3) What specific information or specifications should be grouped into each freeze point? (This may be only a preliminary list at first, with agreement by all parties that the list will be reviewed and modified at some future date).

4) What process will be used to manage change

before each freeze point (informal process), and what process will control changes after each staged freeze (formal process)?

5) Finally, an agreement is needed on how post-freeze changes will impact cost, schedule, resources, etc. Will the customer agree to increasing the project schedule or budget if they violate the freeze (a process called "indexing"), perhaps in return for a late-delivery penalty clause?

*Step 2* – When discussing the type and content of each staged freeze, consider the suggestions in Figure M6.3. Generally, I recommend no more than three freeze points for a project specification, but this depends on the nature of the project, its complexity and duration, and the pain associated with change. Keep it simple at first, particularly if you have never tried a staged-freeze before.

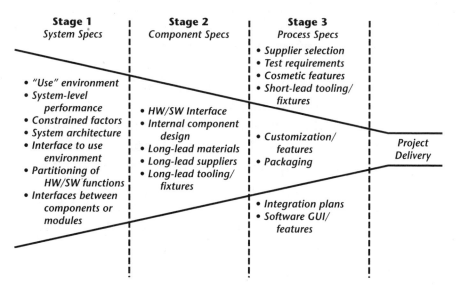

**Figure M6.3:** Some recommendations for the staged-freezing of a specification for a physical product. Typically no more than three freeze points should be identified for a specific document to avoid confusion and unnecessary turbulence.

***Step 3*** – Get an agreement in writing at the end of your meeting (or series of meetings . . . we have to be realistic here). Proceed with the execution of your project. Notify all involved stakeholders when a freeze point approaches, and provide them with a feed-forward of the frozen requirements as they currently stand. You might consider scheduling a "waste-free" review of the soon-to-be-frozen requirements (see Method #5). Try to get a handshake that the frozen items are acceptable, but if this is not forthcoming, don't delay the freeze. It is critical that all parties adhere to this process as though it is law. If you or your management "blink," the customer will lose respect for the staged-freeze and you will be back to fighting each change battle as it comes.

***Step 4*** – If a change is requested (by any party) after a freeze point, execute the change control process that was established in Step 1, above. The key here is to use this formal mechanism to identify the cost and schedule impact of the change, to interrogate the justifications for the change, and to push back whenever possible to eliminate trivial or low value requests.

***Step 5*** – At the end of the project, you might consider reviewing all specification changes that were processed during the effort and identify ways to reduce those disruptions in the future. Should the mix of frozen requirements change? Should more time be allowed before formal release of a given spec? How did the customer / management / team behave? Record your lessons learned and fold them into the next deployment of this countermeasure.

## How to Measure Success

The best measure of success for this countermeasure is the number of months saved in the overall project schedule due to its use. Compare the actual completion date of your project to the one that was planned prior to staged freezing. Or contrast a completed staged-freeze project to previous projects that did not use the process.

You could also track the number of formal requirement changes executed during the project and compare it to the number of informal changes typically experienced on past projects. Did the staged-freeze process indeed corral changes into low-pain periods? Finally, consider polling all stakeholders after the project is complete to gather their impressions. Was the customer frustrated by having their hands tied, or did they appreciate the discipline and clear structure that staged freezing provides? Ultimately, it is the customer's acceptance that will determine the success of this method, so "measure" their reactions. Don't make the mistake of believing that customers are always happier if they are kowtowed to. Respect for a project team is gained through professionalism and demonstrated performance; leave the sucking-up to the sales force.

## Method #6 at a Glance

# Staged-Freeze Specifications

**Overview** – Project durations can be significantly reduced by performing tasks in parallel rather than serial. To avoid the risk associated with this approach, however, a method is needed to control (i.e., freeze) changes that could result in wasted time and effort. The staged-freeze method enables early starts on critical-path tasks with minimal increase in risk.

## Waste-Slashing Benefits
1) Reduces overall project cycle time by enabling parallel task execution.
2) Channels change imposed by customers and other stakeholders into low-pain segments of the project.
3) Provides a means to arbitrate the impact of change by identifying points beyond which change must be formally approved.

**When to Apply** – The best time to implement this method is at the onset of a project. Negotiation between customers and the project team (or amongst the team itself) on freeze points should be performed early in the execution of a project.

**Who Can Use It** – This method is best used by either the project manager or other negotiating authority.

## Typical Implementation Profile

|  | Low | Med. | High |
|---|---|---|---|
| Non-Recurring Cost | X | | |
| Recurring Cost | X | | |
| Time to Implement | X | | |
| Need for Mgmt. Champion | | | X |
| Short-Term Benefits | | X | |
| Long-Term Benefits | | | X |

# Visual Communication and Control

> *"This report, by its very length, defends itself against the risk of being read."*
> —Winston Churchill

You've heard it all before; "A picture's worth a thousand words." But has it occurred to you how wasteful it would be to use those thousand words *instead* of a picture to communicate? Written language is just one form of human symbolic communication, and as I've mentioned before, it is both the most flexible and the most inefficient. Fortunately we have at our disposal a plethora of choices for symbolic language, although most of us don't realize it. Colors, icons, pictures, and graphics all have the ability to convey information in a more precise and efficient way than words ever could. Visual communication takes advantage of the human brain's natural structure. The recognition and processing of complex images has been a forte of Homo sapiens for a million years or so.[1] By comparison, written language is the new kid on the block.

In many cases, symbolic communication can be a catalyst for team efficiency. Let's say, for example, that you are the general of a Roman army (a bit of a stretch, I will admit). You've deployed your five legions across a mile-wide plain in Northern Italy in anticipation of a life-and-death clash with invaders from across the Alps. A quarter-million strong, these barbarians threaten to sweep southward down the coast and sack Rome itself if your defensive stand is not successful. Now here's the problem; your five legions add up to only about thirty thousand combatants. With hordes of Germanic warriors attacking from all sides, how can you hope to hold your ground, let alone prevail? (I'll bet you're wondering how this relates to visual communication, aren't you?)

The great Roman general, Gaius Marius, found himself with just such an "opportunity" in 96 B.C.E. Outnumbered eight to one, the outcome was what you might expect . . . a rout. What you might not expect is that *the victory went to the Romans.* Wild and fierce as the Germanic tribesmen were, they fought as poorly organized rabble. The legions, however, hardened through years of training, discipline, and battle, fought as one. Now here's the visual communication part: For Roman tactics to succeed, Gaius Marius needed to deploy his orders and coordinate his troops over a mile-wide battlefield with virtually no delays or misunderstandings. How was this possible?

Amidst the din of battle and across great distances, verbal commands were all but useless (although audio "symbols" such as horns and battle cries could be effective). However, from the days of Troy, visual methods were used by the Greeks and Romans to achieve superior battlefield communication. Flags of various colors and patterns were used to trigger pre-defined tactics and movements. Tall staffs carried the insignia of each century (a sub-division of a legion consisting of a hundred men) so that the general and his officers could see troop locations from a great distance. Even the color of the plumes in the helmets of Roman legionnaires carried information about rank, role, and responsibility. Today, you might try to solve Marius' problem using cell phones and pagers, but I'd sell my villa on the Appian Way first.

There are enumerable ways in which visual symbols can improve the efficiency and accuracy of project communication, as shown in Figure M7.1. Two of the most powerful techniques are described as countermeasures in the following sections, but opportunities are everywhere. Models and prototypes can serve as "boundary-spanning objects" that provide a common focus for team learning, knowledge sharing, and assumption checking.[2]

Physical or graphical icons can quickly highlight the identity and purpose of tasks, components, or modules.[3] In each of the listed examples, words are made unnecessary by a clear visual representation. When Apple Computer introduced the Macintosh operating system, for example, they didn't need to explain what the purpose of the "trash can" was; dragging unwanted files to the now familiar icon was obvious to even a complete novice.

I will grant that visual communication is not likely to save your project; it is a lubricant intended to grease the wheels of project interactions. Take this method as far as your interest and creativity will allow. To really get your visual juices flowing, I recommend you do some reading. There are some excellent books available on visual communication,[4,5] but one I regard as mandatory reading for any project manager. *The Visual Display of*

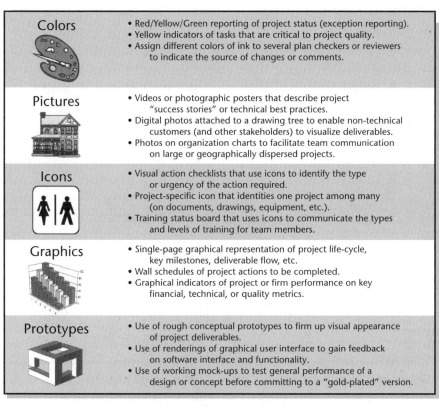

| Colors | • Red/Yellow/Green reporting of project status (exception reporting).<br>• Yellow indicators of tasks that are critical to project quality.<br>• Assign different colors of ink to several plan checkers or reviewers to indicate the source of changes or comments. |
| --- | --- |
| Pictures | • Videos or photographic posters that describe project "success stories" or technical best practices.<br>• Digital photos attached to a drawing tree to enable non-technical customers (and other stakeholders) to visualize deliverables.<br>• Photos on organization charts to facilitate team communication on large or geographically dispersed projects. |
| Icons | • Visual action checklists that use icons to identify the type or urgency of the action required.<br>• Project-specific icon that identities one project among many (on documents, drawings, equipment, etc.).<br>• Training status board that uses icons to communicate the types and levels of training for team members. |
| Graphics | • Single-page graphical representation of project life-cycle, key milestones, deliverable flow, etc.<br>• Wall schedules of project actions to be completed.<br>• Graphical indicators of project or firm performance on key financial, technical, or quality metrics. |
| Prototypes | • Use of rough conceptual prototypes to firm up visual appearance of project deliverables.<br>• Use of renderings of graphical user interface to gain feedback on software interface and functionality.<br>• Use of working mock-ups to test general performance of a design or concept before committing to a "gold-plated" version. |

**Figure M7.1:** Several ideas for application of visual communication to facilitate project execution. The footnote to this figure provides detailed references for many of the above suggestions.[7]

*Quantitative Information*, by Edward R. Tufte, is an absolute treasure trove of ideas, presented in one of the most beautiful and informative works I've come across. Give your team and your stakeholders a treat and make this book a part of your improvement library.[6]

## Countermeasure 7.1 – Visual Statusing of Exceptions

I'm willing to bet that you've already used this countermeasure at sometime in your project experience. If not, this is one of those techniques, like the stand-up coordination meetings, that should be mandatory training for any new team leader. The most common application of visual communication in projects is the ubiquitous "red / yellow / green" status chart, such as that shown in Figure M7.2. The goal is to avoid reporting tables full of numbers that take time to interpret and may not send a clear message to reviewers (either customer or management). Instead, the three familiar traffic light colors are used to signify activities that are in good shape (green), a little shaky (yellow), or in deep trouble (red). At a glance, reviewers can identify those areas that demand their attention, while skipping over activities that are proceeding smoothly.

As obvious as this countermeasure seems, there are some

| Task | Responsibility | Status to Plan | | |
|---|---|---|---|---|
| | | Cost | Schedule | Performance |
| PCB Preliminary Design | Harry J. | ↓ | ↓ | ↓ |
| PCB Layout | Harry J./Tom H. | ↔ | ↔ | ↔ |
| Enclosure Preliminary Design | Kathy M. | ↑ | ↑ | ↑ |
| Enclosure Supplier Selection | Kathy M. | ↑ | ↔ | ↑ |

**Figure M7.2:** An example of a project status report that uses visual communication techniques that enable management by exception. Note that the "up / middle / down" arrows correspond to "green / yellow / red" task status. Either symbology works, but arrows reproduce more easily.

subtleties that can make this approach far more effective. First of all, it should be clear to my now-educated reader that using colors instead of numbers to communicate status is an excellent application of information theory. The project leader sorts the status of tasks into three "bins," based on their degree of acceptability (or pathology). The "green" bin holds tasks whose status has not changed, and as such, carry no valuable information. The "yellow" bin holds tasks with some shady character; not a great deal of information value yet, but worth a quick glance. All of the information content of the status report is concentrated in the "red" bin, enabling reviewers to home in on the areas that require immediate attention.

Perhaps a more important subtlety of this countermeasure is that it represents a powerful tool for exception management.[8] By defining quantitative thresholds for the three color bins, customers and management are effectively empowering the team to work within these boundaries. If, for example, a schedule slip of up to one week is considered acceptable for your project, management might allow you to get a few days behind and still report a task as "green." The yellow range might represent one to two weeks of schedule variance, while the red light would come on when a task is either ahead (yeah, right) or behind by more than two weeks. The same clear ranges could be defined for cost status, key performance metrics, resource availability, etc.

Here's the real payoff of this countermeasure: If a project team stays within their "green" boundaries, stakeholders can safely empower them to do their work with a minimum of interference. Only when an *exception* occurs (crossing one of the predefined boundaries) should stakeholders become concerned. Trust and discipline are required on all sides, however, to make an exception management strategy work. Start off slowly and work your way toward a more rigorous implementation. Try using the red / yellow / green colors during your current routine status meetings (perhaps in addition to numerical data), and move toward exception reporting once reviewers feel comfortable with the format. Incidentally, you can also use directional arrows to report exceptions (e.g., an "up" arrow is the same as green, a "sideways" arrow equals a yellow, and a "down" arrow is . . . well you get the idea). The good thing about arrows is that they reproduce on a black and white copy or fax machine (or in the pages of this book, for that matter). Take your pick, but if you aren't already using this proven technique, time's a wasting.

## Countermeasure 7.2 – Visual "Help Needed" Signal

Here's a visual technique that I bet you're *not* currently using, yet it can play a vital role in keeping a project on schedule. Picture this scenario. Your team is desperately working to meet a tough deadline. Just as you feel your collective heads rising above the water's surface, one of the key members of your team comes down with a serious illness and is laid up indefinitely. The only possibility for success now depends on your management *immediately* reallocating resources to provide you with a suitably talented replacement.

You call every executive in your company's phone book, but no one is "available" to take your call. You fire off e-mails with red "!" next to them, but no reply is forthcoming. Finally, you make the trek to headquarters and scour the hallways for anyone with enough clout to reassign personnel and save your project. Even after you manage to buttonhole some harried executive and explain your situation, nothing happens. Finally, several weeks later, the subject comes up in a project review and is dealt with . . . too little, too late.

It is tragic that so many projects fail to meet their goals due to circumstances beyond the control of the project team. Although management is notoriously good at cracking the whip, it is often hard to get executives to take prompt action in support of teams. Somehow the required action just slides off them like they are made of Teflon, and fails to get the urgent priority it rightfully deserves. Wouldn't it be great if there was an unambiguous way to signal that the success of your project depends on immediate action by management? A way that would really stick?

Toyota Motor Company developed just such a technique during their monumental rethinking of automobile production.

A typical auto assembly line produces a car every two minutes or so. Hence, it gets pretty expensive if production stops, even for a short time. To protect against such events, Toyota installed "andon" (meaning "signal") lights at critical points along their mile-long assembly lines.[9] These tricolored lamps are mounted on poles so that they can be viewed from a distance, and are used to visually report the status of the line. Green lights mean that cars are popping out at the desired rate. A yellow light is a warning that something bad may happen; a parts shortage, a maintenance issue, etc. Things really start jumping, however, if one of the andon lights goes red, meaning that production is at full stop. The supervisor for that process step is given a short period (about ten minutes) to get the line started again. If they fail, the general manager of the factory is immediately notified. Amazingly enough, if the factory manager cannot get things moving in just a few hours, the problem is escalated directly to the CEO of Toyota!

This visual control concept can work quite well in a project environment, as shown in Figure M7.3.[10] A white magnetic board could be set up at "headquarters" that displays all major projects (or a web page could be used, provided that it is not ignored). Next to each project is a location for a color-coded symbol. Again, red / yellow / green are the logical choices (unless, of course, your executive team is conveniently color blind), but other information could be communicated through additional symbols or colors. Remember, the point of this signal board is not to make trouble for project teams, or to provide more opportunities for micromanagement. It is designed to help teams get through obstacles that they cannot overcome without some senior clout.

In one firm, such a board was set up in the executive suite, and each senior staffer was assigned a project to monitor, including the Chief Financial Officer and the CEO. Every day the board is checked, and if a project symbol turns a nasty color, the appropriate executive must take immediate action to get things back on track. Even if they are not able to fix the problem themselves (as might well be the case for the CFO) it is still their responsibility to find someone who *can* solve it. In this way, both managers

| Project | Contact | Next Milestone | Status |
|---------|---------|----------------|--------|
| Project A | Jane A. | Preliminary Drawings | ↓ |
| Project B | Mike B. | Final Acceptance Test | ↔ |
| Project C | Tom C. | Package to Ship | ↑ |
| Project D | Jean D. | Project Kick-off Meeting | ↑ |
| Project E | Carol E. | Critical Design Review | ↑ |
| Project F | Tony F. | Customer Sign-off | ↓ |

**Figure M7.3:** A project "call for help" board that might be posted in the executive suite. The idea is that when a project's symbol turns negative (either down arrow or red icon), executives must provide immediate support to get the stalled project back on track.

and project professionals work together to protect the interests of the firm. I suppose you could say that this countermeasure converts the "executive coating" in your company from Teflon to Velcro.

## Step-by-Step Implementation

Although implementation of visual communication techniques is fairly straightforward, let's walk through how you might establish red / yellow / green, exception-based status reporting for your project. We'll assume (naively, I'm sure) that none of your managers or customers have ever seen this technique before.

## What You Will Need

Not a lot of "what" needed for this implementation, other than some knowledge of past history. Try to arm yourself with good examples of previous projects that could have benefited from visual statusing. To be successful you will need to convince project stakeholders to abandon the old reliable "by the numbers" reporting in favor of exception management. The only way this will happen is if all parties can agree on clear boundaries for reporting schedule slips, budget overruns, etc. Based on past experience, how much latitude can reasonably be given to teams before things start really going south for the winter?

## Who You Will Need

Whomever is demanding routine status reporting must be involved in this implementation. The easiest way to begin using this countermeasure is to reach an agreement with stakeholders on exception ranges (i.e., the definitions of red / yellow / green) at the kick-off of a project. Unless you have a formal company policy on status reporting, agreement on format and approach should really be between you and your overseers, so don't go looking for people to ask permission. Forgiveness, if necessary, is far easier to obtain.

*Step 1* – For the first attempt at visual statusing, I would stick with the "big three" status topics: cost, schedule, and performance. For cost, determine the upper and lower pain thresholds of your management (we'll assume that management is your project's prime stakeholder from this point forward.) The upper limit will very likely be the current budget for the task, although some flexibility for minor overruns might help avoid trivial "red" signals. A lower limit should also be established, since money not needed by one task is almost certainly needed by another task, or even by another project within your firm.

*Step 2* – Continue the negotiating process with management by addressing schedule exception limits. Here, you might try using a rule of thumb that I've found valuable: Allow a schedule variance of ten percent of a task's planned duration before triggering a red signal, unless the schedule slip will impact a contractual milestone. If a contractual milestone is involved, a "zero tolerance" policy must be adopted for slips in schedule.

*Step 3 –* Finally, consider which performance parameters are critical to the success of your project. Keep this to just one or two key metrics at first, but expand the list as needed throughout the project. If you have no flexibility in your specification, then a red signal is triggered anytime a mandatory requirement is in jeopardy. Usually, however, there will be some trade space in which to maneuver, so see if you can build in some wiggle room for each key parameter before hitting the panic button with management.

*Step 4 –* Once the exception ranges have been agreed upon, create a "strawman" version of a monthly status report that uses visual symbols instead of numbers. Have your management make comments and changes to your strawman, and then start using the format as your baseline approach. Note that things typically go pretty well if green symbols are aplenty, but be prepared to explain yellow warnings. More important, for every red symbol you should have a recommended "get well" plan ready to present to management.

*Step 5 –* As you and your stakeholders gain experience with the method, tweak and modify it as needed. Don't abandon the approach just because of one or two minor miscommunications. Learning takes time and patience, but the benefits in terms of time saved, clarity of message, and focus of valuable management attention, is well worth the investment.

## How to Measure Success

The benefits of this method are obvious. It is the disbenefits that we have to watch out for. Although they are not quantitative metrics, the perceptions and comfort level of your stakeholders are the real test of this countermeasure's success. After each status meeting, you might try asking your management or customer how they feel you could improve your reporting methods. Don't immediately cave in and return to boring slides and detailed numbers. As a temporary appeasement, I suggest using both numbers and visual symbols, so that some time can be saved skipping over the healthy tasks. Remember that stakeholder satisfaction is what determines project success. Be careful not to push so hard for waste elimination that you foster mistrust on the part of those who control your team's fate.

# Visual Communication and Control

**Overview** – Words are both the most flexible and the most ambiguous means of communication. Anytime we can use visual symbols, icons, colors, graphics, pictures, etc. to communicate a message, we have an opportunity to reduce errors, save time, and improve understanding.

## Waste-Slashing Benefits
1) Reduces "access time" for information.
2) Can help increase the power of a communication.
3) Errors and misunderstandings can be dramatically reduced.

**When to Apply** – Anywhere and everywhere in project communication. The only caveat is that the visual "language" must be understood by all parties involved in the communication.

**Who Can Use It** – Anyone.

## Typical Implementation Profile

|  | Low | Med. | High |
|---|---|---|---|
| **Non-Recurring Cost** | X | | |
| **Recurring Cost** | X | | |
| **Time to Implement** | X | | |
| **Need for Mgmt. Champion** | X | | |
| **Short-Term Benefits** | | X | |
| **Long-Term Benefits** | | X | |

# Standard Work Methods and Templates

*"There is no useful rule without an exception."*
*—Thomas Fuller*

F ar be it for me to violate one of my own lean rules and repeat myself. Therefore, rather than describe again in detail the *four levels of standardization* and the *need for inclusivity*, I will simply refer the reader back to Chapter 4. In the interest of saving you time, however, I will provide a quick recap.

Standard work should be thought of as a continuum, rather than either black or white – standardized or uncontrolled. On the most rigorous end of the spectrum are detailed recipes, or standard work instructions, that force conformity and precision.[1] Since most project work requires a bit more flexibility, we can relax our rigor just a bit and create templates (for documents or data) and guidelines (for tasks or design elements). These provide a starting point for all project teams, and establish an "envelope" for the acceptable execution of work.

If a project activity requires empowered creativity to be performed successfully, a checklist can be created to remind team members of factors that are critical to quality, or that reflect lessons learned from previous projects. Checklists don't actually standardize work, they simply keep it from slipping on a banana peel. Finally, for those aspects of project execution that require hard delineation between right and wrong, a set of project "rules" can be established. Much like the system of laws in our society, they protect the project from specific negative behavior by defining a region of empowerment and a region of exception.

The other mandate that was presented in Chapter 4 (see Figure 4.2) involved the need for standards to be tiered and inclusive as they are deployed throughout a company. A good analogy for this structure is again provided by our legal system. Federal law supercedes all others (in the USA, at least), but is typically fairly general and subject to interpretation. State laws tend to be more specific and are often adapted to the unique needs of each state's constituency. Local laws are even more detailed, and reflect regional needs and neighborhood concerns. Although state and local laws provide most of the guidance for our behavior, they must be aligned with Federal law to remain valid and enforceable.

The same concept applies to the deployment of standards within a firm. Global engineering conglomerates such as ABB - Asea Brown Bovari, for example, gain tremendous benefits from establishing a commonality of work methods across countries and cultures.[2] ABB recognizes, however, that global standards must be highly flexible and adaptable to be successful. Each regional business unit is empowered to adapt global practices to their specific needs, within predefined limits. This flexibility is further extended to each project team, with the same requirement for upward alignment. Without the economies of scope and learning curve advantages gained by such a structure, ABB and other diversified global concerns would have an impossible time controlling their quality of output and coordinating multi-regional projects.[3]

Well, so much for the review. Since it is likely that you have had your fill of conceptual banter by now, I will change my presentation format slightly for the remainder of this method. Each of the following countermeasure descriptions provide several applied examples of how standardization can reduce waste and improve project consistency and quality. For those readers who hunger for more of my snappy narrative, fear not. There are still four more methods to come.

## Countermeasure 8.1 – Standard Work Methods

Why do you think cooks use recipes? It is not because they can't make something edible without them; any good cook can improvise a passing-fair meal. Recipes enable a chef to capture an especially delicious concoction for future use. Perhaps even more important, they allow other cooks to create the same tasty dish with very little effort. Without recipes, most of us would be limited to rudimentary gruel, and even the best chefs would suffer from unwanted variability in the quality of their fare.

The situation is no different in project work. Once an efficient method has been established for a repetitive activity, why reinvent the wheel? A standard work method is just a recipe that enables anyone on a project team to perform a given task with the skill of an expert. Naturally, only routine activities are suitable for such extreme standardization, but a few opportunities immediately come to mind.

Most projects demand the formal release of drawings or other controlling documents. Although the content of these data items should be unencumbered by restrictions, the release process is routine, and conformity is actually an advantage. Defining a recipe for drawing release would enable any team member to perform the task without fear of errors, inconsistencies, or other *faux pas.*

Similarly, issuing a purchase order for materials or services is a turn-the-crank activity that is ripe for standardization. We wouldn't want everyone who buys something to use a different P.O. format, or a unique set of terms and conditions. The same holds true for entering data into an information system, or processing a capital request. When the task is routine, and variability is an enemy, having a step-by-step set of work instructions makes good sense. Save the originality and creativity for more challenging endeavors.

## Countermeasure 8.2 – Guidelines and Templates

Our opportunity horizon expands considerably when we move from regimented standard work methods to flexible guidelines and templates. These time-saving tools enable project team members to gain a head start, while encouraging a healthy bit of conformity and consistency. If your firm executes a large number of projects, for example, it might make sense to have several project-plan templates available for team leaders to utilize.[4] Each template could service a different category of project: different industry sectors, different customer types, internal versus external projects, etc.[5] As with all templates and guidelines, these "project plans in a box" must be tailorable to the specific needs of each project. Moreover, if your firm wishes to have its projects conform to global project management standards, (such as the Project Management Institute's Project Management Body of Knowledge [PMBOK]), then project-plan templates are an excellent starting point.[6, 7]

On the design side of project work, there are numerous opportunities to apply templates and guidelines. Naming conventions for software, for example, establish an explicit pattern for designation of variables, modules, objects, etc.[8] Similarly, hardware designers could define naming conventions for component and sub-assembly drawings that would facilitate rapid access and enable design reuse.[9] In the world of product development, design rules and guidelines for manufacturing processes allow design engineers to incorporate the capabilities of production processes into their creations.[10]

Templates and guidelines create a "default structure" that can be quickly adapted to specific needs. It is imperative, however, that project teams feel empowered to "violate" these standards if they encumber value creation. If a violation is deemed to be necessary, an informal exception review can be held to decide the issue. As with all attempts at the standardization of creative work, value must come first and conformity a very distant second.

## Countermeasure 8.3 – Checklists

There is simply no end to the potential uses of checklists in project work. Since checklists don't require any significant effort to use, they place a negligible burden on team members' time. The benefits, however, can be enormous. Every deliverable on a project should have an associated checklist that itemizes important issues, risks, quality constraints, and customer mandates. Design reviews can have their own checklists that provide reminders of what topics or concerns are critical to project success.[11, 12]

Projects that involve integration, construction, assembly, or on-site installation could benefit greatly from a checklist that identifies critical interfaces, tests, checkpoints, inspection points, and other quality assurance considerations. As you might imagine, developing such a checklist takes time and experience. A new project team should begin the process by holding a brainstorming meeting prior to project kickoff, but as the integration or construction process progresses, new items should be added in real time. In this way, a legacy of learning is captured for subsequent project teams. Firms such as Hewlett-Packard, for example, have evolved high-value checklists over multiple projects, giving them a substantial advantage over neophytes.[13] As a mechanism for capturing lessons learned and reusable knowledge the checklist is unsurpassed, so the time to start building these treasure troves is now.

## Countermeasure 8.4 – Work Rules

This last countermeasure is best understood by analogy to the "laws of the land." Every society has a code of laws by which its citizens must live, and in a real sense these laws both reflect and help create the culture of that society. A country such as Singapore, which has a very strict set of laws, will tend to develop a culture of conformity. Nations with laws that allow a higher degree of personal expression will tend to encourage more diversity of thought . . . at the expense of discipline.

This is not a lesson in political science; it is a lesson in how to change the culture of your project, and of your entire firm. Every project team should establish a set of "laws," in the form of explicitly documented work rules, at project inception. These rules do not need to look like the Code of Hammurabi; a few simple directives can help define exceptional behavior and avoid major negatives. In Chapter 8, I will discuss how this idea can be extended to the enterprise as a whole.

Can a single-sentence work rule help avoid project waste? Here are but a few examples. On a project I managed back in the days of the Strategic Defense Initiative ("Star Wars" in the popular vernacular), my customer discovered that by contacting various members of my project team directly, he could sneak in added scope and hear early rumblings of upcoming problems. Fine for him, but a disaster for our project. My team members loved the attention that these calls represented, but didn't understand that they were being played against each other and against the interests of our firm. I solved the problem with a simple rule that I suggest every project manager consider: "There is only one point of contact with the customer, me, and if any other contact is made, it must be directly reported to me." This rule ensures that all communication with the customer is consistent, and that there is no confusion over scope, requirements, problems, etc. If your customer is trustworthy, you can relax this rule a bit, but at least you have it "on the books" if it is needed.

Other rules that can help define an efficient work culture for your project team might include: 1) only a single point of contact with the procurement organization, 2) no late arrivals at meetings, 3) no verbal instructions (there should be written documentation of any project-critical communication), 4) no sole-source suppliers, 5) all overtime must be approved by the project manager, and so on. The goal is not to oppress the masses. These rules form a set of exception limits. If a limit must be exceeded, permission for the violation must be gained.[14] In this way, all team members are guided toward conformity where it is needed, but are left to their own devices where free expression is desirable.

## Step-by-Step Implementation

Don't miss this step-by-step implementation – it is one of the most valuable in this book. One of the most powerful techniques for improving project efficiency is to create a standardized "project directory," as shown in Figure M8.1. This tailorable directory, which can be implemented on a file server or an intranet page, represents a focal point for all project work. Every deliverable for a project should be represented in this "tree" (very much like the work breakdown structure of a project, for those readers with a more formal project management background). In addition to a deliverables directory, you will also want to establish a "standardized" planning directory that will serve as a repository for all project planning and control information. Note that these two directories can become the heart of the "virtual project room" described in Method #4.

## Example of a
## Standardized Project Directory Template

**Figure M8.1:** Graphical representation of a standardized "project directory" template. This directory captures all planning and deliverable data items in an efficient format, and enables project teams to better focus on value-creating activities.

The benefits of such a standardized structure are manifold. First, by definition, any work that involves creating or updating one of the items in the deliverables directory is value-added. By inference, any other work may prove to be waste. Hence, the directory represents a centralized focus for team value creation, and is an excellent waste discriminator. A second advantage is gained by the elimination of redundant information. By tailoring this flexible template to the specific requirements and nature of a project, we can avoid repetitious boilerplate. The "tree" approach segregates out common information (such as hardware / software descriptions that apply to every document and deliverable on a project). Such common information is created only once, and then efficiently shared by all items in the directory.

The final advantage of this powerful technique is the ability to capture historical project information in a common format. Although the template should be tailored to the specific needs of each project, the common structure enables comparisons of work hours, durations, and other costs across multiple projects. Estimates for future projects can now be based on something that resembles actual experience. With a bit of scaling and manipulating, your firm can use this common structure as an actuals-based estimating tool for any new proposal activity.

## What You Will Need

You can build a project directory for a single project, but the greatest benefits are achieved when a template is created for use on all projects within your firm. For now, let's take the easy route and assume that you are setting up a directory for your own team's use. All you will need is your contract (or other requirements document that itemizes the deliverables you must create). If your project is similar to previous efforts, it might also be useful to gather the final lists of deliverables from those as well.

## Who You Will Need

If you are going to set up an intranet page to handle your project directory, you may need an IT professional to help you get started. If you are simply setting up a file directory on your local server, you probably don't need technical support. I suggest that you create a "strawman" version of both the planning and deliverables directory yourself (assuming that you are the project manager or team leader), and then have a brief review of the structure with your team. Don't worry about getting it perfect the first time; this is a living structure that should evolve as your team gains more detailed understanding of how to meet the customer's requirements.

*Step 1* – The best time to establish a project directory is at the onset of your effort. You will begin by setting up the deliverables directory. Comb through your contract or requirements document and make a list of every physical or information item that must flow outward from your team throughout the duration of the project. If you have a work breakdown structure established, this will be an excellent starting point. Include status reports, design reviews, plans, bills of materials, procurement documents, inspection reports, regulatory submittals . . . everything that must be created to achieve project success. Organize these items hierarchically, so that similar items are grouped into logical sub-directories. Physical items such as structures, systems, hardware prototypes, etc. should still be captured in the directory, even if only by a placeholder. Your goal is to be as complete as possible.

*Step 2* – Now look for common information or "boilerplate" that would be repeated in several of the deliverables. Carve out this redundant information and create a sub-directory to hold it all. These items need only be created once, and then shared by the entire team. Examples include descriptions, overviews, organization charts, flow diagrams, terms and conditions, and so on.

***Step 3*** – Once you have a good first iteration of your deliverables directory, identify which items will require a detailed plan in order to be executed efficiently. Remember that planning is both essential and non-value-added – a real paradox. The right amount of planning will give you optimized results, so don't assume that every deliverable needs its own plan. Start with the master schedule, statement of work, and budget, and expand them into greater detail only if you feel that the task warrants it. Treat every detailed plan as though it is just a chapter in your overall plan. Don't have team members create stand-alone quality, installation, construction, test, and manufacturing plans, for example. Instead have each responsible team member create a very focused and lean file within the project's planning directory.

***Step 4*** – Now gather your team together and hold a review of the project directory. This meeting is important, since in a real sense you are establishing all the work that must be done to complete your effort. Once a "final" version is agreed upon, assign responsibilities for every plan and deliverable in the directory. Determine the schedule for completion, and compare it to the project's master schedule. Reconcile delivery dates and start creating value. As the project progresses, revise the directory to capture omissions or changes, and delete any items that prove to be non-value-added. Again, this directory should be a mirror image of your project work, so as you evolve your tasks and deliverables, make sure that the directory evolves as well.

## How to Measure Success

The success of standardization efforts is best measured by compliance. If standards are not used, they are worthless. If standards constrain employees to performing low-value work, they are worthless. If standards fail to save employees time and / or improve project quality, they are worthless. Only standards which avoid these pitfalls will be effective and valuable. Perhaps the best way to tell if a standard method or template meets the above criteria is to poll your team members and ask whether they feel that the standard is helpful. Surprisingly, this subjective assessment is extremely important, since the decision as to whether an employee will comply with standards is made based on subjective impressions. Keep those standards that are readily accepted, modify those that are marginal, and cast aside those that are soundly rejected. And in all cases, be sensitive to that fragile entity called creativity; it is difficult to inspire, and all too easily destroyed.

## Standard Work Methods and Templates

**Overview** – There are a surprising number of opportunities to "standardize" project work; not the creative parts, but the dreary, repetitive activities. The use of several levels of standardization enables project teams to choose the appropriate degree of conformity and flexibility.

### Waste-Slashing Benefits
1) Eliminates wasted time "reinventing the wheel" on repetitive tasks or activities that occur on every new project.
2) Reduces errors and misunderstandings.
3) Enables new team members to get up to speed quickly.
4) Creates a structure which can capture lessons learned.

**When to Apply** – Whenever there would be a positive payback for investing in standardization. Typically this method applies to recurring activities; the more frequent the recurrence, the more value will be gained through standardization.

**Who Can Use It** – This can be used at any level in the organization from project team members to the entire enterprise.

### Typical Implementation Profile

|                          | Low | Med. | High |
|--------------------------|-----|------|------|
| **Non-Recurring Cost**   | X   | X    |      |
| **Recurring Cost**       | X   |      |      |
| **Time to Implement**    | X   | X    |      |
| **Need for Mgmt. Champion** | X | X  |      |
| **Short-Term Benefits**  | X   | X    |      |
| **Long-Term Benefits**   |     | X    | X    |

# Risk Buffering and the Critical "Core"

> *"Nothing is so fatiguing as the eternal hanging on of an uncompleted task."*
> —*William James*

"There must be some way out of this mess," thought Ian as he completed his third loop around the deserted courtyard of ACME Gas and Electric's corporate headquarters. Today had been a double shocker, the impact of which he was still trying to absorb as he paced in the yellow glow of the walkway lanterns. First, his most trusted team member, Jim Pitt, had dropped a bombshell. No way could Jim's team complete installation of the new power breakers in time to meet the customer's "go live" date. A fifty-acre natural gas refinery finished and ready to start pumping . . . but no power to drive the pumps! Without the power substation Ian's team was constructing, his oil-company customer would lose *a million dollars a week*. And without the breakers, there would be no substation. Zero warning, zero indication from Jim of a possible delay. It seemed that the schedule slip was as much a surprise to Pitt as it was to Ian.

But his day got even worse. Late in the afternoon, he was told that his system test plan was in limbo, due to a lack of engineering resources. Now even if he could work some magic and get the breakers on line, he wouldn't have the resources to complete the final testing in time. At least two weeks of slip seemed inescapable, with a month the more likely outcome.

The fertilizer was certainly going to hit the air-circulating device when all of this came out.

What infuriated Ian the most was that he had communicated his needs for months in advance, and was assured that the test plan would be completed before it was needed. He didn't even put the darn thing on his critical path "watch list." Somehow, an activity that should have had adequate slack time ended up being in neck-and-neck competition with breaker installation as the pacing item for his project. So much for MS Project and all that critical-path management stuff. He had been blindsided and still couldn't figure out why. Now all he could do was minimize the damages and try to deflect the blame from his team onto himself. It's a good thing public utilities never go bankrupt . . . .

Why is it that project tasks are routinely late? It is too easy to spout platitudes about Parkinson's law,[1] and simply blaming bad estimates doesn't cut it either. There are two real, tangible reasons for the vast majority of schedule slips on projects: failure to recognize and plan for technical risk, and a lack of adequate resources to staff critical-path tasks.

The countermeasures described in this section, along with those included in the two methods that follow, address the frustrating reality that project schedules are often not worth the magnetic media they are stored on. Bad estimates are made every day, for a variety of reasons. The usual culprit is unbridled optimism, but often task leaders will give shorter-than-realistic time estimates in response to pressure from management. In Tracy Kidder's landmark book, *The Soul of a New Machine*, a project team member observed, "If you say you're gonna do it in a year and you don't take it seriously, then it'll take three years. The game of crazy scheduling is in the category of games that you play on yourself in order to get yourself to move."[2] Whatever the reason, I cannot deny that bad estimates are legion, but we can fight back . . . we have the technology.

The two catastrophes that Ian faced in the above vignette resulted from two distinct sources. The first, a slip in the integration of some new-technology power breakers, was caused by not recognizing the technical risks involved and therefore not providing a "shock absorber" in the schedule to mitigate those risks. The second disaster resulted from Ian not recognizing that a critical-path schedule is meaningless unless adequate resources are available to staff each task. A resource "buffer" that ensured the availability of needed resources could have alleviated some of the pain, and possibly saved the project.

In recent years, a new project management methodology known as "Critical-Chain Project Management" (CCPM) has been gaining adherents because it addresses the realities that almost every project manager must contend with.[3] Risks due to technical uncertainty or resource availability are managed through strategically placed buffers, with the size of the buffer being proportional to the level of risk. Although a great deal of literature has been published on this subject, the core ideas of CCPM are really quite simple. I've taken the liberty of stewing down these concepts into some straightforward work methods and countermeasures. Those readers who are interested in a purist's view of CCPM should refer to the several excellent references I've provided in my Notes section.[4] For the rest of you, let's see how we might have saved Ian and his team from a fate worse than layoff.

## Countermeasure 9.1 – Managing the "Critical Core"

The first step in teaching Ian a lesson in reality-based project management is to explode the old myth about the critical path. As the old saw goes, "the critical path is the sequence of tasks that have no slack time . . . a slip along the critical path means a slip to the entire project." While this is certainly a true statement, it doesn't go nearly far enough if we are to avoid the fate of Ian's project team. First of all, it is a rare project that has a single, well-defined critical path. Sure we can always find one by asking our PM software to do its thing, but in any complex project there are often several (or dozens) of possible critical paths, each with a duration that is nearly equal to the longest pole. If we focus on just a single set of critical tasks, we can easily be blindsided by supposedly non-critical activities that slip their way into the limelight.

Instead, I suggest that project managers blur their vision a bit, and consider a "critical core" of tasks, as shown in Figure M9.1. I define the critical core as those activities that are either pacing the project, or are within striking range of being the pacing item. In other words, tasks that could conceivably be schedule-drivers should be treated differently from those tasks that cannot reasonably be expected to impact final delivery. The schedule success of a project is determined by managing risk and resource availability of this core suite of tasks, not just a single serial pathway. In CCPM, the concept of the "critical chain" is defined as the pathway that has the highest risk of slippage when resource availability is considered.[5] I simply suggest that several runners-up be included in the team leader's peripheral vision so that there are no surprises when risks and uncertainties enter the picture, as shown in Figure M9.2.

### The "Traditional" Critical Path (a nice ideal)

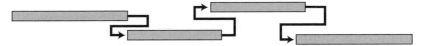

- A single serial pathway that determines the duration of a project.
- A slip along the critical path causes a slip to the project end date.

### The "Critical Core" (a reality on most projects)

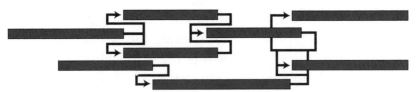

- Multiple pathways, each of which MIGHT determine the duration of the project.
- Which pathway drives schedule is determined by resource constraints and other risk factors.

**Figure M9.1:** It is useful on most projects to consider a broader vision than the traditional critical path. All tasks that are potential schedule-drivers should be included in a "critical core" of activities that receive the lion's share of project management attention.

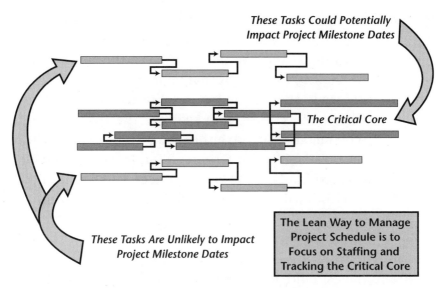

**Figure M9.2:** The focus of project management efforts should be on controlling technical risk and assuring that there are adequate resources for the critical core.

Before we move on to addressing both technical and resource risk, let's consider a few "lean rules" to follow when planning a project using the critical-core / critical-chain concept:

***Rule #1*** – Don't waste time doing detailed planning of work that will take place a year from now. A detailed planning window of three months is more than adequate on most projects; the rest can be tracked at the forty-thousand-foot level, using key milestones and high-level work packages.[6, 7]

***Rule #2*** – Schedule high-risk tasks as early as possible in a project (this is a good critical chain rule-of-thumb).[8] The reason is that if these high-risk activities begin to slip, you will still have the maximum schedule remaining to accommodate the problem. Remember that time cannot be bought back or inventoried. If things get away from you at the end of an effort, your only recourse will begin with an apology.

***Rule #3*** – Strengthening any link in the chain (or task within the critical core) other than the weakest one does nothing to improve the strength of the whole chain.[9] In English, this means that your attention as a project manager should always be directed at those tasks within the critical core that are the highest risk to schedule. Beefing up either the technical approach or the availability of resources for those weakest-link tasks will bolster the entire project. Padding non-core activities will do little or nothing to protect you.

## Countermeasure 9.2 – Core Value Milestones

Really, Ian should have seen it coming. Jim Pitt and his breaker-installation team had begun work several months earlier, and from the very beginning the reports of progress seemed a little too rosy. After one month of effort on what was supposed to be a four-month task, Jim's status report blithely stated that his team was "twenty-five percent complete." At the halfway point, guess what? The breaker effort was reported to be fifty percent done. A site tour by Ian at about this time, however, showed virtually no progress. Not one of the eight massive breakers that were to be installed had even arrived yet, and no preparatory groundwork had been started. A bit more healthy skepticism by Ian at this point might have yielded a portent of what was to come. Instead, he "fully empowered" his team to report status as they deemed appropriate. Bad move.

What was needed to avoid the first of Ian's twin challenges was a method for *objectively* measuring the progress of Pitt's task. Percent complete is generally a meaningless concept. So much so that project managers have a tongue-in-cheek saying that goes, "it's not the first ninety percent of a project task that kills you . . . it's the *second* ninety percent." Fortunately, there is a far better way to monitor the progress of large and schedule-critical tasks. To do this I will steal (and greatly simplify) a page from what is called "Earned-Value" (EV) project management.

My adaptation of EV is really quite straightforward (unlike

the formal system, which like critical chain, tends to be a bit arcane).[10] By defining objective intermediate milestones throughout a long-duration task, it is possible to detect and anticipate schedule slips weeks or even months before they actually occur.[11] For example, Ian could have sat down with Jim Pitt before his critical task began and defined several intermediate points at which progress could be measured, as shown in Figure M9.3. The first point might have been the release of a breaker installation plan, the second might have been the completion of groundwork at the site, and the third through sixth could have represented the installation of the four pairs of big breakers. A last milestone might represent completion and signoff by the inspectors. A total of seven *serial, objective, incremental measures of real, value-creating progress.*

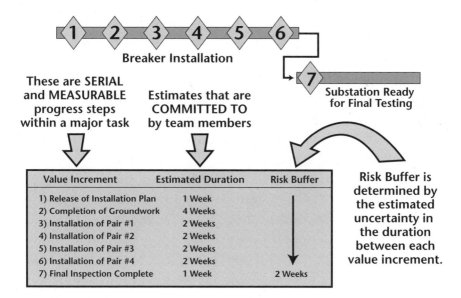

**Figure M9.3:** An example of how Ian (the project manager in my vignette) could have used objective incremental value milestones to track progress on the breaker installation task. With an early warning of schedule slip, Ian could have taken proactive measures to protect the completion date of his project.

As the task progressed, Ian could have asked that progress be reported based on which intermediate milestones had been completed. By assigning a planned completion date for each measurable event, a slip in the overall task would have become apparent in time to add resources, turn up the heat on Jim's team, etc. This general approach to progress tracking is considered mandatory in aerospace and defense, is in broad use in construction and engineering, and has even worked its way into the software and high-technology sectors.[12, 13] The key ingredient is unambiguous and objective incremental milestones. It is easy to argue over percent complete, but hard to deny that a circuit breaker the size of an SUV is still in its crate rather than carrying the customer's juice.

### Countermeasure 9.3 – Risk Buffering

Incremental value milestones give a project manager predictive information about the potential for future schedule slips. They do not, however, protect the project against those delays. Wouldn't it make sense to have some "shock absorbers" built into a project schedule that could help absorb both technical and resource-availability risks? When combined with value milestones, this buffering strategy can transform a run-of-the-mill project schedule into a predictive and robust plan with a high probability of success.

This is the central idea of CCPM: Integrate risk buffers into a project schedule that are sized in proportion to the degree of uncertainty of each critical-core task. The buffers come in two flavors, technical and resource related. Technical risk buffers protect those activities that may slip due to a lack of knowledge or experience, or resulting from pushing the limits of new technologies. The resource variety of buffer looks essentially the same, but guards against a lack of available resources to accomplish a given task. In either case, low risk implies a small or nonexistent buffer, while high risk demands a more substantial schedule buffer. An example of how incremental value milestones (Countermeasure 9.2) and risk buffers can be used to track and protect a complex task is shown in Figure M9.4 for the case of our fictional vignette.

There are a number of suggestions in the literature for how

to size buffers, and perhaps more important, how to protect them from being removed by management or discounted by the team. The most important points are summarized in the following set of rules:

*Rule #1* – Risk buffers in a project schedule should always be inserted just prior to major customer-driven milestones.[14] Placing a buffer after every critical-core task is actually wasteful. It is better from an overall schedule standpoint to gather up the buffers for a series of tasks and create a combined buffer that protects each major milestone or deliverable.[15]

*Rule #2* – Technical and resource-availability risk buffers look the same on a project schedule; they appear as another task that is added onto the end of a major activity. Technical risk buffers should be sized according to uncertainty, and the tasks with the largest buffers should be "front-end loaded" in the project master schedule as much as possible.[16, 17]

*Rule #3* – Resource risk buffers should be sized according to uncertainty in the availability of adequate staff to meet the planned completion date. If a particular individual or functional discipline is known to be in high demand, the risk of getting the people you need would be high. If you have a dedicated team with qualified people standing around waiting for work, your resource risk is very low. Note that there is much more we can do to ensure that adequate resources are applied to critical-core tasks. Methods #10 and #11 provide several proven techniques for reducing resource-availability risks.

*Rule #4* – It is imperative that your risk buffers be protected from shortsighted behavior on the part of both management and your team. Management is notorious for

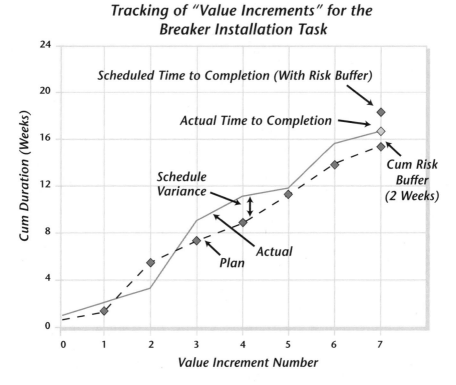

**Figure M9.4:** A graphical way of representing both incremental value milestones and risk buffers for a critical-core task. This diagram enables rapid predictions of schedule slips so that proactive measures can be taken in time to save your project's schedule.

subtracting out contingency budgets and schedule pads.[18] Any slack time that directly impacts final delivery is considered unnecessary by many executives. Yet these same execs seem mystified by the poor schedule performance of their project teams. Management must be educated on the need for buffers, and should become a partner in sizing and placing them in your project plan.[19] From the team's perspective, buffers should be shown explicitly on the project master schedule, and should be treated *as the property of the team*.[20] If an individual task leader consumes some of the team's buffer, they are putting the overall project at higher risk. Peer pressure can help dissuade team members from sucking up the buffers into the duration of their individual tasks (where Parkinson's law will render them ineffectual).

## Step-by-Step Implementation

In this section, we will address Ian's first problem; the slip in schedule of Jim Pitt's breaker-installation task. Using the template provided in Figure M9.5, we will create a tracking plan for this critical-core task. Ian's second challenge, assuring adequate

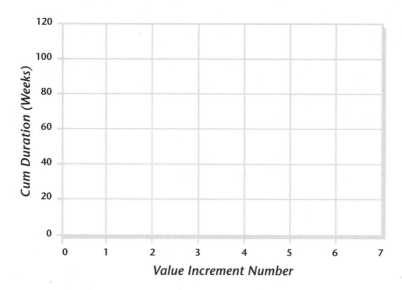

### Critical-Core Task Tracking Plan

| Milestone # | Milestone Description | Duration | Cum Duration |
|---|---|---|---|
| 1 | | | |
| 2 | | | |
| 3 | | | |
| 4 | | | |
| 5 | | | |
| 6 | | | |
| R | Risk "Buffer" | | |

**Estimated Time to Completion =**

Figure M9.5: A template that can be used to establish incremental value milestones and a risk buffer for a critical-core task. The step-by-step directions for its use are provided in this section.

resources were available to complete the test plan, will be dealt with in the two methods that follow.

## What You Will Need

The main thing you will need is a clear picture of the steps required to complete the task involved. In Ian's case, he would need to understand, at a high level, the order of work required to install the four sets of twin breakers. This knowledge need not be detailed, and gathering it should not involve micromanagement: Just a high-level, objective view of the series of events. He would also benefit from having some schedule "actuals" from previous projects available so that he could compare the time estimates provided by Jim Pitt with prior experience.

## Who You Will Need

The "who" is easy. For each major task within the critical core of your project, you need a face-to-face sit-down meeting with the associated task leader. Ian and Jim, for example, should have spent a half hour of quality time identifying objective milestones and determining the optimal size of risk buffers. Again, we are assuming for this example that there were adequate resources available on Jim's team to actually do the work. The schedule slip was entirely a result of technical risk; in this case, the team's lack of familiarity with a new variety of breaker.

*Step 1* – Once you have arranged a *tête-à-tête* with an appropriate task leader, begin by establishing a "rough-order-of-magnitude" estimate for the overall duration of the task. Don't go into too much refinement yet; this will happen as a natural byproduct of establishing incremental milestones. Jim's initial estimate was sixteen weeks, which seemed reasonable, at least on the surface.

*Step 2* – Now walk through the execution of the task. What is the first essential milestone that must be achieved for the task to be on its way to completion. It is vital that the milestones you select be unambiguous and measurable. Jim might have tried to pass off "Installation Planning" as an incremental milestone, but how would Ian know whether it had been completed? This is really a percent-complete estimate in sheep's clothing. Instead, Ian should insist on "Release of Installation Plan" as the first serial milestone, since there can be no argument about whether a plan is released or not.

*Step 3* – So it goes through the rest of the task. Step-by-step you would walk through the work involved, identifying several incremental milestones along the way. It is usually a good idea to establish at least one per month, but the number could be more or less depending on the duration of the task and the length of the overall schedule. For Jim's four-month task duration, at least four milestones should have been defined, but given the high technical risk, a few more would be warranted. Once the milestones are chosen, determine estimates for the duration of each step. These durations should add up to something close to the original total-task estimate; if not, spend some time iterating back and forth until a resolution can be reached. The task leader must be comfortable with the estimates for this tracking approach to work, so don't try to strong arm your teams into overly optimistic durations.

*Step 4* – Finally, we must add a risk buffer to the end of each critical task. This will appear on the project schedule as a separate and subsequent task, but will be sized based on the risks of the prior work. Here is where Ian really dropped the ball. Instead of whining about how "critical-path management doesn't work" he should have recognized the technical uncertainty along his critical path and planned for it. Neither Jim Pitt nor his team had ever worked with the new breaker design being installed, and there were significant differences between the new and old versions. A little soul searching here about realistic schedule assumptions would have made it clear that at least a two-week shock absorber would have been appropriate.

*Step 5* – As Ian's project progressed, he would require Jim's team to report only their objective progress against the agreed-upon incremental milestones. A slip in any milestone would be compared to the overall risk buffer for the task, and if the buffer was in danger of being fully consumed, immediate action would be required to bring the project back on track. In this way, the tracking method described here can be used as a tool for exception management: Schedule slips need to be reported only if they consume more than X percent of the allowed risk buffer for that critical-core task.

## How to Measure Success

Ian could easily measure the schedule variance of Jim's team by noting the planned versus actual completion dates for each incremental value milestone. The consumption of risk buffers is also a good indication of how well team members are hitting their schedule marks. I've used incentives to encourage the protection of risk buffers. Any team member or task leader that completes their critical-core activity without consuming part of *the team's* risk buffers receives a tangible pat on the back: dinner for two, a couple of baseball tickets . . . and no, the reason for the second ticket is not to allow the project manager to go along.

| | |
|---|---|
| | **Method #9 at a Glance** |

# Risk Buffering and the Critical "Core"

**Overview** – Managing the "critical path" of a project is not sufficient to ensure that a project will meet its schedule. This method provides a simple approach to monitoring *real* progress on critical-core tasks, and offers a way to buffer tasks from the uncertainty and risk that often causes schedule delays.

## Waste-Slashing Benefits
1) Reduces schedule slips due to technical risk or poor estimates of task duration.
2) Enables risk and uncertainty to be accounted for in those tasks that define the critical core (those activities that are on or near to the critical path and can potentially impact the overall project schedule.)

**When to Apply** – This method is best applied during the planning phase of a project, but could be implemented mid-project if schedule slips are out of control.

**Who Can Use It** – Task leaders and project managers.

## Typical Implementation Profile

| | Low | Med. | High |
|---|---|---|---|
| **Non-Recurring Cost** | X | | |
| **Recurring Cost** | X | | |
| **Time to Implement** | | X | |
| **Need for Mgmt. Champion** | | X | |
| **Short-Term Benefits** | | X | |
| **Long-Term Benefits** | | | X |

# Dedicated-Time Staffing and "Superteams"

*"All organizations are at least fifty percent waste – wasted people, wasted effort, wasted space, wasted time."*
*—Robert Townsend*

R ecall from the previous section our depressed project manager, Ian, and his twin schedule nightmares. His first debacle was caused by a failure to recognize and compensate for technical risk (risk buffering) and a lack of objective metrics to track task progress (incremental value milestones). So much for getting the power breakers installed on time. Now what could Ian have done to avoid his second catastrophe; inadequate resources available to complete the test plan in time to "go live?"

If you are fortunate enough to work in a project environment in which team members are 80 to 100 percent dedicated to one project at a time, much of this discussion will seem irrelevant. Revel in the knowledge that you are in the profound minority. For the vast majority of readers who are forced to either share resources across several projects, or must beg resources from functional departments, have I got some ideas for you. Admittedly, some of the countermeasures described in this section require buy-in by upper management to be deployed broadly. Don't let that dissuade you. You can start small with these techniques and work your way up to changing the world once you have some success under your belt.

Let's begin by identifying the target. The following statement defines the ideal allocation of resources for any project-driven enterprise:

*In an ideal firm, employees are assigned to those activities or projects that are the highest-value opportunity at any given time, are given a clear work plan that establishes their day-to-day priorities, and are protected from disturbance so that their work plans can be executed efficiently.*

Does this in any way resemble your firm's resource management approach? Unfortunately, for many firms, the above statement would read more like, "In our company, resources are applied to whichever project is in the most trouble this week, people are given no clear priorities other than to 'just do it all,' and their work can be disturbed by anyone at any time." The sad truth is that most firms do not actually manage their resources at all; they let the individual workers try to sort it out for themselves. As a result, individuals who must multitask are in a constant state of turbulence. Each time the phone rings or there is a knock on their cubical, value-creating work grinds to a halt while priorities are reshuffled. Set up to do a task on one project, stop in the middle to run to a meeting for a second project, return in time to get that status report out on a third project, and . . . where was I? It is hard to believe that any work gets done – in fact very little does.[1]

Several surveys have been conducted of firms that are infected with high levels of multitasking, including informal studies that I've conducted at my client firms. The results are consistent and disturbing: Most project team members spend less than twenty percent of their time working on any one project.[2] Furthermore, employees who must divide their time among three or more projects with no clear prioritization or work plan report that their value-creating productivity drops to *essentially zero*.[3]

Never fear. The following countermeasures are designed to help achieve high levels of productivity and schedule control, even in a heavily multitasked environment. They all address the same fundamental goal; give workers undisturbed blocks of time to complete priority work, and make sure that there are enough workers to staff all high-priority projects.[4] A simple goal, but one that requires *discipline and cooperation* to achieve.

## Countermeasure 10.1 – Dedicated-Time Staffing

Imagine a workday in which all of your tasks were clearly prioritized. Everyone in the firm, from your team leader to the CEO agrees that if you work on Task A first and Task B second, you are maximizing your value to the firm. Now dream on a bit. Suppose that you could move down your priority list in such a way that your work efficiency and output were maximized. Ah, and the icing on the cake. You are allowed to close your door, send your calls to voice mail, and work on value-creating tasks for large chunks of your workday without fear of interruption. If such a dream were to come true, you would have far less reason to come in early, stay late, and drag yourself in on the weekends, right?

| Typical Multitasking Environment | With Dedicated-Time Staffing |
| --- | --- |
| • No Clear Prioritization | • Prioritization of Work |
| • Impossible Workloads | • Sane Workloads |
| • Chronic Overtime | • Overtime as "Reserve Capacity" |
| • Low Morale | • Creating Value Improves Morale |
| • "Just Do It All" Syndrome | • Realistic Project List |

**Figure M10.1:** Comparison of a typical multitasking work environment with the concept of "dedicated-time staffing." The goal of this approach is to allow employees to work high-priority tasks without interruption for substantial periods of time.

I won't belabor the nightmare that is the obverse side of the above fairy tale: Too many projects, too few people, no prioritization (because that would give employees an excuse not to "do it all"), and interruptions that border on the absurd. To turn our nightmares into sweet dreams, we must achieve what I call "dedicated-time staffing," as shown in Figure M10.1. This does not imply that employees only work one project at a time. It simply means that they are assigned a task that is high value, and are left alone to get that work done before they must switch to another task or project.[5] As trivial as this sounds, it is the essence of team productivity.

In yet another attempt to make this material practical, I'll describe how to achieve dedicated-time staffing in your firm by responding to the excuses that I've heard most frequently from my professional students:

*Excuse #1* – I shouldn't have to micromanage my team's time.

> Horsefeathers. It is *your job* as project manager to get the work done on time and on budget. If you aren't helping your team organize and prioritize their project work, and making sure that resources are on task, what *are* you doing? It should be the unalienable right of every project manager to allocate resources within his or her project (a right that is conferred and reaffirmed every time your team members get a paycheck.)

*Excuse #2* – My team must also service outside customer calls and sustaining field support. Those always take priority.

> A valid concern, but still no excuse. There are several ways to handle this situation. If the required support is generic in nature (i.e., several different employees could handle typical customer or field support issues) then designate one or more people to be "on-call" for a set period. This could be as simple as giving them a beeper whose number is defined as the "on-call" number. The project manager would

select those team members that are on less-than-critical tasks for on-call support, thereby protecting the time of employees who are driving the project's schedule. As resource priorities shift, on-call duties would shift as well. If the support work is unique in nature (only one employee has the required knowledge) then determine how much delay in response is acceptable. That way, those uniquely talented employees have a chance to finish the project work they have started before jumping through hoops for some other customer.

Another approach to balancing customer / field support work with project work is to define "quiet-time" periods that are protected from interruptions. The entire team would be allowed to do project work in the mornings, for example, and would then be available to support the field or the factory in the afternoons. For another approach to protecting your people's time, see Countermeasure 10.2.

*Excuse #3* – I share my team members with several other important projects, and must slug it out with the other project managers on a daily basis.

Doesn't that sound crazy? You all work for the same firm, but you must constantly battle for resources down in the trenches. Me thinks someone isn't doing their job – someone whose job title has a three-letter acronym. Granted, it is unlikely that you can pop into work tomorrow and point out to your executives the error of their ways . . . and keep your job. You can, however, work cooperatively with other project managers to level resource demands and establish multi-project work plans for employees in high demand. See Countermeasure 10.4 for more details.

*Excuse #4* – All this won't make a difference. We have ten-times more projects than we can handle.

Unrealistic demands breed disenchantment. There is a critical point of overload at which people simply cease to try.

If your management has piled project after project onto a finite group of employees, eventually those workers will recognize that their leaders are disconnected from reality. From that point forward, the coupling between strategy and execution is lost. Executives live in a dream world in which every opportunity that crosses their path is another entry on the balance sheet, while employees wander about their daily work in a haze of frustration and confusion. See Countermeasure 10.3 for the bitter medicine that can remedy both executive denial and team disenfranchisement.

### Countermeasure 10.2 – Team "Filters"

Just exactly how brave are you? If you've got a modicum of courage, this countermeasure will not just *add* productivity, it can *multiply* it. The idea is simple (but potentially career limiting if care is not exercised . . . hence the need for a stout heart). As team leader or project manager, you interpose yourself as a "filter" for any disturbance that might distract your team from its value-creating work plan. I'll illustrate this technique with a personal anecdote.

Once upon a time, defense budgets were fat and the need for strategic weaponry urgent (at least that is what we all believed at the time). My firm was contracted by the Defense Research Projects Agency (DARPA . . . a very lean-and-mean organization) to produce a prototype night-vision system for use as a demonstration unit. The funding was essentially unlimited, but whereas a typical project of this sort would have taken a full year, my group was given *two months*.

"Impossible," I screamed as I was awarded the honor of managing this albatross. "I'll only take this on under one condition – that I be allowed to isolate my team, suspend all the rules, and act as a demigod." I assumed that these demands would frighten my management into moving down to the next candidate on the list. Unfortunately, there wasn't any list.

With my terms agreed upon, at least in theory, I proceeded to organize my team. We would hold daily stand-up coordination meetings, establish prioritized work plans, and *stick to them* to our dying breath. In the past, my team members had been called upon by every manager and executive who had a bee in their bonnet, most often to perform tours and demonstrations for admirals and generals. Now all of those requests would be filtered through me first, as shown in Figure M10.2. My team was instructed to *nicely* redirect any such requests to my overloaded voicemail box, where they would be dispositioned based on their priority and impact on our schedule.

As painful as this was to enforce (my stock certainly took a short-term nose-dive among executives) the results were astonishing. A twelve-month prototyping effort was completed in *less than two months*, and the quality exceeded all expectations. Moreover, the vote from my team was unanimous; the use of a "filter" to screen, organize, prioritize, and disposition interruptions was key to our success. Fortunately, stocks are really long-term investments, and my portfolio doubled after this project's results became known.

You need not take this filtering idea to an extreme, as I did. Even gaining agreement from certain parties within your firm to confer with you first before contacting your team can be a big

**"Filters" protect the dedicated time needed for team members to create value!**

**Figure M10.2:** Cartoon that illustrates the idea of "filtering" the interruptions that team members face in their daily work. The goal is to reduce the disruptive impact of unplanned requests from customers, the field, or the factory.

advantage. This way, if a specific individual is working on a critical-core task, you can either suggest alternatives or try to schedule the interruption at a convenient break point in their project work. Again, this is an opportunity for you to actually add some value as a team leader. Too bad they don't award medals for this kind of valor.

## Countermeasure 10.3 – Resource Prioritization

Here's a little quiz to measure your aptitude as a senior executive. First question: You have just won the first prize in your local supermarket's sweepstakes – a one-minute shopping spree. You can cram anything you can get your hands on into your shopping cart, but you only have sixty seconds. What strategy would you use:

A) I would load my cart with economy-sized bags of potato chips since I know my whole family would like them.
B) I'd go for a balance among the four major food groups.
C) I'd make a beeline for the meat, cheese, and non-prescription drugs.

If your answer was "C" you have good executive potential. Next question: You have been given a one-month license to mine for gold in Yellowstone National Park. Reserves there are rich, vast, and well-marked, but you only have a small team of workers to assist you. Would you:

A) Start digging at the entrance, since it would take the least time to get there.
B) Dig near the campgrounds because many campers lose pocket change and you might get lucky.
C) Focus your team on the richest reserve and work your way down the list in priority order.

If you selected "C" again, good job! You are just one step away from being a prime executive candidate. Last question: You are made general manager of a business unit that performs project work. Your team is the best there is, but competition is fierce and margins are getting squeezed. How would you allocate your finite resources:

A) I would empower my employees to work on whatever project they found to be the most interesting.

B) I would tell my team to work on every project equally, because we can't afford to turn down any opportunity.

C) I would create a prioritized list of projects based on their potential to build our firm, and focus resources on those high-value opportunities in priority order.

In this case the correct answer is either "A" or "B." What's that you say? The right answer should be "C?" You obviously have no executive potential. Go back to doing real work and leave the tricky decisions to the big whigs.

The above is just a silly quiz, but if executives were measured by their actions, you would find that the vast majority are answering "A" or "B" to that last question every single day. I once met a general manager who had a team of twenty project engineers assigned to complete over *sixty projects*. When I suggested prioritization, the response was, "I refuse to prioritize, because that will just give people an excuse not to get everything done."[6] A quick check of timecards from the previous three months, however, showed that a mere ten projects had received any attention at all. Only after confronting the GM with this hard reality was a prioritized list forthcoming.

When faced with finite capacity and excessive demand, the only two sensible solutions are to either increase capacity or prioritize work.[7] A simple process such as that shown in Figure M10.3 can make a monumental difference in a firm's balance sheet, while simultaneously improving employee morale. I don't suggest that you prioritize every project and task down to the very bottom of the list. Instead, I recommend that you select the top fifty percent of your project work for prioritization. These projects would become the primary focus of your firm's resources and management's attention. The second tier of project work would be performed only after the high priority list is completely serviced. These priority projects would be treated differently: They would have the right to reserve critical resources, for example, as will be described in Method #11.

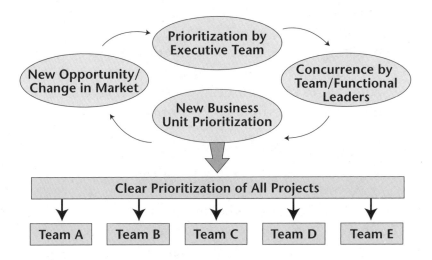

**Figure M10.3:** The need for business-unit-wide prioritization of projects can be satisfied with a process like the one shown above. Keep this simple and flexible; the purpose of the priority list is to resolve conflicts in resource allocation that cannot be solved in any other way.

The ranking of your priority projects can change from week to week (please don't change them day to day), but during each week, everyone in the company should know what they must work on first.[8] Here's an important point, however. The goal of prioritizing projects is not to let Project #1 beat up all the other projects for as long as it is on top. The priority list should only be used when all other means for staffing projects has been exhausted, and a critical project still does not have adequate resources to meet their commitments. Resource-leveling techniques such as the one described in Countermeasure 10.4 can help avoid the need for high priority projects to "pull rank" on a regular basis.

Finally, a look to the future – your future, that is. By projecting forward your business unit's needs for various skill sets, you can give your organization a chance to be proactive in resource management, rather than reactive.[9] A simple histogram, such as the one shown in Figure M10.4, can provide top-level visibility of upcoming resource bottlenecks. Granted that individual workers are not interchangeable parts, but even projecting the demand for some broad categories of talent can yield valuable insight into when your resource tap will run dry.

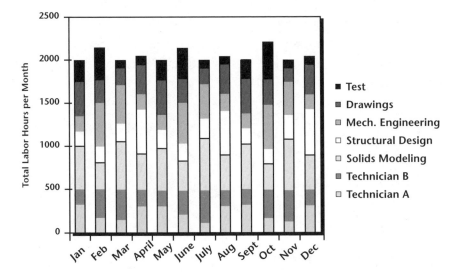

**Figure M10.4:** A simple histogram such as the one shown here can give project managers visibility into future resource bottlenecks. This can enable proactive solutions, such as cross-project resource leveling, outsourcing, or limited overtime.

## Countermeasure 10.4 – Superteams

Much of the waste associated with the multitasking of project team members results from the "many-bosses" syndrome. Most of us are familiar with the archetypical form of this malady; a matrix organization in which employees are torn between loyalty to their functional manager and dedication to their project manager (see the quote at the beginning of Chapter 7). As if two bosses were not enough, in many firms, project workers are sublet to several projects simultaneously. No small wonder these shared resources feel like an abused wishbone at Thanksgiving dinner.

This countermeasure provides at least one way to reduce the negative impact of the many-bosses syndrome. Its effectiveness hinges on the recognition that even though one or more employees may be shared between projects, not all of their work is of equal priority at any given time. In a sense, the superteam concept I propose is really just dynamic, multi-project resource leveling.[10] I'll illustrate this with an example. Consider a team of six structural design engineers that specializes in developing truss-and-girder frameworks for bridges. This team typically works as a unit, but due to an excessive workload, all six members are assigned to service three different and competing projects, as shown in Figure M10.5.

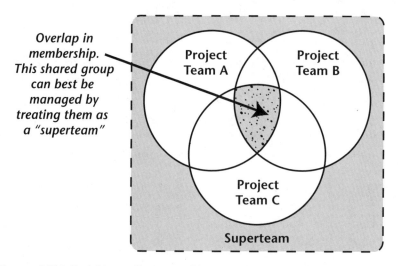

*Overlap in membership. This shared group can best be managed by treating them as a "superteam"*

**Figure M10.5:** A Venn diagram of intersecting sets of employees on project teams. For those of you who have forgotten your grade-school math, this means that several project teams overlap in their membership. This situation can be managed effectively using the superteam concept.

Here's the problem. Each project manager wants to "own" these shared resources.[11] Constant battles erupt over who gets what work done when, and always the employees are caught in the middle. Fortunately, there is a simple solution to this ubiquitous problem. When there is a great deal of overlap in team membership among several projects, the associated project managers should treat these shared resources as a "superteam" that must accomplish the goals of *all projects* in a coordinated way. For the above example, the three project managers would convene a brief weekly meeting with all six design engineers in attendance. The group would go over the tasks that are scheduled for the superteam in the upcoming week, and prioritize them independent of which project they service. The workers themselves would provide input to these work plans and can sanity check any assumptions. Once the work plan is in place for the superteam, it is executed without change unless an emergency occurs that might require adjustment by upper management. If there is an irresolvable conflict among the three projects, the priority number (assigned in Countermeasure 10.3, above) is used to resolve the issue. You might even consider establishing a "trading" process within the superteam: One project would loan resources to another and receive credit for a "worker to be named later."

Rather than expecting employees to figure out how to manage their complex, multi-project workloads, why not use cooperation and negotiation? It is certainly far better than running upstairs to visit the "elephants" for resolution every time there is a priority conflict. Besides, like we used to say in aerospace, "You can get the elephants to stampede, but you can't determine which way they'll run." In the step-by-step discussion that follows, I describe how to identify, organize, and manage a superteam.

## Step-by-Step Implementation

The following steps illustrate how you can begin using the "superteam" concept to optimize the productivity of workers in a multi-project, multitasking environment. I will use a simplified example, but feel free to generalize and adapt any idea presented here to work within your specific industry, team structure, or company culture.

## What You Will Need

All that is needed to initiate a superteam is an awareness of which members of your current team are heavily committed to other projects. Unfortunately, if each team member is multi-tasking on a different set of projects from their teammates, the superteam concept won't work. The general rule is that a group of several workers must be shared among a common set of projects. Gather up the project schedules and task descriptions for each shared employee. These will be necessary to coordinate task priorities among the conflicting projects.

## Who You Will Need

The "who" is very important. A superteam meeting must include the impacted project managers and all the workers that are shared among the represented projects. If you cannot get all involved project managers to cooperate in managing the superteam, the effectiveness of this method will be greatly diminished. Fortunately, project managers should have a strong motivation to work together; fear that they will be on the short end of the resource priority stick at some point in the future. It might be necessary to get an executive champion to help you herd the kittens into the first superteam meeting. Hopefully, if all goes well, the benefits will fuel long-term cooperation.

*Step 1* – Set a time for your first superteam meeting. You will need to educate the involved parties as to the purpose of the meeting, and get their buy-in first. Try to make it clear that the goal is to accomplish just a few simple things:
- Avoid multitasking waste by establishing weekly work plans for shared employees.
- Move tasks and shift schedules to enable all critical-core work to be done in a timely manner for all projects involved.
- Identify impasses where available resources are simply not adequate to do the critical work. Hopefully this will allow some proactive and cooperative action, such as hiring an outside contractor or instituting some short-term overtime.

*Step 2 –* Once the meeting is convened, spend five minutes per shared worker deciding on what is the optimal use of their time. Keep the environment positive and flexible. If this degenerates into a polarized contest between hardheads, the method will fail and the multitasking waste will remain. Only use the business-unit-wide prioritization of each project as a last resort to break deadlocks. Keep the meeting short – a half-hour is more than enough.

*Step 3 –* Document the agreements reached *in real time*, either on a laptop computer (a spreadsheet can be created for this purpose), or on one of those printing white boards. Get everyone in the meeting to agree to the documented work plans *before leaving the room*. Then follow up with an electronic copy to all meeting attendees and any functional manager or executive that is directly impacted.

*Step 4 –* After a week, hold another meeting. Begin by asking everyone whether they think the approach worked well during the past week, and how it might be improved. Proceed to adapt your approach and continue the meetings. Use the standard "lean meeting" rule: If the meeting isn't solving an important resource allocation problem, discontinue it. It can always be trotted out again when shared workers begin to feel their joints separating from the pull of too many bosses.

## How to Measure Success

On-time completion of intermediate project milestones is an unambiguous metric of success for all of the above lean countermeasures. Also, the capacity to handle multiple projects and the average cycle-time per project should reflect the elimination of multitasking waste. The benefits of business-unit-wide prioritization of projects would actually be visible on the balance sheet if you know how to find it.

As with all of the methods in this book, however, don't become obsessed with measurement. Sometimes the best measure of whether you are improving is a subjective estimate by the people directly involved. Don't be afraid to simply ask employees whether these measures help maximize their work output, keep the confusion down, or otherwise improve their chaotic workdays.

## Method #10 at a Glance

# Dedicated-Time Staffing and "Superteams"

**Overview** – This method offers several practical tips for avoiding the waste of multitasking in a multi-project environment. Techniques are provided for protecting team member's work plans, leveling resource demands across projects, establishing priorities across multiple projects, and projecting future resource shortfalls so that proactive measures can be taken.

**Waste-Slashing Benefits**
1) Reduces the productivity drain associated with multitasking.
2) Enables the most important opportunities for your firm to receive needed resources on a priority basis.
3) Provides an advanced look at future resource requirements.

**When to Apply** – Most of these countermeasures can be applied to any project, at any stage in project execution.

**Who Can Use It** – Task leaders and project managers, managers of program offices or project management offices.

**Typical Implementation Profile**

|  | Low | Med. | High |
|---|---|---|---|
| Non-Recurring Cost | X | X | |
| Recurring Cost | X | | |
| Time to Implement | | X | X |
| Need for Mgmt. Champion | | X | X |
| Short-Term Benefits | | X | |
| Long-Term Benefits | | | X |

# The Reservation System

*"Waste of time is the most
extravagant of all expenses."*
—Theophrastus

This method is really a one-trick pony . . . but it's a very neat trick. Have you recently visited one of the Disney theme parks? Since I grew up in the shadow of the Matterhorn (the one in Anaheim, not the one in the Swiss Alps), my family visited the original Disneyland on a regular basis. As a young and budding scientist, I can remember standing in one of those interminable lines and being frustrated by a sign that read, "Your wait will be one hour from here." Thanks for nothing. If the Disney folks knew that our wait would be one hour, why did I have to stand in line? After all, they could put a bowling pin with my name on it in line as a placeholder, and I could just show up at an agreed-upon time.

Forty years hence, and many millions of hours of park patron's time wasted, Disney has seen the light. Their new Fast-Pass system allows you to reserve a time-window during which you can show up at your selected ride and get on with minimal delay. You now can use your new-found freedom to purchase overpriced souvenirs and gobble down empty calories. The same idea has been in use for years at restaurants, theaters, airports – anywhere that capacity (in the form of seats for these examples) is desired at a specific time. You could show up at your town's most tony restaurant on a Saturday night, for example, and hope for the best. Or you could do the sensible thing and reserve a table for four at 8:00 p.m.. With the latter approach you enjoy a timely dinner, whereas with the former you park your carcass and pray for leftovers from happy hour.

The following two countermeasures address queues and wait times for any needed capacity: internal resources (human or otherwise), materials or services from suppliers – anytime there is a lead-time to be overcome. The general rule can be stated as follows:

*If the amount of capacity for a needed resource is known, and the arrival time of the need is well-established, queues and wait times can be eliminated through a reservation system.*[1]

Restaurants reserve tables to avoid long waits by customers. Only those without foresight must suffer a two-hour starve-a-thon. For your dinner reservation to be effective, however, you must know both how many chairs you will need and when you will arrive. You *do not* need to know exactly who will be at dinner, or what they will order. The reservation is for *capacity at a specific time*, it is not the same thing as buying dinner. A few possible applications of the reservation system in project work are listed in Figure M11.1. This is by no means a complete list; the potential for using this method to avoid delays is unlimited.[2]

**Figure M11.1:** Just a few of the opportunities to apply a reservation system to avoid unnecessary delays in project work.

## Countermeasure 11.1 – Eliminating Queues and Wait Times

A simple idea with lots of power. Suppose that you need to have a dozen drawings created by the drafting department at some critical point in your project schedule. Unfortunately, this department is run as a shared-resource center with a non-priori-tized waiting list.[3] You submit your job form along with all the necessary information, and your drawings will be completed at some time in the future, depending on the amount of work in the queue ahead of you. There are two big problems with such an arrangement. The first is that you won't have "all the necessary information" until just before you will need the drafting work per-formed. If you begin your wait in line from that point in time, you will definitely slip your schedule. The second problem is that you don't know for sure how long the queue will be, so you can't even plan for a well-defined lead time in your downstream schedule.

I've stated before that first-in-first-out queues are the worst way to allocate shared resources in an enterprise. This is because the queue is mindless of priority; it treats every job as equal to all others. If, however, we have established some priority pro-jects, as recommended in Method #10, we have an opportunity to use them as "queue-busters." Suppose that the top five high-priority projects in your firm were allowed to make reservations for any shared resource. All that would be required is a written notification in advance of the amount of capacity required and the planned arrival time, as shown in Figure M11.2. It would not be necessary for the job to be ready for submittal; the final infor-mation package could be made available on the day that work begins. As the reserved time approaches, a courtesy contact could be made to confirm the reservation and adjust for minor changes in capacity and arrival time.[4] The work then arrives on schedule and the capacity is immediately available.

Obviously, there are a few potential problems with this tech-nique. First of all, what if you are early with your job? Then you would receive the first available resource after that person has finished the job they are currently working on. Suppose you arrive late? If you are using this system with an outside contrac-tor or supplier, if you don't use it, you lose it . . . and pay for it.

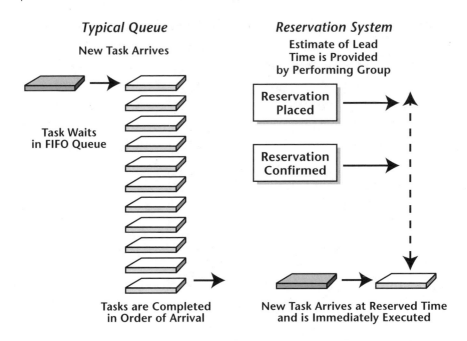

**Figure M11.2:** A schematic representation of the reservation system. All that is needed by the "reserver" is knowledge of how much of a resource will be needed and when that need will occur. It is not necessary to precisely define the work to be done in advance.

With an internal resource center, such as the drafting department I mentioned above, the reserved resource would simply pull the first job off of the "lower priority" stack and begin work. When you arrive with your tardy task, you will be serviced by the next available person. This is the main reason for not prioritizing every project in your firm. By creating two (or more, if you dare) tiers of priority, the first tier gets immediate service, while the second-tier projects form a backlog and buffer for reservable resources.

## Countermeasure 11.2 – Reserving Key Resources

This concept of making reservations for key resources can be extended to the availability of any team member, any equipment that might be a bottleneck, or even setting aside face-time with your executives to approve incremental funding or subcontracts.[5] The trick is to only allow a subset of your over-all project list to make a reservation. If you give every project equal access to this system, you will actually create more waste. With the second-tier work serving as a buffer, there is never a risk that a resource will be without useful work. By giv-ing the highest value projects reservation rights, you are assured that those heavy hitters will be able to maintain schedule and budget.

Try this with the less-than-full-time members of your team. Could you reserve slots of time with their functional depart-ments that would be clear of all interference or other priorities? This would only be appropriate if that person was on a critical-core task (and therefore impacting project schedule).[6] In this way, you can buffer your project against the loss of key person-nel at high-pain points, without having to lock away your val-ued workers from all other suitors.

As with all resource-optimization methods described in this book, a degree of maturity, cooperation, and negotiation is need-ed to make them work. Even if these qualities are currently lack-ing in your firm, a small-scale implementation, say to reserve test equipment or CAD system chair-time, can be a good initia-tion. Remember that the most complex mega-project can be brought to its knees by the lack of an available draftsperson or test system. What's that old saying that goes, "For the lack of a nail, the shoe was lost, for the lack of a shoe, the horse was lost . . . ?" Somewhere along the line, the kingdom was lost, but then I'm sure that they didn't have a reservation system for black-smiths back in those days.

## Step-by-Step Implementation

I'll keep this short and sweet. The following are some simple steps that will allow you to make a reservation for work capaci-ty at a shared-resource center (any functional group that behaves like a "black box" from the viewpoint of your project team). Remember that the onus is on you to show up on time and to accurately know how much capacity you will require.

## What You Will Need

You will need a good estimate of required capacity and a reasonably good idea of when you'll be ready to initiate the job. If you are involved in a heavyweight project, you might consider padding your capacity estimate a bit. Don't abuse this, however; if every hot project over-committed capacity, the system would become quite inefficient. Same point with arrival times. You shouldn't make a too-early reservation and then hope that the shared resource will "hold your table" while you drag in late.

## Who You Will Need

Who "owns" the shared resource? All you will need is an agreement with that person as to how the reservation will work. Follow the steps provided below:

***Step 1*** – Contact the shared-resource owner and suggest the reservation system. This can be done informally unless the system has been implemented as a formal process across your entire business unit. Reach an agreement on how you define capacity (by hours, by bodies, by drawings, etc.). Then determine the capacity you will need, and the estimated arrival time of your work. Finally, agree on a time prior to the need date at which you will confirm your reservation.

***Step 2*** – As the need date for the reserved resource approaches, recalculate the capacity you will require, and adjust your scheduled arrival date. Contact the shared-resource owner with this information, and adjust your reservation accordingly.

***Step 3*** – Show up with your work and get immediate service. If you missed your marks on either capacity or timing, however, don't be surprised by the wait you must tolerate. Remember that even at its worst, the reservation system will still provide high-priority projects with better service than a FIFO queue could ever achieve.

## How to Measure Success

What was the promised lead time without a reservation? What is the actual lead time with a reservation? Subtract the two and you have a nice waste metric. Also consider measuring the amount of shared capacity used (or left unused) by priority projects, the on-time arrival of reserved work, and the accuracy of capacity estimates. For a high-volume shared-resource center, these data can represent the inputs to an optimization model that can drive the day-to-day operations of the group.

# The Reservation System

**Overview** – High-priority projects deserve different treatment than lower-priority ones. This method enables high-priority projects to reserve needed resources (people, equipment, etc.) so that there is no waiting or lead time.

### Waste-Slashing Benefits
1) Avoids negative schedule impact of waiting and lead times.
2) Avoids schedule slips due to uncertainty in resource availability.
3) Enables resources to be applied to the highest value opportunities for the company.

**When to Apply** – Anytime resources are in short supply or where a first-in-first-out queue exists to allocate needed resources.

**Who Can Use It** – Any team member, task leaders, project managers, and functional resource or equipment managers.

### Typical Implementation Profile

|  | Low | Med. | High |
|---|---|---|---|
| Non-Recurring Cost | X | | |
| Recurring Cost | X | | |
| Time to Implement | X | | |
| Need for Mgmt. Champion | X | X | |
| Short-Term Benefits | | X | |
| Long-Term Benefits | | X | X |

# The Value-Added Scorecard

> *"There are three kinds of lies: lies,*
> *damned lies, and statistics."*
> —Benjamin Disraeli

This final method is not a project management technique at all – it is a way to monitor your progress in implementing the other eleven methods. Even though I've provided you with some ideas for measuring the success of these waste-reducing countermeasures, I have some reservations as to whether those metrics actually capture the whole story. Project management is not a "factory" process in which statistical measures can define excellence to a high degree of accuracy. Much of what we do in project work is subjective, qualitative, or otherwise hard to put a yardstick to. If we fool ourselves into believing that one can apply statistics to such things we are in danger of drawing some wrong conclusions.

Yet another problem with rigorous quantitative data-gathering is that it is inherently *non-value-added*. After all, if we could just improve ourselves without measurement, would our customers know the difference? Ah, but you recoil in disbelief. Could I be suggesting that we shouldn't measure our improvements? Not exactly. I *am* recommending that measurements be carefully selected, that the effort to gather data be tightly constrained, and that we not lose sight of the goal – to reduce, rather than increase, unnecessary work.[1] That being said, we do need some way to monitor our progress. I propose here a simple, low-waste supplement to labor-intensive data gathering that can work for many types of improvement initiatives.

As we discovered early on in this book, waste in projects can be hard to identify, difficult to quantify, and generally a pretty slippery beast. Only after developing the waste-sensing talents of yourself and your team can you choose appropriate initiatives and understand the difference between value and its opposite. Why not use that newly found insight to metric your team's improvement over time? I suggest a simple scorecard approach, using subjective numerical ratings, that can track your team's assessment of their own success.[2] This scorecard approach can be tailored to any situation, and can be used as a barometer for virtually any type of waste. It takes just five minutes or so per week to capture the data, and you won't have to hire a team of statisticians to analyze the results. Granted, it should be used in conjunction with other performance measures, but this simple technique can significantly reduce the need for a much more wasteful tracking process.[3]

## Countermeasure 12.1 – The Value-Added Scorecard

Let's not overcomplicate this. In Chapter 9, I will provide you with several ways to identify which countermeasures will give your team the biggest bang for their improvement buck. Once you have such a list of initiatives, just jot them down on a scorecard such as the one shown in Figure M12.1. The diagram lists seven different areas that this fictional team felt were important sources of waste. I suggest that you begin your improvement journey with only three or four, and work your way up to a more aggressive plan once you have some success under your belt.

Each week in your stand-up coordination meeting (even if you have more frequent meetings, once per week is sufficient), spend five or ten minutes going through the items on the scorecard. For each improvement area, ask the team to score as a group the level of waste you are still experiencing. For example, the first item in the figure focuses on meeting waste. You could simply ask, "How wasteful were our meetings this week?

| Improvement Initiative | Waste Score (1=No Waste, 5=High Waste) |
|---|---|
| Wasted Time in Meetings | |
| Late Core Deliverables | |
| Incomplete Core Deliverables | |
| Project Website Not Up-To-Date | |
| Wasted Time on Preventable Errors | |
| Wasted Time on Non-Core Tasks | |
| Poor Communication / Other Waste | |

*These Can Be Any Type of Waste that Has a High Impact on Your Project*

*Scorecard is Updated Weekly in Stand-Up Meeting*

*Scores are Subjective 1-5 Ratings – Generally a Consensus of the Team*

**Figure M12.1:** Example of a project team value-added scorecard. Waste-elimination initiatives are selected by the team based on their potential to positively impact project success. Ratings are performed weekly by the entire team and the subjective scores are used to maintain focus and encourage improvement.

Did we follow the lean rules for collaborative meetings? Did we utilize our stand-up coordination meetings effectively? On a scale of one-to-five, how do we stand?"

The one-to-five subjective rating scale is the key to this simple approach. Define a score of "five" as "boy we really stink" – in other words, your team hasn't done a thing to implement their lean countermeasures. Define "one" as "we've got this one licked" – it's time to add a new improvement initiative to your priority list. Any score in between should reflect the progress (or the lack thereof) toward waste elimination. Typically, a new initiative would begin at "five" and work its way down to a consistent "one," at which point it should be dropped from the scorecard. Backsliding will show up as an increase rather than a decrease in score.

Get the group to agree on a score for each item on your scorecard. If consensus is not forthcoming, spend a few minutes hashing out disagreements. If there is real discord, schedule a separate meeting to work out the problems. This is rare, however. Most of the time, the group will see things in a fairly uniform way. Once all scores are recorded for the week, capture them in some visible way (see Figure M12.3 for a simple "stacked-histogram" graphic) so that the team and management will be exposed to the scores on a frequent basis. As time goes by, your aggregate score should consistently decline, until you reset your scorecard by adding some new improvement initiatives.

Speaking of management, what about the waste that they cause? If your management team is really a partner in your improvement process, they shouldn't resist having a scorecard of their own.[4] Of course, your team needs to be politically correct, but a monthly rating of management's impact on project work, such as that shown in Figure M12.2, can be an effective communication tool. When there is disagreement about whether management is really being wasteful, have an improvement meeting and agree on a lean compromise. If your firm is blessed with first-rate executives, they will not object to having their scores posted in a visual format right next to your team's internal ratings, as shown in Figure M12.3.

**Figure M12.2:** Example of a management value-added scorecard that a project team might create to highlight sources of waste that are outside of their control. This scorecard can serve as a communication tool between executives and their teams.

Metrics are only useful if they are used. Discuss with your team and with management how the scorecard results will impact their future behavior. If the scores fail to improve over time, are you going to shrug and say, "Well, I guess waste isn't so bad after all?" If management is causing consistent waste, will there be tangible action, or just a brush-off? One final warning: Grade inflation (or in this case, deflation) is a real problem with any subjective rating system. One way to avoid this is to agree on some semi-quantitative threshold for each point on your five-point scale. For example, if meeting waste is a real problem, you could agree that "five" equals your current number of team-hours spent in meetings, and that each point lower in score implies a ten-percent reduction. Don't use this as a hard-and-fast rule, just a touchstone in case your team seems to be changing their scores much more rapidly than they are changing their wasteful ways.

### Step-by-Step Implementation

I find it hard to believe that you need a step-by-step description of this method in addition to the above discussion. If you are still insecure about how to define waste and track its demise, go back to Method #1 and start over again. By the time you get to this point a second time, you will be a fire-breathing waste-slasher, and you won't have a problem implementing this simple tracking method. As for me, I just can't wait to adapt our twelve powerful lean methods to the incredibly important special case of new product development. Won't you join me in Chapter 7?

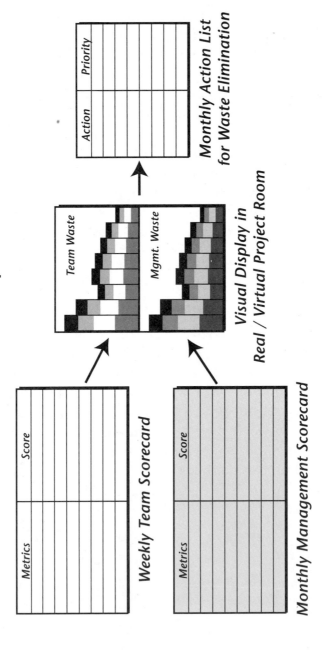

**Figure M12.3:** How the whole simple system works together. Team scorecards, along with management scorecards if you dare, are used as a metric for waste-reduction progress, and potentially as a source of new initiatives for continuous improvement.

## Method #12 at a Glance

# The Value-Added Scorecard

**Overview** – Implementing improvements is challenging, and teams often backslide after an initial success or two. This method describes a simple, subjective scorecard that can be used to monitor progress in waste reduction. Visual graphics are used to allow project teams and their management to be partners in driving lean methods into an organization.

## Waste-Slashing Benefits
1) Allows teams and management to keep improvements from stalling out or backsliding.
2) Couples with the systematic improvement methodologies described in Chapter 9.

**When to Apply** – At the onset of an improvement initiative, or as a corrective measure when backsliding is observed.

**Who Can Use It** – Anyone who is trying to implement lean methods within a team or an entire organization.

## Typical Implementation Profile

|  | Low | Med. | High |
|---|---|---|---|
| **Non-Recurring Cost** | X | | |
| **Recurring Cost** | X | | |
| **Time to Implement** | X | | |
| **Need for Mgmt. Champion** | X | X | |
| **Short-Term Benefits** | X | | |
| **Long-Term Benefits** | | X | |

# PART III

## The "Special Case" of New Product Development

# Creating a Lean Product Development Process  7

I have good news and bad news. The good news is that virtually every waste-slashing idea you've learned so far in this book is directly applicable to "projects" that involve the development of new products. In this chapter, I will present an overview of how our twelve lean methods can be applied to your new product development (NPD) process. These techniques are currently in use in dozens of my client firms, and have proven to be extremely effective at cutting time to market, while improving schedule predictability and resource utilization.[1]

Now for the bad news: There is no way I can do this topic justice in a single chapter. An optimal NPD process can be (and, in fact, *should* be) significantly different from industry to industry, product to product, and customer to customer.[2] It is this diversity that makes the concept of "best practices" even less appealing for NPD than for the more general case of project management.[3] For example, the ideal process for designing new cars will likely make sense only for high-volume products requiring tremendous upfront capital investment and high recurring touch-labor content. It is unlikely that the same development process would be effective for a software firm whose products involve a high degree of customization, minimal capital investment, and essentially no recurring touch labor.

With this caveat in mind, here's how we'll proceed. I will present a broad-brush overview of how lean methods can be applied to new product development.[4] The details of how these techniques can be tailored for various industries and products, however, will have to wait for my next book (which will be a follow-on companion to this literary masterpiece).[5] For the time being, we will explore four "facets" of new product development: the overall process, the "fuzzy front end," the "project in the middle," and finally, design for lean manufacture, as illustrated in Figure 7.1. The goal will be to identify what is different and unique about NPD, and to guide the reader in adapting the twelve lean methods to this very challenging special case. By the way, you don't have to wait for another book to begin using these practical tips. I hereby give you permission to think for yourself and take some initiative while I'm off giving birth to the next opus.

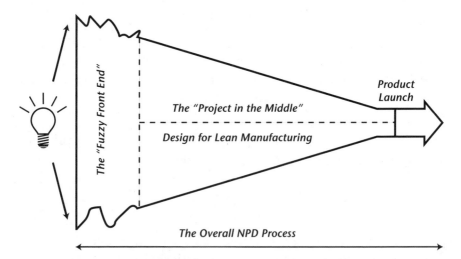

**Figure 7.1:** A graphical representation of the four "facets" of new product development that are discussed in this chapter. The goal is to highlight those aspects of NPD that are unique, and to guide the reader in applying our twelve lean methods to this challenging type of project.

## Facet 1 – Leaning the Overall Process

There are several aspects that are "different" for new product development when compared to more general project efforts. The first is that it is actually a *recurring process*. Projects are inherently unique in nature, so establishing a "project process" only makes sense if you plan to execute similar projects on an ongoing basis. This is clearly the case for NPD. Hence, we will learn how to build an optimal development process that can be executed repeatedly with great speed and efficiency. (Note that the other main "differences" associated with NPD will be covered in the sections that follow.)

It is worthwhile to spend a moment considering the evolution of the NPD process over the past century, as shown in Figure 7.2. The main reason for this retrospective is to allow you to place your firm's current methods along a "best practices" timeline. Are you still in the dark ages? Have you taken some of the major steps that can bring your firm reduced cycle time and higher product quality and value? Once you know where your firm resides, you can begin considering what your future target should be. Again, let me warn you that best practices are often highly industry and firm-specific. I will make some broadly applicable recommendations, but many of the suggestions that follow will have to be filtered by your own good sense and judgment.

### Evolution of New Product Development "Best Practices"

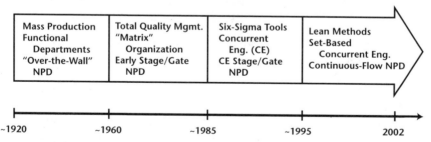

| Mass Production Functional Departments "Over-the-Wall" NPD | Total Quality Mgmt. "Matrix" Organization Early Stage/Gate NPD | Six-Sigma Tools Concurrent Eng. (CE) CE Stage/Gate NPD | Lean Methods Set-Based Concurrent Eng. Continuous-Flow NPD |
|---|---|---|---|
| ~1920 | ~1960 | ~1985 | ~1995 | 2002 |

**Figure 7.2:** An evolutionary timeline of NPD process "best practices" and improvement philosophies, beginning with the early days of mass production and leading to our present level of understanding. Note that the dates shown are approximate, so don't panic if your personal experience disagrees with my timeline.

Well, it all started with Henry Ford and Fredrick Taylor. Ford revolutionized manufacturing by defining an optimal model for low-mix, high-volume production. The assembly line was the key, and its success depended on division of labor and specialization. As mass production began to permeate all aspects of Western economic life, a sociologist / economist named Fredrick Taylor saw the need for an organizational design that would match the efficiencies of the Ford-era factory. He proposed what is often referred to as "scientific management theory." Basically, this is the same specialization and division-of-labor stuff that Ford had instituted on the assembly line: strong functional departments, white-collar and blue-collar workers . . . this should start sounding familiar. Believe it or not, the vast majority of manufacturing firms today are still organized in exactly the same way. Here's the problem; *it doesn't work for rapid product development.*

Strong functional organizations are anathema to lean NPD. The reasons are obvious if you think about it objectively. Is there any one department in a functional organization that can design a new product? Clearly all functions must be involved at some point in development, but in a "silo" organization, this is accomplished by throwing deliverables "over-the-wall" from function to function. As long as product life expectancies are measured in decades and new products can gestate at a glacial pace, a functional organization can hide its inadequacies. Once speed and cost become primary competitive factors, the "over-the-wall" process shows itself to be the dinosaur that it is.

In the sixties and seventies, the limitations of the old functional structure became apparent. Global competition and rapid technological change drove firms to find a better answer. The concept of the "matrix" organization emerged from this need, offering an (albeit oversimplified – see the quote at the beginning of this chapter) answer to how cross-functional development work could coexist with functional silos. It turns out, however, that the matrix organization is the "dirty little secret" of modern industry. We all know it really doesn't work like the advertisements say, but what other option do we have?

The first real breakthrough in defining an effective cross-functional new product development "best practice" was the advent of the stage / gate NPD process (aka, phases and gates, tollgates,[6] etc.), as shown in Figure 7.3.[7] Based on a successful approach developed for high-risk defense-department megaprojects, the idea seemed quite logical. Establish several "gates" along the timeline of a development project where a list of "gate deliverables"

### Over-the-Wall Product Development

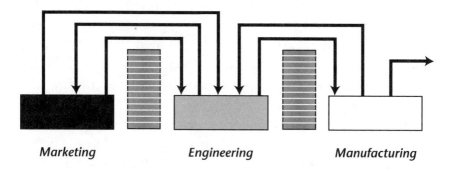

Marketing          Engineering          Manufacturing

### Stage/Gate Product Development

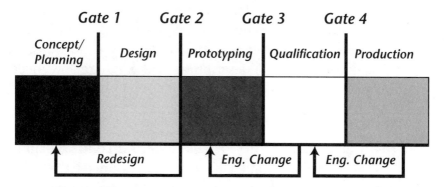

**Figure 7.3:** Diagrams of the antiquated "over-the-wall" NPD process, and the much-improved stage / gate process. This is not the end of the story, however. Applying lean methods to NPD can yield a "continuous-flow" process that is far more efficient and flexible than stage / gate.

are reviewed. If these deliverables are deemed to be acceptable, the project moves on to the next stage. If they are rejected (due to excessive risk, errors or omissions, unacceptable profit margin, etc.), the firm must decide whether to revise the deliverables and take another shot at the gate, or to cancel the project.

The great thing about stage / gate NPD is that it can serve as a set of "training wheels" for an organization that is making the transition from strong functional silos to a cross-functional team environment. The concept of "concurrent engineering" (CE) emerged at about the same time as stage / gate, and is highly synergistic with it.[8] Activities that had previously been performed in serial, over-the-wall fashion, could be executed in parallel by CE teams (also known as Integrated Product Teams).[9] The stage / gate process serves as a "policeman" to ensure that each function works on the appropriate deliverables during each stage of the project. Not so bad, right?

The drawback is that the stage / gate NPD process is inherently wasteful. It is really just a sequence of large time batches, each of which can be a massive roadblock to the flow of value. Moreover, the fundamental assumption on which it is based is flawed. Product development does not follow a clean, sequential set of stages. In an optimized process, the critical path should drive the project schedule. It should not be driven by some arbitrary structure that forces the entire team to wait at each gate until the slowest task is completed. In its most anal form, stage / gate can be more of a hindrance than a help, as is illustrated in the following (totally true) description of the gate-review meeting from hell.[10]

## Why the Stage / Gate NPD Process Needs a Lean Overhaul

"This gate review is called to order," announced Carl in a loud and officious voice. After things settled down, he placed a transparency of the review agenda on the viewgraph projector and continued. "First of all, who's here and who's missing?" A quick perusal of the room made it clear that this meeting was off to yet another rocky start. Of the six NPD "gate keepers" that held the future of Star Data Systems in their hands, only four were present. As usual, marketing had not deemed these "mundane" proceedings to be their highest priority. Without marketing present, a follow-up review would be needed before the GalaxyStar product could move from the Specification Stage into the ever-popular Prototyping Stage. Carl Miller, the VP of manufacturing and titular head of the meeting, was livid. "This is the third time we've tried to get this product off of top-dead-center," he fumed. "I'm tempted to get the CEO on the phone right now and let him know how great his stage / gate process is working."

Carl had a point. The GalaxyStar data router was to be the flagship of a new product-line for his firm. Yet it had become embroiled in what seemed like an endless battle to move from stage to stage in Star Data System's stage / gate NPD process. First of all, there were *seven gates* that had to be cleared for a new product to enter production.[11] At both the first and second of these gate reviews, some trivial missing deliverable had caused a shouting match about "the integrity of the process." In both cases, the project was essentially put on hold awaiting those final boxes to be checked off. Thus far, there had been three-months worth of unnecessary delays – and there were still four more gates to go!

Now, with time-to-market already compromised, the gate-review team was heading for another nightmare. There had always been bad blood between the heads of engineering, marketing, and manufacturing. In the old "over-the-wall" days, there was enough distance between them to keep tempers from flaring. Now that concurrent engineering was the big thing, Carl and his engineering counterpart, Carol Campbell, were at each other's throats on a regular basis.

"Look Carl," hissed Carol from the far end of the conference table, "I'm getting pretty sick of listening to you gripe about this process. It is company policy, it's in our ISO 9000 manual, and our guys in Engineering are fully on board. *Exactly what is your problem?*" That last question was delivered with enough heat to sear the eyebrows of the other attendees at the meeting. Everyone in the company knew that the job of General Manager was soon to be open, and both Carol and her alliterative nemesis, Carl, were running for it like mudslinging politicians. These gate reviews had become a king-of-the-hill game in which the loser was the future of the company.

"I'll tell you what my problem is," snapped back Carl, already flushed with anger, "Your glorious Engineering team has given my Manufacturing Engineers nothing but garbage since the Concept Stage. Well, I've had it. I'm not going to sign off on one more incomplete deliverable, just to let your precious designers off the hook. In particular, I want to see a completely costed bill of materials before your geniuses spend one stinking hour on prototype design. Now who has the problem?"

As nasty as this interchange may have sounded, it was nothing compared to the meetings that were held a year later when it became apparent that the GalaxyStar product was going to be an also-ran in the marketplace. This true (but sanitized) story highlights several of the limitations of the stage / gate process, at least when it is implemented without some good common sense.[12] Holding up the NPD process because you can't get the right gatekeepers in the room for a review is pathetic at best. Likewise, unabashed political infighting is a sure sign of a lack of leadership, discipline, and responsibility in a firm. Even more mundane forms of stage / gate waste, such as forced serial actions, waiting for slow gate deliverables, and the inevitable loop-backs when changes occur, can mean a death sentence for a new product.[13]

If your firm uses a stage / gate type process, take heart. Most implementations are not as demented as the one described above. With a few simple modifications, and a new attitude toward how products should be developed, your stage / gate process can be transformed into a lean and effective methodology. And don't let me hear you complain about ISO 9000 not letting you make needed improvements. Excuses are like shields for waste; don't let your fear of change prevent you from doing what's right.

## A New Attitude – Continuous-Flow Development

Let me suggest to you a new way of thinking about product development. We are going to build a lean NPD process by considering the nature of the product itself, rather than being driven by the org-chart *du jour*. Once we've established the optimal way to develop a high-value product, we'll consider how to make it work within a typical "matrix" organization. I am, however, going to stipulate one thing right from the start: You must (let me repeat . . . *you must*) utilize cross-functional teams to develop your new products,[14] and *they must be led by a "heavyweight" team leader.*[15] This means that once a new product initiative is launched, the appointed leader is empowered to guide the team without undue interference by functional managers. Even for small projects with part-time team members, this factor is critical to success.[16] If your firm is still using functional managers to control the flow of work in new product development, you are hereby notified: Your organizational structure is near to extinction, and no one will be putting it on the endangered species list.

Now then, what is it about the nature of a product that should drive the new product development process? Clearly we must consider the technologies embodied in the product, the manufacturing processes to be used in production, the range of intended customers, and the overall business case that makes it a profitable venture. The above considerations can be thought of as defining an "envelope" in which the new product must reside to be a viable entity. The envelope is quite large in the early conceptual stages of development, where many possible solutions and trade-offs can be considered. As the process progresses, decisions must be made: Certain aspects of the product must be fixed in stone to enable downstream work to proceed. The range of options narrows, but we still have room to perform trade-offs and evaluate alternatives. Only when we must commit to capital investments (e.g., tooling, fixturing, long-lead items, etc.) should we make our final decisions and go "cut metal." What I've just described could be envisioned as a "narrowing funnel," as shown in Figure 7.4.[17]

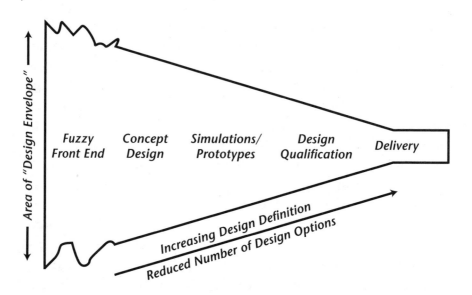

**Figure 7.4:** The "narrowing funnel" perspective on new product development. As a new product design moves from early concept stage to final product launch, decisions are made that narrow the funnel. These decisions reduce the options open to designers.

So we want our process to look like a funnel . . . how does this get us to market? The next step we must take is to define the critical linkages and internal team deliverables that must be created to enable a successful product launch. This list might include:

- Marketing Requirements Specification
- Engineering Design Specification
- Engineering Prototypes
- Manufacturing Process Development
- Production Prototypes
- Test Reports
- Launch Package
- etc., etc., . . .

These deliverables are at the heart of the value stream for your development project, and will form the critical core (or path, if you prefer) of your project plan. At the points of handoff for each critical deliverable, your funnel will narrow. (Note that the linkages between these critical-core tasks should follow the lean guidelines of Method #2 – Customer-Defined Deliverables). Prior to releasing a marketing requirements specification, for example, lots of options can be considered. After release, Engineering will be hard at work, and major changes will result in wasted time and effort. If you've been paying attention, this should sound familiar to you (see Method #6 – Staged-Freeze Specifications). Indeed a combination of tight linkages between critical-core tasks and the use of staged (or progressive) freezing of the design itself will yield a highly efficient NPD process. This "new attitude" toward product development, in which the critical-core value stream defines the process, is referred to as "continuous-flow product development."

Now let's fill in some details. How do we verify that the critical deliverables are complete and acceptable? Rather than holding arbitrary gate reviews that force the creation of lots of unnecessary paperwork (and in some cases, even "dummy deliverables"), why not harness the gate structure to review critical project hand-offs? Lay out your critical-core schedule, define the key hand-offs, and then place reviews prior to the hand-off points. The reviews can include a vetting of the deliverables themselves, a progress report on other parallel tasks, and a check against the business case to re-verify the economics of the project. You might consider using the suggestions in Method #5 – The "Waste-Free" Design Review for these new, lean gate meetings.

Now what about freeze points? Again, they should be aligned with the hand-off of critical-core deliverables. Basically, the entire NPD process should be aligned with these hand-offs, since they are at the heart of value creation. I generally suggest at least three freeze points be defined in your process: 1) Freezing of the customer or user interface (form, fit, function), 2) Freezing of component definition and / or system partitioning, and 3) Freezing of design aspects that impact long-lead materials or tooling. The first freeze could be imposed simultaneously with the hand-off of a marketing requirements specification. The second could be scheduled in sync with the release of an engineering design

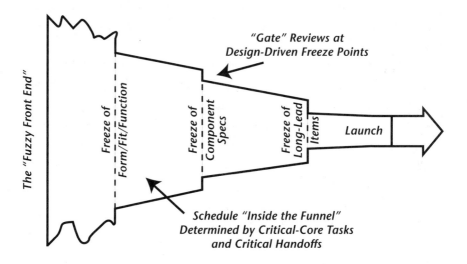

**Continuous-Flow Product Development**
*(One of Many Possible Implementations)*

*The "Fuzzy Front End"*

*Freeze of Form/Fit/Function*

*Freeze of Component Specs*

*Freeze of Long-Lead Items*

*"Gate" Reviews at Design-Driven Freeze Points*

*Launch*

*Schedule "Inside the Funnel" Determined by Critical-Core Tasks and Critical Handoffs*

**Figure 7.5**: Conceptual diagram of the "continuous-flow" new product development process. A narrowing funnel provides the general structure, with several freeze points identified that enable parallel work to begin, thereby shortening development cycle times. Note that there are many ways in which this general structure can be adapted to meet specific company needs.

specification (along with flow-down requirements), and the third could be aligned with the acceptance of prototype test data. You can use more freeze points if you wish, but just be careful not to overcomplicate the process. Remember that the only reason to freeze design elements (and thereby limit your range of downstream options) is to allow parallel work to begin, thereby reducing your overall time-to-market.

So there we have it, as shown in Figure 7.5. We are envisioning here an idealized process that resembles a critical-core project plan, with lots of design options at the beginning and narrowing to a final configuration at the end. The "funnel" would have some discontinuities in it that are driven by freeze points in the design process. Several "gate reviews" could be held at critical hand-off and / or freeze points. They would serve the same purpose as the old-fashioned kind, except that they would be scheduled based on the nature of the value stream rather than being arbitrarily imposed from on-high.

Note that several things are absent from this continuous-flow NPD process. There are no "stages" *per se*. This reflects the reality that product development is anything but serial.[18] Why define stages that serve no purpose other than to corral work into artificial time batches? If we can execute stages in parallel, then so much the better. Also missing are the stonewall gate reviews. Instead, work continues uninterrupted on all tasks except the ones whose hand-off is being reviewed. The rule is to never slow down the value stream unless a major problem is identified. There is a lot more to say about the continuous-flow process, but at the highest level, that's the picture I'd like you to form in your mind.

Before we move on to discuss the internal workings of the continuous-flow process, I'd like to describe the way one firm instituted lean product development. In fact, they sort of invented it. That firm is Toyota Motor Company, and their approach to new product development is a classic example of how methods that may seem counterintuitive on the surface can actually be very lean. Remember that NPD is really still in the Dark Ages when it comes to efficiency. New thinking is what it takes to break down the barriers erected by our mass-production forefathers.

## Toyota's Approach – Set-Based Concurrent Engineering

"Good morning Mr. Algernon, please make yourself comfortable." A small, portly man in an ill-fitting suit was led to the place of honor at the head of an oval conference table. The year was 2030, a time of great opportunity for entrepreneurs. Yet despite an exponential growth in technical capabilities and industrial capacity, most firms were still using the same, antiquated methods for developing new products. Mr. Algernon was the latest victim of these ossified methods. This fact was evident in the apprehensive look on the little man's face as he was being fawned over by a customer-comfort robot.

"My name is Charlie Logan, and I'm head of Sales here at GeneCrafters, Inc. Can Freddie here bring you some more coffee before we begin our presentation?" Logan nodded toward the floating basketball-shaped gadget that was hovering too close to the prospective client's head for comfort. Algernon waved away both the offer and the comfort-robot, looking even less at ease than a moment before.

"I'd really like to get down to business." The customer shifted in his well-padded leather chair. "I've already wasted six months of my time with your illustrious competitor, and truthfully I'm ready to pack this whole idea in." The competitor that Algernon was referring to was ACME Genetics, one of the first bioengineering firms to begin offering genetically engineered animals for all occasions. After two decades of debate, the insurmountable moral and ethical issues over genetic manipulation of species had been put to rest (this is, after all, a science fiction tale). Now virtually anyone with enough funds could have the animal of their dreams, or at least that's what the advertisements claimed.

"Since you've obviously had a bad experience with 'the other guys,' why don't we begin with you describing what has left you so frustrated." Charlie Logan had gone through this process with several former clients of ACME, and knew what he was going to hear. Nonetheless, he put on his best "really interested" face and settled in for another sad story.

"I'll make it short and not so sweet," began Algernon. "I had this bright idea for a new type of farm animal. Combine the food-producing features of several species into a single, compact little barnyard beast. This way, even people with small rural properties could produce the same range of fresh-food options as larger commercial farms." A quick pause for a belt of coffee, and he continued. "I thought I made it very clear up front with ACME that I was looking for something unique and original. The only requirements that were etched in stone were that the animal must be food-producing and about the size of a large goat."

"Things went badly from the start." Algernon pulled a crinkled diagram out of his briefcase and slide it across the table to

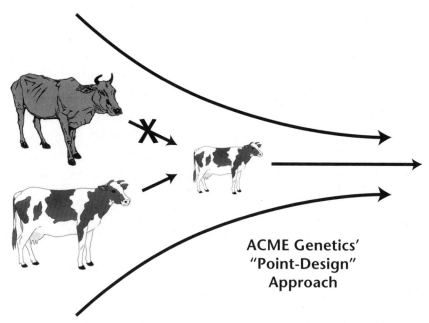

**Figure 7.6**: A graphical representation of the "point-design" NPD approach used by ACME Genetics. The primary limitation of this process is that it narrows the "funnel" too early, potentially missing value opportunities. Once the design team converged on a "cow concept" it would be unlikely that a "chicken concept," for example, would be considered.

Logan (you can take a peek at it in Figure 7.6). "Somehow, no matter how hard I tried, I couldn't get them away from the 'cow concept.' Big cow, small cow, steer, longhorn, milk cow, you name it. Lots of choices, and all of them bovine. True, they were willing to engineer the milk and meat flavors to my specifications, but when I asked them to 'think out of the box' they threw it back in my face. If I couldn't tell them what was missing from the design, then I must be satisfied with the solution. They should really rename their firm 'Cows-R-Us.'"

It was clearly time for Logan to intercede. Algernon looked to be ready to bolt for the door. Time to captivate this disenfranchised customer. "Let me show you the GeneCrafters product development approach and let's see if it might work better for you." Logan touched an orange pad in the corner of the black-glass conference table and a bright projection display came to life on the wall behind him. (You can view the graphic he displayed in Figure 7.7). "After reviewing your request for quotation, we developed this strawman concept for your custom-animal project. At GeneCrafters, we never propose 'point designs' to our customers. We've discovered that most of our customers have unarticulated needs and benefits that don't come through in initial requirements documents. Proposing a single-point solution to those early requirements often results in the complaints that you've expressed. Moreover, even our own design teams find that considering only a narrow range of options, such as the cow *du jour* from ACME, can limit our opportunities to innovate. Hence, we use a 'set-based' approach to product development."

"In the early stages of our development effort, we might, for

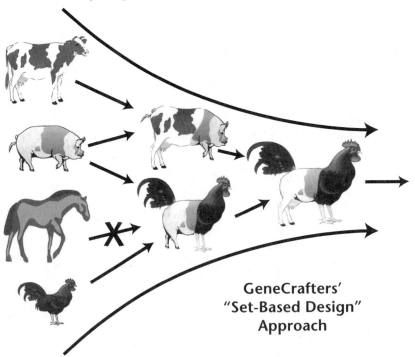

**GeneCrafters'
"Set-Based Design"
Approach**

**Figure 7.7:** Presentation given to Mr. Algernon by GeneCrafters, showing their "set-based design" approach. By considering a set of several conflicting design options up-front, a higher-value concept is created. Delaying design decisions until as late as possible in the process keeps options open and results in less-disruptive change.

instance, offer you enhanced versions of several familiar barn-yard animals. We actually use independent teams to generate these concepts, and then have each team present their creations to you for review. Conflict and debate are encouraged, and trade-offs and compromises are continuous. You have the opportunity to hear a broad range of benefits and options, and can down-select the most desirable ones for the next phase." Logan paused to observe his client's body language. Clearly he had Algernon's interest, but there was still skepticism oozing from every pore.

Algernon took advantage of the pause to insert a question. "This sounds great in theory, but the cost of running four differ-ent design teams in parallel must be prohibitive. Money is defi-nitely a consideration on this project, and I doubt I can afford your high-brow process."

"Actually, just the opposite is true, Mr. Algernon." Logan began to feel a bit more confident; the client had asked just the right question. "We don't go very far down the road with these early prototype concepts. Just enough detail to tease out a more accurate picture of what you really desire. Once we have some feedback, we narrow the options, spend a bit more time on refin-ing the designs, and again seek your input before finalizing." Now Logan could see the expression he was hoping for on Alger-non's face – that "I'm almost ready to open my wallet" look.

"Let's talk about this concept diagram you've displayed," said Algernon, his eyes turning upward toward the projection dis-play, his tone far more relaxed. "Can you really put together the best features of a chicken, a cow, and a pig all in one animal?"

"Frankly, so could ACME," replied Charlie Logan, already adding the commission for this sale to his monthly tally. "The technology is not the problem; we do stranger things every day. The problem is in the process itself. Without considering a broad and often conflictory set of design options up-front, our thinking narrows too quickly to a 'solution.' It's in the argu-ments among our concept teams, and the reaction you have to these debates, that real value is created. Casting a big net early on avoids us missing a high-value opportunity. By delaying decisions until later in the process, we keep our options open and avoid looping back when we discover that we were premature in freezing a design."

"Ok, you've hooked me," responded Algernon, now looking like a new man. "If you can really deliver a cow-chicken-pig creature, my little business will be a huge hit. With bacon, sausage, ham, eggs, butter, cheese, and milk all coming from the same beast, it will be like owning a 'Grand Slam' breakfast on four legs!"

And with that, the sale was made. Toyota Motor Company is a pioneer in this so-called "set-based concurrent engineering,"[19] but automotive case examples tend to be highly industry specific. The underlying principles, however, are applicable to any sector. When a customer's needs are not well understood, it may be more efficient and more valuable to offer a "set" of conflicting design options, while delaying design-freeze decisions as long as possible. Rather than a "point-design" funnel that narrows right from design kick-off, try keeping options open and gathering continuous feedback from the customer or market. There may be no better way to draw forth unarticulated needs and benefits, thereby assuring a successful, high-value product.

### Facet 2 – The "Fuzzy Front End"

Without question, the most frustrating, annoying, and downright intractable aspect of new product development is initial requirements definition. Whereas the typical project is assumed to begin with a contract, a charter, or at least a specification or statement of work, NPD often begins with nothing but an idea . . . and a "fuzzy" one at that. Indeed, divining customer needs and defining initial requirements can be more of an art than a science.[20] The more ambiguous and challenging the customer need, the more cost and time will be required to specify a viable product solution.[21]

Since there is no pat answer to the fuzzy-requirements conundrum, many firms drag their feet during the early stages of product development.[22] In fact, over half of the total time from idea proposal to product launch can be spent vacillating on needs, features, options, and performance trade-offs.[23] During this time, the "market clock" keeps ticking away, and future revenues and profits are evaporating with each tick.[24]

I certainly don't have a simple answer to this cosmic problem. Short of clairvoyance, there is no closed-form solution. I can, however, identify the three key elements of a lean requirements-definition activity. They are, in order of importance:

1) An iterative feedback process between the product design team and the customer(s) or market(s).
2) Use of real, tangible models, simulations, prototypes, strawmen, etc., that can evoke gut-level customer reactions, capture tacit desires, and evolve as new learning takes place.
3) Involvement of the CEO and executive team in reviewing the new-product business case, and fully committing the organization's resources to a successful development effort.[25]

The first requirement is beyond essential. Only the customer can serve as the arbiter of a product's value (despite the protestations of design engineers that they "understand the customer's needs better than the customers themselves"). The degree of ambiguity in requirements determines how many feedback iterations are needed, and how close together they should be. For cut-and-dried products with clear solutions, only a quick market test is needed to ensure that a product design is on track. A brand new product, in a new market, that utilizes new technology, is a poster child for almost continuous prototyping and testing with lead users or focus groups.

The second mandate given above follows directly from the first. If frequent feedback is essential, then a means to gain that feedback efficiently is a must for lean NPD. The solution here is the use of physical, visual, tangible prototypes (or other variations on this theme). There is strong evidence that customers will be far more capable of articulating their needs when confronted with a visual model to challenge their senses.[26] Sitting around a conference table with piles of specifications and engineering drawings is typically far less productive than arguing over a physical prototype.

This leads us to the final requirement I have suggested. Involvement of executives in the NPD process is most valuable when the business case for the proposed product is still in a state of flux. Once requirements are defined, interference by a well-meaning VP or CEO will almost certainly generate an avalanche of waste. Let the executives get their two-cents worth in during initial idea screening and project funding meetings. Once the "project" of NPD is defined and the requirements have converged, executives should swagger back to their inappropriately pretentious offices and try to look busy.

If we agree that early customer feedback is essential, and that the way to get it is through visual prototypes of some sort, how then do we get customers to join the party? The possibilities are endless, but I've illustrated a few highly effective strategies in Figure 7.8.[27] The first of these techniques is often referred to as "probe-and-learn" market testing: When a market need is sensed by a firm, the general concept is explored through multiple variations on a theme. Several possible designs for a new kitchen appliance, for example, might be rendered on a 3-D CAD system. These early concepts could then be presented to potential customers for feedback. If a clear winner emerges, that design (or perhaps several minor variations) would be refined and retested in the marketplace. The process would continue until a resonance with market feedback is obtained.

There are a number of possible fora to gather probe-and-learn data from customers. Focus groups are the traditional approach, but these gatherings of potential users often degenerate into staged and choreographed affairs run by less-than-objective facilitators. Even trade shows are a bit too artificial for my taste. It is easy to love something in the "out of context" atmosphere of a trade show. I prefer to bring the models or prototypes to where the customers live. Demonstration projects, alpha-test sites, giveaways, even having employees take prototypes home and try them with friends, have all shown high value when it comes to gathering feedback.[28]

| Strategy | Advantages | Disadvantages |
|----------|------------|---------------|
| Probe-and-Learn | • Very flexible<br>• Provides multi-dimensional feedback | • Feedback may be slow<br>• Suitable venues may not be available in your industry |
| Set-Based Design | • Encourages constructive debate and innovative thinking | • Requires significantly greater staffing at the early stages of product development |
| Indwelling | • Allows for the deepest understanding of the customer's needs and use environment | • Can be costly and time-consuming<br>• Suitable opportunities may not be available in your industry |

**Figure 7.8:** Several useful strategies for gathering early customer feedback on design concepts and product requirements, including probe-and-learn, set-based design, and indwelling.

The next strategy on the list, set-based design, was described in the previous section. This approach closely resembles probe-and-learn from the customer's perspective, but emphasizes the creation of conflicting design options as a way to stimulate creativity and ferret-out unspoken customer needs. At each level of the product design, several disparate options are considered and the advantages of each are weighed. Nice strategy if you can afford it. In the real world, there are few products that are grand enough for the full Toyota-type implementation. Ford used this approach, for example, to develop the highly successful new Mustang. Three conflicting design concepts were considered: the "Rambo," the "Schwarzenegger" and the "Bruce Jenner." The idea was to try variations on the Mustang theme and determine which combination of power, comfort, styling, etc., would meet with the greatest customer enthusiasm.[29]

On a far more humble scale, I've used a combination of probe-and-learn and set-based design to develop the book you hold reverently in your hands. I began this process five years ago by developing a dozen possible outlines for a professional development workshop. I included in my "set" everything from soft-skill, tree-hugging type material, to the hard and practical lean material you have come to know and love. Without a single viewgraph to back me up, I sent these disembodied outlines to a number of universities and professional associations. Only half of my "prototypes" received any attention, so I immediately dropped the losers and cobbled together a strawman course for the winners. It only took one pilot session of the remaining six possibilities (and the associated feedback from student surveys) to narrow the field to three. After refining all three workshops to a point of reasonable maturity, I decided to drop a very successful Lean Supply-Chain Management course, and focus on the body of knowledge presented herein.

A final approach that can yield excellent results is referred to as "indwelling." The idea here is to turn your design team into pseudo-customers. If designers have had the chance to walk a few miles in the customer's shoes, it will be far easier for them to formulate desirable solutions. This can be accomplished in several ways, but usually it involves placing design team members into the customer environment in some way and allowing them to experience it for themselves. When Nissan decided to attempt the development of a Eurocar, they sent fifty of their top designers to Europe for six months to test-drive competitors models on actual European roads and tracks. The result was a far better understanding of how Europeans view driving, performance, style, handling, etc.

In another interesting example, Matsushita, the Japanese consumer-products giant, used indwelling to educate their designers about how to develop the first automated breadmaking machine.[30] Early prototypes for this product produced bread . . . if you have a very loose definition of bread. After a few chipped teeth and upset stomachs, the design team realized that there must be something about breadmaking that was eluding them. They got three of their designers jobs at one of Tokyo's finest bakeries for three months, where they made bread with their hands day in and day out. After this indwelling experience, the first redesign of their breadmaker produced excellent results (of course their innovative capabilities may have been stimulated by a fear of being sent back for another tour of duty).

If shipping your employees off to work in the trenches is not a viable possibility, you can consider bringing the indwelling environment to you. The office equipment manufacturer, Steelcase, for example, has established a prototyping center at one of their sites that enables customers to create full-scale models of various office configurations.[31] In this way, designers, marketers, and customers can collaborate on the ideal solution, and test their concepts in real time. Whatever approach you choose, there is no substitute for early customer feedback on some form of visual model or prototype. If your firm can't converge on initial requirements, it's probably because you aren't asking the opinion of the people that really matter.

## An Adaptation of Method #1 – Testing for Customer Value

All this schmoozing with the customer is great, but it sure would be useful to have an analytical tool that could help you capture and prioritize the insights you gain. Fortunately, we can develop such a tool through a simple extension of Method #1 – Testing for Customer Value. Naturally, the tool that I will describe is lean and efficient. It is certainly not the only alternative, however. A number of approaches to value estimation and value engineering have been described in the literature, most notably Quality Function Deployment (QFD).[32] You are welcome to dig deeper if you have the interest, but I've found the tool described below to be effective and nearly waste-free.

Recall from our earlier Method #1 description that we identified three "tests for value:" performance overshoot, excessive complexity, and the least-discernable-difference test. For the purposes of this product-specific chapter, I will modify these general tests slightly. First, let's consider the performance-overshoot test. The problem with most attempts at gathering customer feedback is that the customer is confronted with only a single option for key performance parameters. This reflects the all too common "point-design" affliction of many design teams. If you consider Figure 7.9, however, you will see that offering a single performance level to a customer gives you little insight into their sensitivity to that parameter.

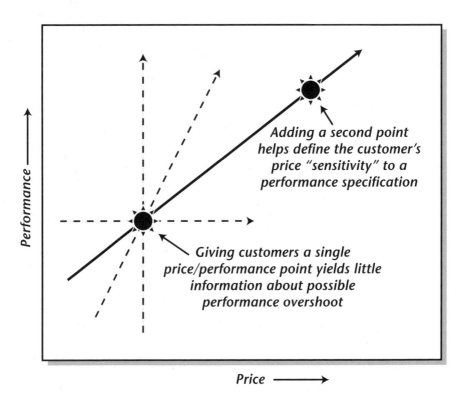

**Figure 7.9:** Testing for performance overshoot requires that customers be given at least two price / performance points to consider. A single-point design provides no feedback into the customer's willingness to pay for increased performance. By offering two points along the price / performance curve, you can determine the "slope of the line" and thereby identify when you are in danger of performance overshoot.

Far better to propose two or more "points" to your customer and discover the "slope of the line" between price and performance. A flat line implies that the customer is not interested in improving the parameter under consideration, and won't give you a nickel for your added cost and risk. A near vertical line tells you that even a small improvement will yield a significant increase in price. We will call this the "Two-Point Overshoot

Test." This test is appropriate for performance requirements that appear to be triggering the customer's salivary glands (forgive me for equating your precious customers with Pavlov's dogs). When purchasing a car, for example, your buying decision might be driven by horsepower, appearance, or handling. Improvement in these key requirements could potentially elicit a higher price.

A second test, derived by modifying the idea of excessive complexity, I will call the "Good Enough?" Test. In this case, we are looking for performance attributes that are not high on the customer's wish list, but are necessary for the product to function properly. These design elements need only be "good enough" to achieve market acceptance. Any cost or risk in these areas that goes beyond this threshold of mediocrity will not be rewarded. Hence, we will create a good, solid design at the lowest possible cost. Using our car example, this test would be appropriate for, say, the car's battery or tires. Most of us would not pay more for a better car battery, and generally couldn't care less about the tire's performance specifications (unless you've recently run afoul of a certain notorious SUV). As long as the battery starts the car and the tires keep you safe, you're not really interested. No point in gold plating these attributes; good enough is good enough.

My final test is related to the concept of the "least-discernable difference." In this case, we are interested in discriminating between valued features and those that are below the customer's radar screen. In Southern California, for example, most high-end cars come standard with cruise control. Can you imagine a more useless feature for those of us that spend much of our lives parked in traffic on Los Angeles freeways? If I were offered the choice between having cruise control included in my vehicle and saving a dollar off the price, I would take the dollar without thinking twice. Hence, I will call this final indicator the "Pay a Dollar More?" Test. (If you are interested in case examples that illustrate these tests, I've provided several references in the Notes section.)[33]

Now, armed with the three tests described above, we can begin classifying the various requirements of your product into bins and applying the appropriate test. To do this I will use an approach similar to QFD, but without the waste that is often associated with this well-worn tool. Initially created to capture the "voice of the customer," QFD (also known as the "House of Quality") can be an excellent method for mapping customer needs into product requirements.[34] Unfortunately, however, this tool seems to have mutated over time from a straightforward technique into an obese time-waster. A QFD that relates a modest number of customer needs into a handful of requirements can be useful. However, a QFD that maps twenty customer needs into forty or fifty requirements is a waste of time. It seems that in many cases the House of Quality has evolved over time into a Mansion of Quality.

Hence, I propose a "lean QFD." Those of you with experience in using the original version can adapt my suggestions as you see fit. If you have no experience in this area, so much the better. You won't have any bad habits to break. A lean QFD is just a two-dimensional matrix, as shown in Figure 7.10. To use this tool, begin by determining the top three benefits that the customer desires. These should be phrased in the customer's language and must drive their decisions about product acceptance and price. If at all possible, you should build this matrix with your customers present, so that they can verify their needs and help you fill in the scores. Note that I only show three benefits in my matrix. This reflects my firm belief that simplicity should reign in any discussion of needs and benefits. Customers don't use a forty-by-forty matrix to make their buying choices, so why should you?

Next, list the most important (or expensive) requirements of the product along the vertical axis. You can include in this area any attribute that you think needs interrogation, and even consider several conflicting approaches to see how they score. Again, use your customers as a guide for the selection of requirements. Utilizing a one-to-five subjective ranking system, fill in each square in the matrix. A "one" implies that the requirement in that row does not have a significant impact on the benefit listed in that column. A "five" indicates a very high impact. Scoring is best done collaboratively with both the customer and the design team present.

**Testing for the Value of Product Features or Attributes**

| | | Key Benefits (1 to 5 Scale) | | | Value Ranking (AxBxC) |
|---|---|---|---|---|---|
| | Feature/Attribute | A) | B) | C) | |
| List in order of descending time or cost impact on project. | 1) | | | | |
| | 2) | | | | |
| | 3) | | | | |
| | 4) | | | | |
| | 5) | | | | |
| | 6) | | | | |
| | 7) | | | | |
| | 8) | | | | |
| | 9) | | | | |

| Value Ranking | Value Test |
|---|---|
| 125-27 | Two-Point Overshoot Test |
| 27-8 | "Good Enough?" Test |
| 8-1 | "Pay a Dollar More?" Test |

**Figure 7.10:** Example of a "lean QFD" that can be used to map customer benefits (that determine price and acceptance) into product requirements. Those requirements that have a high aggregate score should be given the Two-Point Overshoot Test. Middle-of-the-road scores can benefit from the "Good Enough?" Test, while the lower scoring requirements should be evaluated using the "Pay a Dollar More?" Test.

Once the scores are in, multiply together the three numbers across each row. The result will range from 125 (all fives) to one (all ones). This combined score is a good indicator of how to categorize your requirements. A score from 125 to 27 implies that the given requirement is a price driver, and the Two-Point Overshoot Test should be applied. A score between 27 and 8 indicates a low correlation between price and performance; a good candidate for the "Good Enough?" Test. Finally, a score below eight shows little impact on customer benefits, and may be something that can be eliminated through the "Pay a Dollar More?" Test.

Obviously, this is a very subjective tool, and the scoring and categorization will not be precisely accurate. Use your good judgment and common sense. If the scores don't seem reasonable, try changing your choice of benefits (or the wording thereof). Once this tool has been used at the very highest level, you can drill down to sub-assemblies and components and apply this method at a more detailed level. You may never bring customer needs into sharp focus, but hopefully this method will remove a bit of "fuzziness" from your requirements-definition process.

### Facet 3 – The "Project in the Middle"

Here's my thinking on product development. Before requirements are well-defined, product development is a strategic and somewhat chaotic process. Some of the chaos can be averted by applying the methods described above, but at some level the process needs to be flexible and creative. Once a reasonable set of requirements has been defined, however, and an acceptable business case identified, it is time to go into action. From the point of requirements definition to the launch of the product into rate production, the activities of the development team should be treated as a *project*.[35] No random walks through functional departments. No disruptive changes (unless essential to retaining a valid business case). And most certainly, no obstructive gates, tollbooths, management indecision, funding bottlenecks . . . you get the idea.

Since the majority of this book deals with lean and efficient project management, it hardly seems necessary for me to reiterate these techniques. I will, however, quickly run through the toolbox and identify any product-development-specific adaptations you might consider. The pace of this discussion will be brisk – this book is long enough already.

The first method, "Testing for Customer Value," has already been discussed in the previous section. Use the three value tests up-front to solidify initial product requirements, but don't stop there. At every design review or freeze point these same tests can be used to verify that overshoot has not snuck in, or that a "good-enough" component has not been gold plated. I also suggest using the tests for value to ensure that internal team deliverables have not overshot or undershot the needs of their associated customers. For example, it might be appropriate to let a test engineer choose between two different possible test-plan outlines, one simple and brief, the other more complete and complex. The two-point test can work for any value-embodying item.

Method #2 – Customer-Defined Deliverables translates into product development seamlessly. Perhaps the only wrinkle here is that since NPD is a recurring process, it would make sense to create some standard templates for each critical hand-off, so that team members have an easy starting point for "strawmanning" their deliverables. Likewise, Method #3 – Urgency-Driven Standup Meetings and Method #4 – Real / Virtual Project Rooms need no translation to work effectively on a product-development project.

The two methods that follow are particularly critical for NPD. Method #5 – The "Waste-Free" Design Review and Method #6 – Staged-Freeze Specifications can work in tandem to define the "funnel" for new product development. Use the Method #5 countermeasure to create highly efficient gate / freeze / design reviews. These meetings would serve as "go / no-go" meetings for senior management, and can be focused on those design elements that must be frozen to allow parallel tasks to begin.

Visual communication is always important, but when physical products are involved, the more visual context that can be created the better. Models and prototypes should be under the noses of designers, executives, and customers from the beginning to the end of NPD. Project metrics and status should be emblazoned in color graphics on every bare wall. A color-coded schedule can be used to focus team members on their respective tasks. The goal in each case is to reduce ambiguity, decrease "access time" for needed information, and to generally stimulate the team's minds to understand, think, and act.

Likewise, the standardization techniques of Method #8 can play a broad and important role in NPD. Since new product development is a recurring process, there is much to gain from creating a shopping cart (or an intranet directory) filled with templates, guidelines, checklists, etc. At a minimum, every deliverable and design review should have a guideline for execution, a template for document creation, and a checklist to ensure that activities are complete and risks are minimized.[36]

A critical core of tasks should be identified for every new product development effort.[37] These activities will be the focus of risk mitigation, resource management, and status reporting. The progress-tracking countermeasures of Method #9 can be invaluable for these purposes. Every task that has the potential to drive the product launch date should have incremental milestones defined and a risk buffer identified.

Finally, resource management during product development is perhaps even more challenging than for other forms of project. The reason is that there are activities that design team members must perform that are not development related and yet may have even higher priority (or at least urgency). I am referring here to sustaining engineering support of products that are already in the factory. It is not uncommon for engineers to be pulled off of NPD tasks on the spur of the moment to go fix a problem that has stopped the production line. What is frustrating about this type of "obstacle to value creation" is that although it is an obstacle for one value stream (product development) *it is an enabler for another* (shipping products and paying the bills).

I've described several ways to handle this resource allocation paradox, but all of them come down to protecting some of your design team's time from disruption. Designate mornings as "development time" and afternoons as "factory-support time," unless the line is completely shut down. Try assigning someone in engineering to be "on-call" for sustaining support, while others are allowed to work on their critical-core tasks. Empower someone with organizational clout to serve as a filter, dispatcher, and resource optimizer. Whatever your approach, if you don't carve out blocks of time that are protected from disruption, your products will migrate through development like a herd of turtles.

Well, there's a quick overview of how Lean Project Management can metamorphose into Lean Product Development. In the next section, we will deal with a final challenge that is unique to NPD: How to design products that achieve the lowest possible production cost while meeting your customer's increasing demands for customization. In the story that follows, I have made the manufacturing folks the heroes. Hopefully, those of you on the engineering side of the building will take up the gauntlet I have thrown and become wizards at design for lean manufacture.

## Facet 4 – Design for Lean Manufacture

"What do you mean, you're shutting it down?" Tina Dobb's voice carried a mixture of surprise and resignation. After all, she had seen this coming for a long time. The X-20 line of industrial sensors had suffered from eroding gross margins since Tina took over as manufacturing engineer for the product family five years ago. In those days, the executives at Sensormation, Inc. had considered the process-monitoring sensors that made up the X-20 product-line to be their brightest hope for the company's future. But despite a growing demand and higher-than-expected sales volumes, the X-20 had failed the ultimate test. It just wasn't profitable. For several years it had hovered at the precipice, but finally in the last two quarters it had failed to meet the minimum five-percent gross margin that was required for a product-line to remain in Sensormation's portfolio.

"I can't believe that you're really going to kill it," Tina groaned, as she slumped into one of the two uncomfortable guest chairs, still not fully accepting the dismal news.

The bearer of this bad news sat on the other side of an old-fashioned, sheet-metal industrial desk; a small, stocky man with broad shoulders and a determined look. Tim Whitney was, without question, the savior of Sensormation, and everyone knew it. He had stepped in as Vice President of Operations three years earlier, at a time when layoffs were a weekly affair. From day one he had moved with speed and tenacity to implement lean manufacturing initiatives at each of the firm's production sites. Their "corporate" facility, for example, had been transformed into a model of efficiency and cleanliness. From Whitney's office, located on a mezzanine that overlooked the entire factory floor, Tina could see row upon row of brightly lit assembly stations decorated with color-coded parts bins. The white, epoxy-coated floor was painted with stripes that identified each major fabrication line, and at every critical process step, a pole towered above the workfloor, topped by a tri-colored light. In all, it was an impressive sight.

"Look, the decision had to be made and you know it," replied Whitney in a matter-of-fact tone. "We desperately need to improve our profit numbers, and the capacity that's being consumed by the X-20 can be used to produce other, higher-margin products. Before I came here, Sensormation was floundering in a sea of red ink. If we don't keep making the tough decisions, we will never move ourselves firmly into the black." Although Whitney's face reflected the firmness and determination that was his trademark, his eyes betrayed compassion for Tina's plight. For five years she had struggled to bring X-20 to full-rate production. She had even recruited two of her former co-workers from a previous employer to join her product team. Now their jobs would be in jeopardy, and Tina would have to move her career back to square one. "Believe me, if there was any other way . . . ." His voice trailed off and he raised both hands, palms up, in a gesture of futility. "I wanted to give you the chance to break the news to your team. Please get them started on the phase-out after the first of the month."

Tim was a good man, Tina thought as she rose to leave. If he thinks the X-20 should be killed, it is probably the right decision. Yet, as she looked out of the large, shatterproof office window onto the factory floor below, she couldn't quite seem to accept it. She noted that all the colored lights on the poles were green – the line was functioning smoothly as usual. As she stared out at the sea of green lights something clicked in Tina's mind. Maybe there was a chance. After all, the factory had been in terrible shape when Tim had joined the company, and look at it now. A Shingo Prize for quality, not to mention a contender for next year's Baldridge Award. Costs down dramatically, inventory turns through the roof, cycle time cut to a third, and all this in just three years. As she turned and began to leave, the idea solidified. She wheeled in place, a look of rebellion in her eyes.

"What if I make you an offer you can't refuse?" She marched up to Whitney's desk, leaned toward him, and planted her fists firmly on its fake wood-grain laminate surface. "What if I showed you a plan that would bring X-20 to full profitability within two years? Would you reconsider your decision?" It was a shot in the dark, but her dedicated team deserved every chance.

"Tina, I know how hard you've worked this problem." Whitney's tone was softer now. "If I thought there was any way to get X-20 into the black, I'd be the first to lead the charge. But you and I both know that isn't going to magically happen. We just can't get our costs down low enough to stay competitive and still capture good margins. It just isn't in the cards."

"Look Tim, you worked a miracle in this factory. How did you manage it with such a defeatist attitude?" Tina could see she had hit a nerve.

"My situation was different," Whitney responded, still the model of patience. "I had the proven methods of lean manufacturing at my disposal. Too bad we can't just lean-out the X-20."

"But what if we could? Remember the seminar that I attended last month on Design for Lean Manufacturing? The instructor presented a bunch of lean design methods that can dramatically reduce production cost." Tina paused to observe his reaction to her challenge. At first, Whitney's expression didn't change. Then she detected a flicker of interest.

"There is nothing I'd like better than to see the Engineering group adopt lean principles," Whitney replied, "but I doubt you'll have much luck. Moreover, it is really too late for the X-20. I think we just have to accept the inevitable."

Tina barely heard Whitney's response. She was already formulating a rescue plan. "Just give me a week. Look, you said yourself that the market for the X-20 is one of the best growth opportunities we have. Why give it up to our competitors if we have even a chance at success? Let me draft a plan for a lean redesign of the X-20. I'll show you just how profitable this product-line can be." She was running on bravado now, since she had never tried anything like this before. Never the shy one, however, Tina charged ahead. "If I can convince you that the margins and return-on-investment would be acceptable, will you back me up and propose it to the board?" She gathered up her best pleading look and laid it on Whitney full-strength.

There was more at stake here than the X-20 line and Tim knew it. Tina was the best he had, and the initiative she was showing here was admirable. Besides, these lean design concepts could be useful in the future. Why not give her a little rope?

"Alright, you win," Whitney relented, "but I hate to get your hopes up. You have until this time next week to put something together, but please don't be upset if it doesn't work out. To call this an uphill battle would be an understatement."

"Thanks, Tim. I really appreciate this." Tina gathered up her stack of production reports and scurried from the VP's office, already wondering how her team would react to her revolutionary new ideas.

Twenty-four hours later, Tina and her five-person team were huddled in the corner of the third-floor breakroom. No conference rooms were available on short notice, and her office was not fit for man or beast, so the breakroom was the only alternative. Since there was no place for a viewgraph projector among the rows of wobbly Formica tables and vending machines, she opted for handouts. Three hastily drawn slides that, she hoped, would capture her team's imagination.

"Well, guys, that's the sad story." She had given the team a quick recap of her conversation with Whitney, and their reactions had been predictable. After fielding a few questions from the disheartened group, it was time to make her pitch. "Now, here are our options. We can accept our fate and try to make the best of it," she began, pausing for dramatic effect, " . . . or we can give it one last shot." She had gotten their attention, but there wasn't much hope in the eyes that met hers. She continued undaunted. "I told a few of you about the seminar I attended last month on principles of lean design. I know most of you have been skeptical about this lean stuff, but I have to tell you, it is our only hope. I've gotten Tim to agree to consider one last chance at rescuing the X-20, so I say we should take him up on it and give it our best effort. How about it?"

She was using all the charm and enthusiasm she could muster, but the response from the team was lukewarm at best.

Well, there was no stopping now. "I'm going to explain three simple concepts to you. What I'd like you to do is to open your minds and give me feedback on each concept. Let me make it clear, however, that minor fixes and penny savings are a waste of time at this point. We need to totally redesign the product-line if we are going to hit the twenty-percent gross margins that our illustrious leaders demand." One of the members of the group raised a hand to interrupt her.

"Tina, we all appreciate you going to the mat for us on this, but frankly, it's just not going to happen. Jim and I have gone over the numbers a dozen times, and there isn't a single one of the twenty models in this product-line that is even close to the margins you're talking about." The voice of doom came from Lydia Jergens, her best friend and compatriot from a previous employer. *Et tu Brute.*

"But that's exactly the point!" Only Tina could turn a death-blow into a segue. "We can't think of X-20 as a collection of individual products. That's why we've failed up until now. We have to think of all twenty models as extensions of the *same common platform*. Take a look at my first slide (shown in Figure 7.11). All twenty of the current models are shown side by side. Do you notice any commonality between them?" Shaking heads gave her the answer she was looking for.

"Exactly! Each model has a unique housing, a unique process run sheet, no common parts, and not a single test that's the same. Yet if we broaden our vision a bit, there are opportunities to achieve very high levels of commonality. Consider the housing for example. The Model D5 has the largest housing of the group. Why not just adapt that housing design to accommodate all twenty sensor models?"

"You've got to be kidding," blurted one of the two design engineers on the team, "that would add material cost to every part! I intentionally designed those housings to be cost-optimized. Now you want to make them *less* cost-effective?"

"Your talking about pennies, Dale," Tina replied, still smiling her most winning smile, "do you have any idea how much money we waste maintaining twenty different housings? Tooling

### The X-20 Line of Process Sensors
### (Side View)

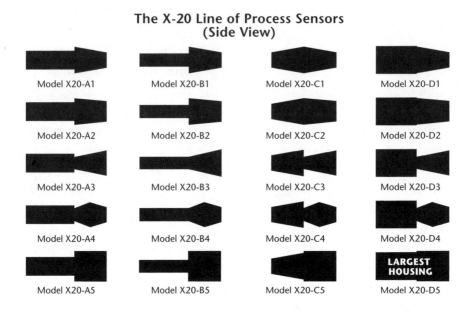

| | | | |
|---|---|---|---|
| Model X20-A1 | Model X20-B1 | Model X20-C1 | Model X20-D1 |
| Model X20-A2 | Model X20-B2 | Model X20-C2 | Model X20-D2 |
| Model X20-A3 | Model X20-B3 | Model X20-C3 | Model X20-D3 |
| Model X20-A4 | Model X20-B4 | Model X20-C4 | Model X20-D4 |
| Model X20-A5 | Model X20-B5 | Model X20-C5 | Model X20-D5 |

**Figure 7.11:** Side-view drawing of all twenty models that make up the current X-20 product-line at Sensormation, Inc. Note that each model has a unique housing, making them expensive to fabricate. By standardizing the entire product-line on the largest housing, a significant reduction in tooling, inventory, and assembly costs can be gained.

cost, inventory cost, handling cost, changeover cost. Plus the volumes of each housing are so low that we haven't been able to justify outsourcing them. With a single housing design, we could increase volumes twenty-fold, and at the same time eliminate all of the waste I just described." To her surprise, a few heads were nodding . . . although the movement wasn't very enthusiastic.

"Now for the next idea." Tina flipped to her next slide (shown in Figure 7.12). "Our sensors come in twenty flavors, but really there are only nine distinct attributes that are represented in different combinations. We have five different "front ends" that do the sensing, and four different "back ends" that transmit the signal to the factory control system. Five times four equals twenty, right?" Heads were nodding in agreement. "Wrong! In the new math of lean design, I can make five times four equal nine." Tina paused to enjoy her dramatic flair, then pushed ahead. "If we standardize the interface between the front- and back-ends of our sensors, we could modularize the product-line. Five front-end modules and four back-end modules. Not only do we reduce the number of sub-assemblies that we produce, but we no longer have to trust our forecasts to determine which models will be needed when. We can inventory the nine modules prior to final assembly, and put together the appropriate front- and back-ends on a build-to-order basis. This way both our lead times and our inventory levels will be cut in half!"

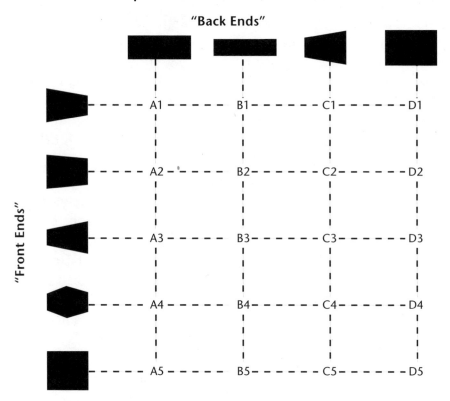

**Proposed Modular X-20 Product-Line**

**Figure 7.12:** By standardizing the interface between the "front ends" and "back ends" of the X-20 sensor line, Sensormation could dramatically reduce the amount of finished goods inventory and at the same time enable rapid-response, build-to-order final assembly.

Well, you had to give them credit, Tina thought, as she paused to catch her breath. One by one she could see the light returning to their eyes. Dale would be a holdout, and that was a problem, but the rest of the team was pretty good at exerting peer pressure. With a little cajoling, Tina was sure Dale would come around. Now for the *pièce de résistance*. She flipped over her last slide (see Figure 7.13).

"The last big opportunity we have is a redesign of the mounting bracket. Right now, we have to customize each sensor based on the orientation that the customer needs for his application. Since this happens early in the build process, we are stuck with unique product configurations and different production routings for almost every order. Why not design a universal bracket that can be mounted at the end of the process? Here again, we enable a build-to-order process, with the bracket orientation defined when the order comes in. Now, ninety percent of the manufacturing process will be identical for every model in the X-20 line, with only the last ten percent being unique to a specific model or a specific order. By postponing the customization of our common platform until late in the process, we capture the economies of mass production, while still being able to customize our products to our customer's needs."

Well, there it was. Still a long road ahead to rally her team and build a viable plan. But there was a glimmer of hope in that cramped corner of the breakroom, and Tina felt certain that her team would come through for her one more time. Of course, Tim would have to buy this lean strategy, but deep down inside she knew that he would relish the challenge. After all, the factory was running smoothly these days, and a warrior like Tim would always rather fight battles than fight boredom.

What Tina discovered in the above story is that good products are not necessarily profitable ones. In fact, by over-optimizing individual models we may actually *defeat* overall profitability. The economics of manufacturing does not favor point designs and unique products. Production costs for a product-line can be minimized only through synergy, commonality,

## Current X-20 Production Flow

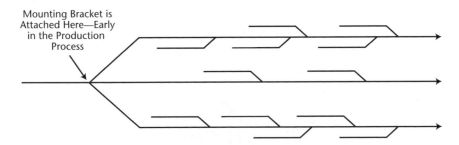

Mounting Bracket is Attached Here—Early in the Production Process

## Tina's Proposed X-20 Production Flow

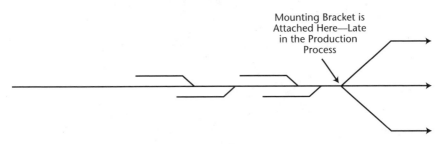

Mounting Bracket is Attached Here—Late in the Production Process

**Figure 7.13:** By postponing the assembly of the X-20 mounting bracket until very late in the production process, the entire product-line will benefit from the economies of mass production while still allowing each order to be tailored to the customer's needs.

and standardization. By intentionally sub-optimizing individual product models (in very minor ways) we can often dramatically improve overall profitability, while still delivering a very successful product.

Unfortunately, a detailed explanation of the cost-slashing methods of lean design is beyond the scope of this book. I will, however, provide you with a brief overview of the possibilities, and guide you to the available literature on each subject. Hopefully, you will follow Tina's example and show some initiative while I'm off writing a book that elaborates on this critical topic.

A summary of just a few of the lean design techniques that can be used to reduce production costs is provided in Figure 7.14. The first and most important method is *target costing*.[38] In these enlightened times, there are still many firms that determine the

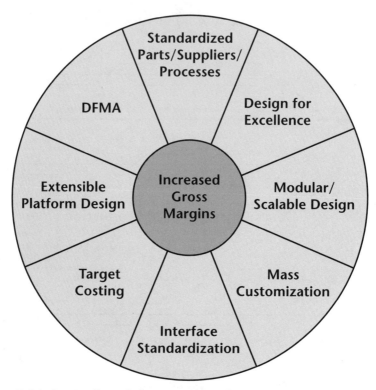

**Figure 7.14:** A sampling of the many lean design strategies that can dramatically reduce production costs and optimize product-line profitability.

price of their products based on the sum of "whatever the costs turn out to be" and "whatever margins we wish we had." Tell me what the problem is with this wishful-thinking price strategy? Come on, you know this one. Right! The *marketplace* determines the price of a product. You don't directly control that side of the equation. Hence, the pricing strategy described above is nonsense. Instead, you must begin by estimating the price that your new product will garner in the marketplace, based on competition, nearest substitutes, etc. You should then subtract off the desired gross margin. What is left is the target cost, and if your new product design cannot meet that target, you have an invalid business case. Time to change your design, change your market assumptions, or terminate the project and move on to a higher-value opportunity.

Once a target cost is established, the next lean opportunity comes at the very earliest stages of product design. Rather than designing for the first market segment that comes along, try a little forward thinking. What are the growth opportunities? How might variety, options, features, etc. enable increased market share and higher revenues? Should the product be scalable to larger / smaller, faster / slower, fancier / plainer versions? By considering how the product-line might evolve in the near future, you can establish a common, reusable platform that can easily be extended into new markets with excellent production economies.[39] Using the largest housing in the X-20 product-line as the common platform for all twenty sensor models was an example of this lean concept.

One of the most powerful strategies for achieving a common, extensible platform is referred to by the oxymoronic name *"mass customization."*[40] This name implies that we can capture the economies of scale that mass production offers, while still gaining the price advantages of a customized product. Indeed, this is not as paradoxical as it might seem. The essence of this strategy is *postponement*. We design our product-line so that customization occurs as late as possible in the fabrication process. Ideally, over eighty percent of production labor and materials are into the product before you can tell what model it will become when complete.

There are several ways to approach the postponement of customization.[41] The most straightforward technique is to let the customers themselves perform the customization. Products that are adjustable or selectable by the user (e.g., those ten-lever ergonomic office chairs that seem to have a mind of their own) are examples of this approach. Alternatively, you could have the products themselves be standardized, but provide a service that customizes the product to specific applications. IBM Global Services has embraced this business model by emphasizing customized services as their core product, and relegating hardware to the backbench.[42] The next best thing to after-delivery customization is to have the customization of the product be entirely in the software / digital domain. This way, the physical fabrication process can be identical for all models in a product-line, with the customization part being achieved through a last-minute download of the appropriate code.[43]

Even if you must customize the hardware itself, the idea of postponement can be a critical success factor. Hewlett-Packard faced a cost dilemma when they introduced their line of low-cost inkjet printers. The printers themselves could work perfectly well anywhere in the world, except that the available power in various countries is radically different. Rather than designing fifty different models of inkjet printers to handle power requirements everywhere from Nairobi to Singapore, HP used a clever postponement strategy.[44] They put the power supply on the outside of the printer (you may remember those big heavy boxes that hung from the power cords of early HP printers). They would then ship standardized inkjet printers to various countries, and separately ship power supplies and cords that were region-specific. The distributors at each geographic location would assemble the final products as they were needed for retail sale. Note that Tina's strategy for late assembly of a universal mounting bracket benefited from this concept of postponement.

A final powerful design technique that Tina recommended to her team was *modularity and interface standardization*.[45] By dividing a product's functions into physically (and digitally) well-defined modules, it is possible to create hundreds of product varieties with a much smaller number of physical elements. In the Sensormation example, nine modules that shared a standardized interface enabled twenty different product configurations.[46] Products such as the Handspring Visor personal digital assistant take modularity to its ultimate potential.[47] With modules that allow the Visor to become everything from a game platform to a digital camera, owners can extend the functionality of their product in a dozen ways at a relatively low cost. In this way, both Handspring and the customer benefit from a modular design strategy.

There are numerous other lean methods that can help reduce the production costs of a new product design. Commonizing on suppliers,[48] sub-assemblies,[49] and components[50] can dramatically impact inventory and procurement costs. Manual assembly labor can be minimized through application of classical Design for Manufacture and Assembly (DFMA) techniques.[51] Even the overall life-cycle cost of a product can be optimized by applying the multifaceted methodology of Design for Excellence (DFX).[52] In each case, the underlying philosophy is the same; standardize, commonize, simplify, and harmonize an entire product-line. If your firm is still living in a world of point designs and zero commonality, take heed. Those companies that take a broad, holistic approach to product-line architecture will have a fundamental cost advantage. You may not have time to recover if such a competitor enters your little corner of the world.

## A Little Help for Your Short-Term Memory

- Product development is a special type of "project" that is actually recurring in nature. Although each new product may be unique, the process that is followed can be standardized, provided that enough flexibility is retained to avoid the loss of innovation, creativity, and value.

- The aspects of product development that make it different from other projects include the fact that the requirements for a new product are often nebulous and "fuzzy," and that the output of the project is a design that can be manufactured at a target cost.

- The best way to reduce the fuzziness of initial requirements definition is to harvest as much feedback from real customers as possible. Strategies for accomplishing this include indwelling, probe-and-learn, and frequent iterative prototyping.

- Once initial requirements are reasonably well-defined, a product development effort can be executed like a normal project, using all of the lean methods described in this book.

- There are some advanced and powerful strategies available for reducing the production cost of new products. All of them involve the ideas of standardization, commonality, simplicity, and product-line-wide synergy.

- Get off of the point-design train before it carries your firm into low-margin oblivion. Challenge your design teams to consider the future evolution of the product-line and create platform designs that possess the cost benefits of mass production and the price benefits of customization.

# Mandates
# for a Project-Driven
# Organization

*8*

*"So much of what we call management consists
of making it difficult for people to work."*
—*Peter Drucker*

I t is a sad fact that most project-intensive firms are organized in exactly the wrong way. Moreover, many firms use incentive systems and management practices that further guarantee inefficiency and (all too often) chaos. The unmistakable evidence of this can be found on almost any night or weekend at your workplace: Lights burning brightly and people shuffling the hallways at times that bespeak of missed dinners with families and long-forgotten golf appointments.

We can do better than this. The methods described in this book represent a starting point for the efficient execution of project work within an organization. However, they can easily be undermined by a management structure that institutionalizes the waste we seek to eliminate. Intrafirm politics and rivalries, strong functional silos, arrogant managers, poor communication, misaligned incentives, nonexistent priorities, continuous interruptions, and so on. I would go on, but it is just too depressing. In this chapter, I will provide you with some hard-nosed advice on how to optimize a project-driven enterprise (call it "tough love for managers"). The goal is to create an organization that supports and nurtures the twelve methods of lean project management, while encouraging a culture of discipline and an intolerance of waste.

In my never-ending search for ways to hold my esteemed reader's attention, I will present this sage advice in the form of a question-and-answer session. Imagine yourself attending a seminar at your local Hyatt Regency. It is late afternoon, you've just downed your fourth stale bearclaw and second gallon of lukewarm coffee, and are filled to the brim with new ideas on how to lean-out your firm. After the instructor flips his final PowerPoint slide, he asks the audience if they have any questions on how to make these great ideas work in their firms. You hesitate momentarily while you check your remaining attention span, and then boldly raise your hand. Here are some of the questions you really should be asking.

## Q1) How Can We Build a Culture of Discipline in Our Firm?

The first step is to recognize the need to do so. For too long we have been suckered in by the "softer" side of organizational management. "Let people be all that they can be, don't disturb their internal harmony, avoid conflict at all costs, embrace the diversity of opinion that surrounds you . . .," and so on. Here's a wake-up call. *There isn't a single team activity that can be executed successfully without structure and discipline.* Would you care to have your local football team "embrace diversity of opinion" while on the field? How about a surgical team that is about to remove your appendix? Maybe it would be better to let soldiers make their own choices about how to attack the enemy.

I'm not suggesting military-style discipline (despite my tongue-in-cheek analogy), but I do recommend clearly defined roles and responsibilities, and a professional atmosphere. Perhaps most important, your employees and coworkers must be willing to respond to directives from management once alternate opinions have been considered. There is a time for discussion and debate and a time for action. Don't be afraid to expect obedience from your employees. After all, they sacrifice their personal freedom everytime they show up for work in the morning. Following directives is part of their job, and you need to let them know it in no uncertain terms.

That being said, we don't desire an authoritarian environment. Far from it. There is a big difference between organizational discipline and Draconian command-and-control management. Instead, we wish to cultivate a set of organizational rules . . . call it a "code of laws." These laws define how individuals work within the organization, but allow considerable latitude for creative thought and diversity of method. A good analogy is the set of rules that have evolved for driving on our highways. There are hundreds of laws on the books to guide drivers toward safe, efficient, and harmonious use of our roads. Yet, despite the considerable discipline imposed by these rules, we have the freedom to drive anywhere we want, at any time we want, in virtually any vehicle we want. A disciplined organization allows freedom where it counts, where it is essential. Rules simply define an envelope in which individuals can create, with the assurance that they are working in harmony with the rest of the firm.

## Q2) How Should We Optimize Our Organizational Structure?

This is a tough one. Not because there isn't a good answer, but because you almost certainly won't like it. The first step is to batter down the functional barriers within your firm. Just take a big old sledgehammer to them like they were the Berlin Wall. (See, I warned you). There are two reliable telltales of organizational inefficiency for a project-driven firm. The first is strong functional departments. The second and related malady is weak team leaders or project managers. This shouldn't be too surprising: If you want to optimize a project-driven enterprise, you have to organize around project work. Here's something that might be a bit unexpected, however. I don't necessarily recommend a classical "projectized" organizational structure. Instead, I suggest working towards a "value-stream" organization.

Before I describe an optimal organizational structure, let's consider the most conservative implementation of a project-driven enterprise. The organization chart shown in Figure 8.1 represents a classic matrix structure,[1] with the addition of a *project office*.[2] Functional departments in this organization still have control over resources, but project managers are given considerable authority once project teams are formed. This is often referred to as the "heavyweight team leader" model for a matrix organization.[3] The problems with this structure are considerable, but it can be fairly effective provided that the project managers have enough clout, and the functional silos don't become bastions of political conflict.

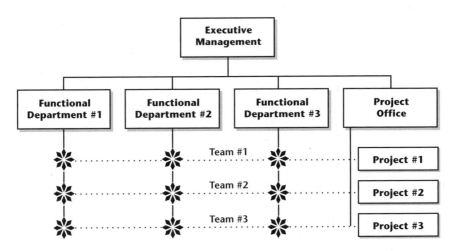

**Figure 8.1:** A typical matrix-type organizational structure. A project office is established to oversee the management of project work, but team members are "owned" by functional departments. The only way that this type of organization can execute projects efficiently is if project managers are given "heavyweight" authority to control their teams once membership has been established.

How might such an organization be improved? First, we need to shift our weight to the other foot, so to speak, regarding where the power in the organization resides.[4] If your firm performs projects for a living, then project work should be front and center in the organization, not an afterthought. A value-stream structure such as that shown in Figure 8.2 accomplishes this by making the project office the focal point for all revenue-generating activity.[5] This particular design, however, has a few unique attributes that make it far more effective and flexible than the "projectized" structure that many large engineering and aero-space firms have adopted.

First, I recommend establishing a *center of excellence* for project management that reports directly to the head of the project office.[6,7] This center facilitates the long-term development of the project management discipline within the firm through standards development, tool selection, training, best-practices benchmarking, and redeployment of available talent. Project managers that are between projects are pulled into the PM center of excellence for a "booster shot," and are used to mentor and train new PM's prior to reassignment.

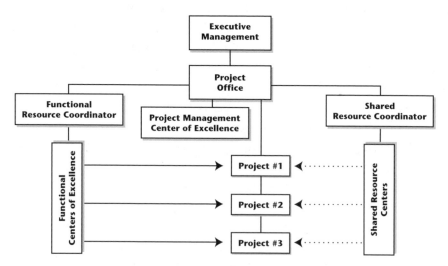

**Figure 8.2:** An optimized "value-stream" organizational structure for a firm whose revenue is primarily derived from project work. The project office is elevated to center stage, with functional centers of excellence and shared resource centers providing the needed staffing for projects. Project managers hold all of the clout in the organization, and have full control of team members while they are assigned to their projects.

The second advantage of this structure is that the clout within the organization is centered on where the revenue and profits are generated. In other words, it is focused on the value stream of the firm.[8] The allocation of resources can be handled in two ways, depending on the nature of the discipline involved.

Those functions that are core to value creation are managed through a *functional resource coordinator* whose role is to manage the allocation of employees to project teams. Each discipline is provided with its own center of excellence,[9] which represents a safe harbor between assignments, and provides for the long-term career development described above. Once an employee is assigned to a project (or projects), however, their fate is in the hands of their PMs.

The final unique attribute of this idealized project-driven organization is the addition of a *shared resource coordinator*. Many of the disciplines that support project work are not needed throughout the life of a project. Rather than assigning these part-time individuals to specific teams, a shared resource center is established for each support function. Typical candidates for a shared resource center include drafting, procurement, information technology, technicians, planners, field support, etc. These shared functions are allocated to projects based on reservations (for priority projects) or on an as-available basis (for lower priority work).

A similar organization chart can be constructed for firms that demand excellence in product development, as shown in Figure 8.3. The primary difference here is the substitution of *product-line teams* for the project office in the previous example.[10] Each product-line team includes all of the disciplines that are needed to develop, extend, support, and maintain their product-line throughout its life cycle. (Note that production operations can be managed under these same teams, or can be pulled out as a separate function, depending on the nature of your product). These teams are semi-permanent, meaning that the membership stays constant over periods of several years. It is a good idea, however, for team members to rotate every couple of years to maintain a healthy level of cross-fertilization. This rotation can be organized by the functional resource coordinator. As market conditions change, teams may shrink or grow, but the focus is always on building *product knowledge and product design efficiency*.

These optimized organizational structures provide all of the benefits of functional departments (*visa vi* the centers of excellence and shared resource centers), but avoid the "two-bosses"

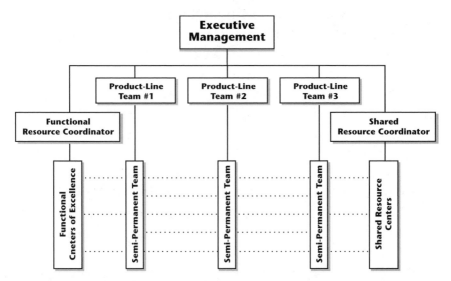

**Figure 8.3:** An optimized value-stream organization for firms whose revenues are derived from the development and manufacture of products. Instead of a project office, product-line teams are established that include all of the disciplines needed to design, support, and maintain each product-line. Resources are controlled by the product-line team leaders, with centers of excellence offering career development opportunities and other support services.

syndrome. In addition, they place the emphasis within the firm on the value-stream, rather than on arbitrary functional departments. As always, you should feel free to adapt these concepts to the specific needs of your firm. Consider them to be a challenge for the future, and a target for your long-term organizational development.

## Q3) What is the Best Way to Handle Rewards and Recognition?

Let's see if we can reason through this one together. First of all, what is the whole point of a compensation system? Answer: To reward employees for their efforts in a way that best supports the growth and success of a firm.[11] So in the language of lean thinking, an ideal compensation program would tie salary, bonuses, and other rewards directly to an employee's enhancement of the value stream. If your firm does project work, it would make sense to reward those behaviors that make projects successful. To encourage such behavior, however, we first need a way to measure it – and isn't that always the rub?

Rather than bore you with lots of discussion on this topic, I am just going to cut to the chase.[12] The effectiveness of your performance measurement system *determines the success of your firm*, plain and simple.[13] Yet the majority of functionally organized firms reward stuff that has almost nothing to do with project success. This is usually because the metrics are inappropriate.[14] If you want to know how fast your car is going, for example, you wouldn't use a thermometer. Here's an approach that I believe works quite well. First, I recommend using a "balanced scorecard" approach.[15] Since project work is multifaceted, using only a single metric as the basis for compensation would be naïve. I like the idea of using (at a minimum) three metrics: one that measures speed, a second that measures cost improvement, and a third that measures quality and / or performance. Since these are analogous to the three constraints of project work (i.e., time, money, and performance) this seems like a logical approach.

Now, what metric could we use for time? How about schedule variance against an employee's project delivery commitments? Using the techniques described in Method #9, you can derive some pretty good quantitative information about adherence to schedule. Unfortunately, this metric won't do the entire job, since employees might be encouraged to pad their task durations to ensure schedule predictability. That's why we need a balanced scorecard. You might also want to include overall project duration as a secondary time metric to avoid team members "gilding the lily."

A metric that measures project costs (or, alternatively, profit margin) can create a push-back against budget padding. I recommend using gross profit margin upon completion of a project contract (or other business-unit-wide measures of profit) as an excellent driver for cost optimization. For product development projects, the average gross margin of the resulting product can serve the same purpose. So now we have two out of three.

The third metric, which must quantify performance and quality, is the trickiest. Depending on your industry, this final metric could be linked to virtually any parameter that your customers would agree is an accurate measure of value. In construction, this could include such things as the number of inspection defects, or the number of items on project punch lists. In aerospace, the metric might be the percentage of proposal wins, number of patents, number of successfully completed deliverables, meeting performance targets, etc. In product development, it might be tied to the ratio of revenues generated by new products versus old products. Whichever you choose, just ask yourself a simple question: "If I had more of this metric, would my firm's performance unambiguously improve?"

In addition to basing pay increases on a balanced weighting of the above three (or more) metrics, we also need a rewards and recognition system that encourages more specific positive behaviors. I have a cleaver trick here. The trick involves the use of a "points system" for employee recognition. Variations on this theme are endless, but here's one that I like. Set a point threshold for receiving tangible rewards (say, 100 points), and award employees points for doing positive things for the company. Solving problems, cutting costs, reducing waste, improving morale or training, submitting suggestions, and so on. You might even consider using a "360 degree" approach in which points are awarded for behaviors that enhance an employee's relationship with upper management, lower-ranking employees, and also their peers. A whole mixed bag of positive behaviors can be encouraged by using this one flexible system. When an employee reaches their point threshold, they can select an award from a set of options. These options might include money, privileges (a preferred parking space or a weekly masseuse), awards (such as a "100 Pointer Club" plaque), or premiums (baseball tickets, desk clocks, etc.). However you decide to implement this system, you need to keep it fun, fair, and achievable.[16] An innovative rewards and recognition system can form the cornerstone of a disciplined and very positive work culture for your firm.

## Q4) Are Tiger Teams and Outlaw Projects a Good Idea?

No. Next question? All right, I'll indulge this topic a bit further. There have been some very questionable ideas put forth by some very bright people regarding the benefits of outlaw projects and the use of tiger teams.[17] If you accept the need for such measures (which are typically designed to circumvent the paralysis within an organization), you have assured that your waste-riddled methods and practices will remain with you forever. Setting priorities for projects is critically important, but designating a "tiger team" or "fast-track team" can send the wrong message to the rest of the firm.[18] Is everyone else on the "slow track"? Why reduce waste in normal operations when the fast-track team handles all the priority work?

Here's a better idea. Use business-unit-wide prioritization in the appropriate way, by making sure that the best opportunities for your company always receive the resources and attention that they need. Use reservations, filters, superteaming, and risk buffers to create *a process that works for all projects*. Put away the Band-Aids and take the steps necessary to achieve lasting and broad-based success. Both the tigers and the outlaws need to be kept from roaming the hallways of your firm.

## Q5) Is There a Straightforward Method for Prioritizing Projects?

Someone smart once said that the toughest part of being a manager is determining what *not* to do. After all, it takes courage to drive a stake in the heart of a wayward project, but no guts at all to keep a dying project on CPR forever. Although we spent considerable time on the topic of prioritization in Method #10, I will walk you through the steps necessary to institute a business-unit-wide prioritization process, as shown in Figure 8.4.

The first step is to identify who will be doing the prioritizing. There is only one viable answer for this; the business-unit executive must be responsible for all prioritization decisions. This can mean that the general manager or CEO does the job directly, or that the task is delegated to a *small* committee of executives. In either case, it is critical that prioritization meetings not consist of endless negotiation and political infighting. It is also important that the decision-makers know to ignore such extraneous considerations as sunk costs, egos, etc. Each time the project portfolio is reviewed, it must be considered with fresh and objective eyes, based on unbiased and current information.

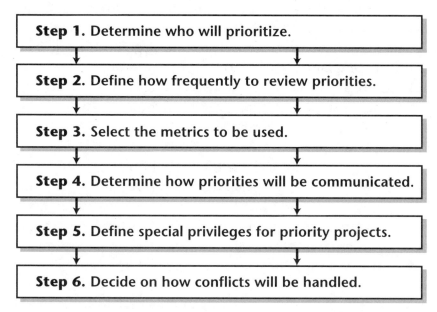

**Step 1.** Determine who will prioritize.

**Step 2.** Define how frequently to review priorities.

**Step 3.** Select the metrics to be used.

**Step 4.** Determine how priorities will be communicated.

**Step 5.** Define special privileges for priority projects.

**Step 6.** Decide on how conflicts will be handled.

**Figure 8.4:** Steps leading to an effective project prioritization process.

This leads us to the second step in achieving an effective prioritization process. How frequently should priorities be reviewed? This is easy. Just consider how often things change in a significant way with respect to the projects involved. I suggest using an exception strategy in which a review of priorities is triggered by the occurrence of specific events (e.g., a major project is completed, a customer complains, a new opportunity presents itself, etc.). A regularly scheduled review can be used for convenience, but the frequency should be based on the effectiveness of the meeting at redefining appropriate priorities. If the priority list doesn't change from meeting to meeting, start canceling some meetings.

Now comes the tough part. What metrics will be used, and in what combination, to determine project priority? Notice that I have assumed more than one metric is needed. A "balanced scorecard" approach can again be very useful here. Try selecting three metrics that weigh projects based on different benefits to the firm (you can use more than three, but don't make this too cumbersome). One might be a revenue-based measure (e.g., the size of the opportunity), a second might be a profit-based measure (e.g., gross margin or total profit), and the third could capture the impact on customer satisfaction (e.g., on-time delivery, customer complaints, service to long-term customers, etc.). Give each metric a subjective one-to-ten scoring (and use weighting factors, if you want to get fancy), and then multiply the ratings together. The result will provide you with a pretty solid differentiation between high- and low-priority opportunities.

But what about all of those traditional financial ratings: net present value (NPV), internal rate of return (IRR), economic value added (EVA), and so on?[19] These can be very useful if your firm is investing its own money in a new-technology-development or internal-improvement project. If your firm primarily does contract work, however, I would cut to the chase and choose simpler, balance-sheet based metrics.[20] Whichever measures you select, you should consider using risk-discounting of projects based on the uncertainty of successful completion.[21] A project that scores high on all metrics, but is very risky, should be downgraded when compared to less uncertain contracts. The Notes section of this book provides some excellent references for performing risk-discounting and other adjustments to your project priority list.[22]

Now that you have a list of priorities, how will they be communicated to your workforce? The most important factor here is credibility. If you publish a priority list, but still send the "just do it all" message to employees, you have failed. Each updated priority list should be broadly circulated to every employee in your firm. I like the idea of having a "priority website" that any employee can visit. However they are communicated, priorities must mean something. Trying to stuff in extra projects rarely results in extra profits when your firm is already running at full capacity.[23] There must be a distinction between high- and low-priority work, with the latter serving as the sacrificial lamb whenever a critical contract is in jeopardy.

To ensure that this occurs, high-priority projects should receive special treatment. I've already suggested several ways to give critical work an edge over mediocre tasks, including reservation rights, protection of team member's time, use of resource-leveling techniques, and so on. Whatever is necessary should be done to ensure that the important stuff gets accomplished on-time, on-budget, and on-target. Hence, there should never be a conflict between high- and low-priority activities; the high-priority work always wins. If there is a conflict *among high-priority projects* for needed resources, all avenues of resolution should be pursued *before* pulling out the priority list. Again, use priority rankings as a tie-breaker, not as an excuse for the top dogs on the priority list to become organizational bullies.

## Q6) How Can We Connect Our Strategy to Daily Project Activities?

There is a common misconception among executives that the way to implement the strategy of a firm is by talking about it. The talking begins in planning meetings, continues through operating plan reviews, and ends with "all-hands" meetings that are supposed to motivate appropriate actions among employees. Moreover, if all that gabbing doesn't do the job and the expected results are not forthcoming, guess what? Some unfortunate mid-level managers are called in for a good talking to.

There is only one way to effectively deploy and execute corporate strategy, and that is to embed the strategy within the structure and work methods of the firm.[24] This is often referred to as "strategic alignment." Some excellent opportunities to achieve alignment of strategy and action are shown in Figure 8.5. The most powerful vehicle for strategy deployment is through the organization of the firm itself. If you say that you want an agile, lithe, gazelle of a company, then get rid of functional silos and rigid organizational boundaries. If you want to move into a new market segment, then create a product or project team whose goal in life is to make that happen. If you don't align an organization with its future objectives (or, in other words, ensure that "form follows strategy"), don't expect employees to take new directives very seriously.

**Figure 8.5:** Opportunities to embed strategy directly into the organizational structure and work environment of a firm.

A second prime opportunity to connect strategy with action is through the prioritization of project work. Priorities determine the allocation of resources and capital, the two life-forces of a corporation. Again, it is not an understatement to say that if your firm fails to set clear and unambiguous priorities, it has essentially no chance of implementing its strategic vision.

The same can be said about compensation and training. If salaries and incentives are not aligned with the critical strategic initiatives of a firm, your employees will go wherever their compensation leads them. You can talk until you are blue in the face about new directions, but without a carrot out there to lead the way, your words will be wasted. Likewise, training represents a tangible commitment by management to a new way of doing things. Expecting employees to somehow figure out on their own how to become different, better, more efficient, etc., is just foolish. Spend some time and money giving your people the education they need. A few hours worth of "saw-sharpening" will make cutting down that new stand of trees a thousand times easier.

Standards can also communicate strategy, or at least reinforce it. If your market strategy requires that your firm be perceived as the quality leader, then your design and production standards must reflect that commitment. If speed is the edge that you seek, then a flexible and waste-free approach to project execution should be embodied in your process documentation. Keep in mind, however, that a wall full of policy and procedures manuals (or, alternatively, voluminous ISO 9000 documentation) is *not* a useful way to deploy strategy. The reason is simple: If people don't use the standards that you establish, they cannot be effective. Keep standards simple and to the point and you will see your teams gradually drift into strategic alignment.

A final avenue to achieving strategy deployment is through improvement initiatives. These are specific objectives that address critical and high-leverage aspects of your firm's operation. A "management by objectives" approach can work well, but you will still need a tool to connect strategy to objectives, objectives to metrics, metrics to actions, and actions to responsibilities. Fortunately, there is a very practical technique that has been in use for several decades. It is called *Hoshin* planning, and it was developed by Japanese firms to achieve high levels of strategic alignment and to enable tracking of progress toward improvement objectives. An example of a *Hoshin* planning matrix is shown in Figure 8.6. Please refer to the Notes section of this book for several highly readable sources on this practical deployment methodology.[25]

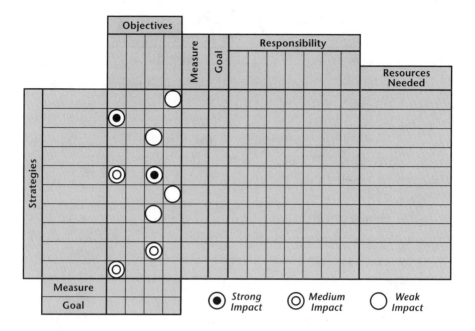

**Figure 8.6:** Example of a *Hoshin* planning matrix that can be used to connect the strategic improvement initiatives of a firm to the daily activities of employees.

## Q7) Is There a Way to Defeat Internal Politics and Infighting?

Politics and infighting are the dark side of any cooperative human endeavor. Organizational wheeling and dealing can destroy trust and morale at all levels of a firm. The fact is that such behavior *must be condoned to exist,* so your challenge is to stop supporting it . . . even if you must stand alone. Politics is a game that must be played in dark corners and shadows. It depends on poor communication for its existence, and cannot survive when exposed to unbiased observers. The solution is to turn the light of communication on brightly in your firm.[26]

A transparent organization is one in which all employees at all levels are given access to all information that directly impacts them.[27] No chain-of-command nonsense. If the CEO makes a pronouncement, every employee should hear that directive in the same words that it was spoken. No conditioning or filtering of information, and no hidden agendas that can misdirect employee's actions.

In a recent *Business Week* survey, 64 percent of employees reported that they don't believe what management says, 61 percent felt that they were not well informed, and 54 percent do not get decisions explained to them well.[28] This tragic lack of trust and communication is in direct conflict with the team spirit and shared vision that are the hallmarks of corporate success. [29]

How can you banish the shadows (and the nasty little creatures that lurk there)? Some of the methods described in this book will serve you well. Stand-up meetings provide continuous feedback and an open forum for conflict identification and resolution.[30] A virtual project room is an excellent way to solidify communication, both internal to and outside of a project team. Communicating priorities clearly will give your people a sense of direction and will build confidence in the ability of their leaders. Whichever way you proceed, please remember that there is no place in a firm for those who are power hungry, deceitful, or untrustworthy.[31] Sweep the dark corners free of these pests and your employees will perform in peace and harmony (well . . . at least they won't have internal politics to blame for their childish spats).

## Some Relief for Your Grey Matter

- A project-driven enterprise must be an enabler for the methods of Lean Project Management. This means that every aspect of the company, from organization to communication, must reinforce a culture of discipline and intolerance of waste.

- Although a "matrix" organization can achieve great things, a truly project-centric firm must go beyond this stopgap approach to implement a value-stream organization.

- Speaking of stopgaps, tiger teams and outlaw projects are a poor substitute for effective prioritization of work and clear communication of strategy.

- Organizational politics and conflict hide in the dark corners of a firm. To banish them, turn the lights of communication and transparency on brightly. The politicos will scurry for cover like so many roaches.

# A Step-by-Step Process for Slashing Waste 9

> *"Success in any enterprise requires the right product, methods, and people, and each must complement the others."*
> —Joseph Burger

Well, oh intrepid reader, we are nearing the end of our journey. At this point you have been exposed to all of the tools necessary to give your team, your division, or your enterprise a lean tune-up. There is just one little piece missing: How do you go about applying these tools in a systematic and efficient way? Not surprisingly, this is the reason why this book has a ninth chapter. Although the twelve lean methods can be applied in an ad hoc sort of way, far more benefit can be derived through one of the two approaches I describe below. So let's all take a nice deep breath, stretch our legs (if you are on an airplane, you will have to settle for reshuffling your cramped limbs), and head for the literary finish line.

## A Lean Project Management Maturity Model

You can think of the deployment of lean project management methods as following a "maturity model" such as the one shown in Figure 9.1. The idea of maturity models has come into use recently as a means of measuring progress in the implementation of new ideas or methods. The Software Engineering

Institute (SEI), for example, has established the Capability Maturity Model (CMM) that describes five levels of sophistication in the development of software.[1] The Project Management Institute (PMI) has a similar model for implementation of formal project management techniques.[2] The simple three-level model I've provided in the figure is tiered based on the scope of your improvement initiative. If your goal is to reduce waste within an individual team, than Level 1 represents a guideline for which methods will provide the most practical value to you. If your quest for speed and efficiency spans multiple projects, a more aggressive Level 2 implementation would be suitable. Finally, if you reside at the pinnacle of a business unit, and wish to slash waste from that lofty perch, an enterprise-wide Level 3 deployment will give you the greatest benefit. Please keep in mind that this model is just a guideline; your situation may require more of some methods and less of others. Use it as a starting point for your lean journey.

## The Lean Project Management "Maturity Model"

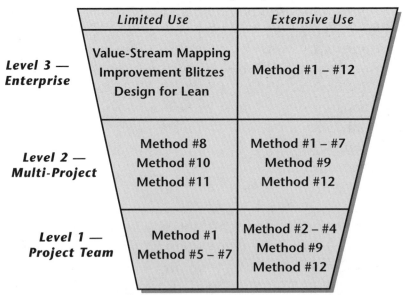

| | Limited Use | Extensive Use |
|---|---|---|
| **Level 3 — Enterprise** | Value-Stream Mapping Improvement Blitzes Design for Lean | Method #1 – #12 |
| **Level 2 — Multi-Project** | Method #8 Method #10 Method #11 | Method #1 – #7 Method #9 Method #12 |
| **Level 1 — Project Team** | Method #1 Method #5 – #7 | Method #2 – #4 Method #9 Method #12 |

**Figure 9.1:** Three tiers of a "lean maturity model" for project management within your firm.

## Immediate Results through an "Improvement Blitz"

There is nothing worse than a bureaucratic, dogma-laden, buzzword-intensive improvement initiative. What a shame to get people all fired up about reducing waste, and then squander their enthusiasm on tedious committees and endless consensus-building. Who needs committees? In fact, who needs consensus? Sometimes you just have to be decisive (at least within your own domain) and make some changes. As long as the outcome is positive, you will hear few complaints. The "Improvement Blitz" technique I describe here is fast, effective, and high-leverage. It is up to you how many people you involve in the blitz, but this is intended to be a freight train not a trolley, so get folks on board or leave them behind. You're hunting for waste and you ain't taking prisoners.

An entire improvement blitz can take place in a single morning.[3] The objective is to identify high-priority opportunities for waste elimination on a specific project, establish an action plan, and assign responsibilities. Improvements should be implemented immediately, and should be considered permanent unless a better way emerges from your experience moving forward. Events of this type are best held at the beginning of a project, but can be called upon anytime there is a critical need. Keep them brief and deliverable-focused; if you don't walk out of an improvement blitz meeting with a healthy list of actions, you've missed the boat.

## What You Will Need

You will need a template for capturing improvement ideas and performing a ranking activity with your improvement team. I've provided an example in Figure 9.2, but there may be a similar form floating around your firm at this very moment. If your company has implemented lean improvement initiatives in other areas of the firm (e.g., manufacturing, accounting, etc.) you may already have something called a *"Kaizen* Event Worksheet."[4] The approach I describe here is just a simplified version of a *kaizen* event (incidentally, *kaizen* means "continuous improvement" in Japanese). Use your existing form or make one up like the one in the figure, and then gather your hunting party and go for the big game.

| Waste Opportunity | Impact | Ease | Priority | Lean Countermeasure |
|---|---|---|---|---|
| 1. Eliminate iteration loop to determine customer needs | 5 | 3 | 15 | Hold "testing for value" negotiation meeting |
| 2. Reduce time to gather strawman requirements | 5 | 2 | 10 | Use a template or checklist to accelerate info. gathering |
| 3. Reduce time required to consult with manufacturing engineer | 3 | 3 | 9 | Use a "feed forward" of info. |
| 4. Eliminate first approval cycle | 4 | 3 | 12 | Use customer-defined template and feed forward of prelim. info. |
| 5. Reduce final approval cycle | 4 | 4 | 16 | Use a reservation system to enable immediate review |
| 6. Reduce time to assign buyer | 3 | 3 | 9 | Implement real-time priority system to eliminate queue |

**Figure 9.2:** Sample template for an improvement blitz event. Other possible formats are referenced in the Notes section of this book.

## Who You Will Need

As a general rule, all parties that will be affected by a change of work methods should be present for the improvement blitz. For example, if you plan to attack your engineering change order (ECO) process, all members of the ECO committee should be involved. I strongly recommend that you focus on a manageable scope for your blitz events. Attempting to improve your entire company in a single meeting will surely result in failure. Better to zero in on a well-established weak spot and be certain of a useful and timely outcome for your meeting.[5] Moreover, a narrow scope implies a smaller group of attendees. This is always a good thing when controversial topics are involved. Keep debate and deliberation to a minimum. You will learn more by trying a new method than by endlessly discussing it.[6]

## Step-by-Step Execution

Begin by doing all the right lean things to set up a collaborative meeting (see Method #3).[7] Select the appropriate attendees, let them know the purpose of the meeting and the expected deliverables, and provide them with pre-work as needed.[8] If you want the best value for your time, it may be useful to have attendees become familiar with the contents of this book. Share your personal copy or break down and invest a few bucks in copies for your team. You might even consider doing some informal training of the lean methods that seem the most applicable to your circumstance.

*Step 1* – Convene your meeting by displaying the blitz template you will be using. Allow a few minutes of questions and answers before beginning a brainstorming session. Remember that there are no bad ideas in brainstorming, so just capture whatever is suggested on a white board or flip chart. You are looking for waste-reduction opportunities within the scope you have defined for the meeting. The suggestions do not have to be phrased in the form of a lean countermeasure; just a description of the waste will do. At the end of the meeting, you can select the appropriate countermeasures and assign responsibilities.

*Step 2* – Perform several minutes of brainstorming (ten to thirty, depending on the size and disposition of the group). You should now have a long, unfiltered list of opportunities. Your next step will be to screen out the low-value suggestions and perform a rank-ordering of the high-value ones.

*Step 3* – You will use a two-parameter ranking system, such as the one described in Figure 9.3. The first parameter (scored on a subjective one-to-five scale) measures the impact of the improvement on your project's success. If project duration is the most critical success factor, for example, then scores for impact should reflect how much time could be saved. The second parameter captures the difficulty associated with making the desired improvement. If the improvement is trivial to implement, you would score this parameter as a five. For very difficult changes, the score would be a one. The product of these two scores is called a "Waste Priority Number" (WPN). Changes that are both easy and have a major impact deserve a high score, whereas improvements that are both wimpy and a pain in the neck should get the lower scores.

*Step 4* – Starting with the highest WPN opportunity, determine how that bit of identified waste can be eliminated. Consider the list of countermeasures provided in Figure 6.1 (see page 90), and determine which of these techniques attack the waste. Note that several countermeasures can often be applied simultaneously. As you identify your improvement approach, begin filling out your blitz template (you can use the same template for the rough brainstorming and scoring, but start with a clean one when you get down to a short list of high-priority opportunities).

*Step 5* – Somewhere in the middle of your priority list you will have to draw a line. Above the line, you will assign action items, responsibilities, and due dates. Below the line, you will archive the results and save them for the next improvement blitz. Don't overextend yourself and your team. It is better to build up steam in the hunt for waste than to burn out support through an over-ambitious first effort.

*Step 6* – Determine who will track the action items to completion, and how you will measure the success of the improved approach. Don't be too quantitative here; a good subjective survey of those people impacted by the change will often provide your most valuable feedback. Be sure to document how it was before, what was changed, what it looks like now, and what you plan to do in the future to maintain or improve it.

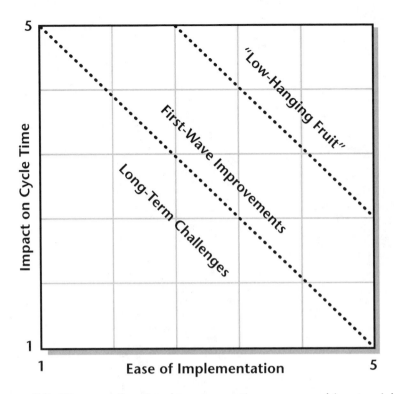

**Figure 9.3:** Diagram showing how two ratings can combine to yield a useful prioritization of improvement opportunities. Both "Impact" and "Ease of Implementation" are scored on a scale of one to five, and the product of these two scores equals a Waste Priority Number (WPN).

## Enterprise-Wide Improvement Through Value-Stream Mapping

The previous "quick-hit" approach for deploying lean methods is intended to be used by an individual team. How then can we apply the material in this book to systematically improve the way *all* projects are executed by *every* team? The answer is value-stream mapping; a simple graphical technique that enables an improvement team to visualize, prioritize, and eliminate waste from any project-related activity. The beauty of value-stream mapping is that it forces you to confront all of the silly, frustrating, and haphazard ways things are done in your firm. In fact, the first step in this more advanced improvement methodology

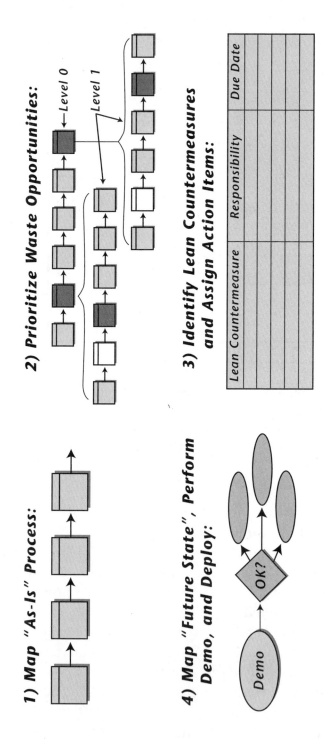

**Figure 9.4:** A four-step process for systematic waste elimination in your firm. An "as-is" value-stream map is created to provide a realistic starting point for improvement. Opportunities for improvement are then highlighted and prioritized. An improvement blitz is then performed to create an action list for waste reduction, and a demonstration project is selected to validate the improvements. Once a new "future-state" process has been verified, it can be broadly implemented throughout your firm.

is to create an "as-is" value-stream map that represents *reality*, with all the hair and warts included.

A four-step improvement process is shown in Figure 9.4. We create an "as-is" value-stream map, and use a "drill-down" approach to identify the highest priority opportunities for waste reduction. Once we have the high-priority targets in our sights, we perform an improvement blitz just like I described in the previous section. A set of countermeasures is identified and action items are generated. We then perform our improvements and document our new, "future-state" value stream. This exercise can still be a one-day affair, provided that you select a project-related activity that is reasonably well-defined and not too controversial. One word of warning, however. I've seen value-stream mapping turn into an overwrought, time-wasting nightmare. The as-is mapping activity is just a means to an end, so keep it simple and informal. Once you have established and tested an improved process, you might invest some time prettying up your future-state map. Even then, I'd rather see a clear and concise high-level map, then a spaghetti diagram worthy of Jackson Pollack.

### What You Will Need

You will need the same things as for the previous "quick-hit" approach, with the addition of any process documentation you might have available. Possible sources include your firm's policies and procedures manuals, ISO 9000 documentation, project standards, etc. What is more important, however, is that you have the right people in your meeting, since *the real as-is process is typically not written down* (usually for a very good reason). Also have available a big handful of colored marking pens, a plethora of two-inch-square Post-It Notes, and a few pads of flip-chart paper.

### Who You Will Need

Invite everyone who plays a role in the process you intend to improve. This is a bit more important than in the previous blitz method, since you are now planning to impact multiple projects, or even your entire firm. Be sure that all possible pathways for the process are represented. For example, if you are focusing on a prototyping process, have representation for both the "rapid-prototyping" pathway, and the "production first-article" pathway. Also be sure to include any approval authorities that can trigger error-correction loops.

### Step-by-Step Execution

The following steps should be executed during an all-day improvement meeting with the above attendees present. As usual, provide pre-work, establish deliverables . . . you know the drill. Note that there are several excellent references available on value-stream mapping.[9] The following is just a simplified overview to get you started.

*Step 1* – Identify the underlying objectives of the mapping effort. In other words, prioritize the importance of project metrics, from an improvement standpoint (e.g., schedule, non-recurring cost, recurring cost, critical resource utilization, etc.).[10] Focus your mapping efforts on pinpointing waste in the high-priority metrics that you've identified.

*Step 2* – Select a segment of your project execution process for value-stream mapping. Ideally, you should choose a segment that has a high impact on the metrics selected in Step 1.

*Step 3* – Create an "as-is" value-stream map for your selected process segment, using the format shown in Figure 9.5. Your goal is to make your map as realistic as possible, so try to capture all the delays and frustrations that may be experienced when this process is active. If you are lacking some needed information, just use your best estimate and continue with your mapping exercise. You can always refine your data later if it becomes necessary.

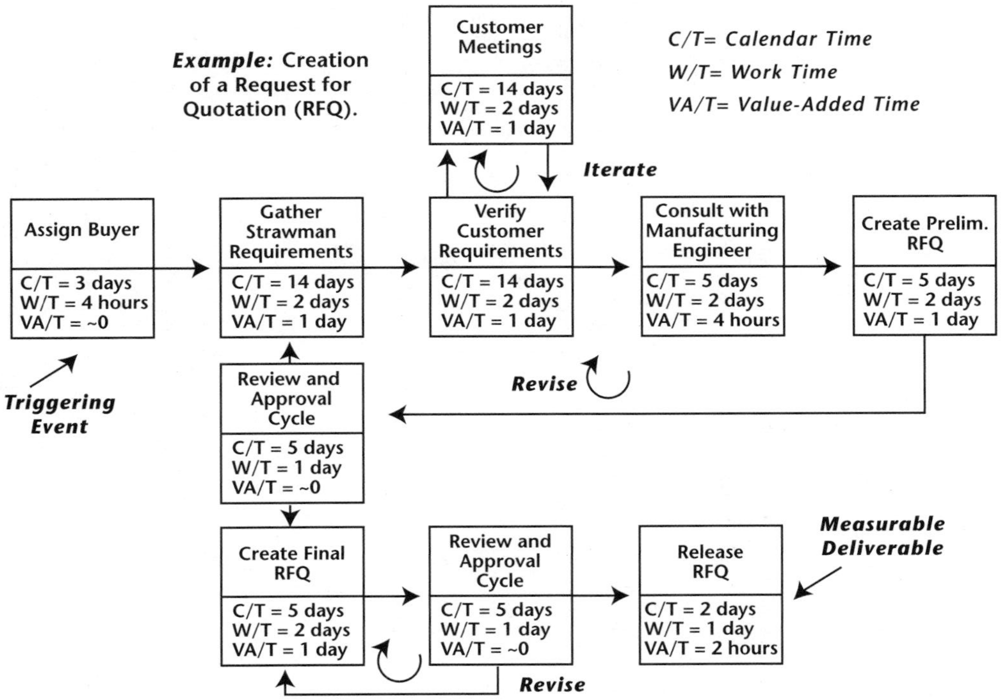

**Figure 9.5:** Example of a value-stream map for a Request for Quotation (RFQ) process. Each process step is quantified by listing three metrics: the calendar time, work time, and value-added time of the step. These metrics can be just rough estimates, since they are primarily used to rank-order improvement opportunities.

*Example:* Creation of a Request for Quotation (RFQ).

$C/T$ = Calendar Time
$W/T$ = Work Time
$VA/T$ = Value-Added Time

*Triggering Event*

Assign Buyer
$C/T$ = 3 days
$W/T$ = 4 hours
$VA/T$ = ~0

Gather Strawman Requirements
$C/T$ = 14 days
$W/T$ = 2 days
$VA/T$ = 1 day

Customer Meetings
$C/T$ = 14 days
$W/T$ = 2 days
$VA/T$ = 1 day

Review and Approval Cycle
$C/T$ = 5 days
$W/T$ = 1 day
$VA/T$ = ~0

Verify Customer Requirements
$C/T$ = 14 days
$W/T$ = 2 days
$VA/T$ = 1 day

*Iterate*

Create Final RFQ
$C/T$ = 5 days
$W/T$ = 2 days
$VA/T$ = 1 day

Consult with Manufacturing Engineer
$C/T$ = 5 days
$W/T$ = 2 days
$VA/T$ = 4 hours

*Revise*

Review and Approval Cycle
$C/T$ = 5 days
$W/T$ = 1 day
$VA/T$ = ~0

Create Prelim. RFQ
$C/T$ = 5 days
$W/T$ = 2 days
$VA/T$ = 1 day

*Revise*

Release RFQ
$C/T$ = 2 days
$W/T$ = 1 day
$VA/T$ = 2 hours

*Measurable Deliverable*

*Step 4* – Start your mapping effort by identifying the beginning and end points of the process to be mapped (what I call the "trigger point" at the beginning and the "measurable deliverable" at the end). Make sure that these are clear, well-defined, and measurable. The magnitude of your mapping effort must match with your team's available time, so be sure to take "bites" that are manageable under this constraint. In general, however, it is better to start with a fairly broad scope, to ensure that "local optimization" will not occur (as opposed to "system optimization," which is your goal).

*Step 5* – Begin your mapping effort at the *highest possible level.* Using your Post-It Notes, identify the major steps within the scope of your process. You will use a "drill-down" method such as that shown in Figure 9.6 to get to the details. Be sure to identify *no more than about twelve steps for the highest level of your value-stream map (in the figure this is referred to as the "Level 0" map).*

*Step 6* – To ensure that you have captured all of the waste in your selected process segment, consider the following questions:[11] Are there any "loops" that typically occur (points at which several iterations are often needed to complete the step)? Are there any "queues" in which your process must wait for execution or action? Are there any approval delays, review meetings, informal approvals, or other control functions involved?

*Step 7* – Each step in your value-stream map should contain three numbers (assuming you are using time as your critical metric). These are: 1) the calendar time, 2) the work time, and 3) the value-added time. If you can't remember how these are defined, see Chapter 1. As always, just use your best estimates. The only purpose for including these numbers is to help you prioritize waste opportunities. Those steps that have the greatest

**Level 0:** Highest level map showing only major steps.

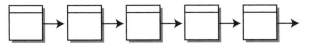

**Level 1:** Highest priority (HP) Level 0 steps are expanded into more detail.

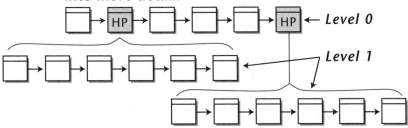

**Level 2:** Highest priority Level 1 steps are further expanded as necessary.

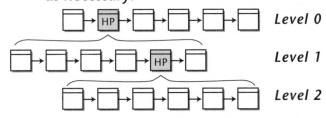

**Figure 9.6:** A technique for "drilling down" in a value-stream map to pinpoint sources of waste. Rather than creating a highly detailed map of an entire process, it is far more efficient to prioritize opportunities at the highest level, and then expand only the high-waste steps into more detail.

calendar time are clearly better opportunities for time reduction than those with short durations. Also compare calendar time to work time, and work time to value-added time. If there is a big difference in either of these two comparisons, you've found a prime candidate for improvement.

*Step 8 –* Now brainstorm as a team to estimate the relative impact and ease of improvement (both on a one-to-five scale) of waste within each Level "0" process step.

Multiply these two scores together to generate a WPN prioritization for your Level 1 mapping. This is just like what we did in the improvement blitz method described in the previous section.

*Step 9*– Expand the highest priority step(s) in your Level "0" map to create a Level 1 map. Again, no more than about twelve steps (if possible) and *only expand the high-priority opportunities*; leave the rest at Level "0".

*Step 10*– Continue to expand into deeper levels, until you reach a point at which a clear improvement action can be identified.[12] *Remember opportunity cost*; the time you spend on value-stream mapping must be focused on high-priority targets,or the exercise will be reduced to mostly waste!

*Step 11*– Create an action and responsibility list just like in the previous section, and go make it happen. Test the improved process using a "demonstration project."[13] This is typically a not-too-critical activity that can serve to work the bugs out of your future-state methodology. Once you have a proven future state, document it for all the involved parties and monitor its progress. Don't be afraid to tweak the process as you move forward; we are always smarter after we have some experience with a new way of doing things.

The format I've suggested for value-stream mapping is about as simple and straightforward as it gets. You can easily make this approach more complex if you feel it is too understandable. Just keep in mind that if you don't find enough waste during your improvement event to pay yourselves back for the time you spend, your firm will actually be worse off. Here is a good rule to follow: Every once in a while, pull your face out of the trunk of the tree long enough to see the forest. You might discover that your biggest opportunity for waste reduction is the bureaucratic way your firm executes improvement initiatives.

## The Last Set of Memory-Joggers

- It is possible to think of the deployment of lean project management methods as following a "maturity model." The first and easiest level of the model reflects improvements to how individual teams function. The second level expands the scope to include multiple projects, while the highest level reflects an integrated lean strategy across an entire business unit.

- The "improvement blitz" represents an easy, quick-hit approach to applying lean methods to your project. This is useful for individual teams, but is too superficial for use as a systematic process improvement technique.

- A more rigorous (and time-consuming) approach involves value-stream mapping to identify the highest priority opportunities for waste elimination. The output is a graphical representation of an improved "future state."

# Some Closing Thoughts

*"Common sense is genius dressed
in its working clothes."*
—Ralph Waldo Emerson

At last we have reached the end of our journey . . . for now, at least. Before I release you into that cold, cruel, wasteful world out there, I feel obliged to give you just a few more words of advice. These thoughts are directed toward those of you with the energy and courage to become change agents within your organization. For the rest, it's been nice chatting with you, and please don't get in the way of your more energetic and courageous coworkers.

*First Thought* – Get your ego out of the way. You can accomplish anything you want in life, provided that you don't take credit for it. Make it other people's idea, make them the heroes, let them feel that they own the solutions you suggest, instead of the ideas being "yours."

*Second Thought* – Take small steps that can be measured and solidified. Attempting change in an organization can often feel like you are trying to get a grip on Jell-O. Flailing around in several directions will get you nowhere. Pick your targets, make tangible progress, and then nail people's feet to the floor (figuratively, of course, and only temporarily – until the next opportunity for improvement comes along).

*Third Thought* – The surest sign of intelligence is the willing admission of ignorance. If you encounter resistance to your suggestions, be sure to listen; you may find that your recommendations are actually wrong-headed. Sometimes we have to admit that we are wrong before we can move in the right direction. Mistakes are no crime, but dogmatism in the face of contradictory facts is punishable by a lack of credibility.

*Final Thought* – Nothing succeeds like success. When it comes to change, people operate in two modes; they are either with you or against you . . . and virtually everyone will start out against you. Find some allies, capture a few minor victories, and then build up a support bandwagon. If success in life is measured by how much impact we have on the world, then being a change agent is one of the top ten ways to succeed. But it certainly isn't the fastest and the pay stinks.

# *Notes*

> *"We work not only to produce but*
> *to give value to time."*
> —*Eugene Delacroix*

## Chapter 1

1. There have been several surveys conducted of this type with similar results. The figure quoted here is an aggregate of informal surveys taken by the author of over two thousand project professionals spanning virtually every industry sector. Naturally, the actual amount of value created by a specific project team or team member is highly variable, but the "one to two hours per day" result is surprisingly robust.
2. Specifically, Methods 9, 10, and 11.
3. For a very practical guide to value-stream mapping, with a focus on "learning to see" waste, see Rother, M. and J. Shook.
4. Womack, J. P., Jones, D. T., and D. Roos.
5. Womack, J. P. and D. T. Jones.
6. For this and other errodite thoughts by this master of human behavior in the workplace, see Maslow, A. H.
7. Womack, J. P. and D. T. Jones, Pg. 15.
8. The "answers" provided in this section are based on a consensus of responses from over three thousand project team members, functional managers and executives that have attended my *Lean Project Management* and *Lean Product Development* seminars over the past several years. Industries represented in these seminars span the full range from construction and public utilities to the cutting edge of high technology.
9. The term "boilerplate" is often used to describe content that is redundant, repetitious, arcane, or otherwise rarely read. Things like the terms and conditions on the back of a purchase order, or the obligatory "capabilities" section of a proposal are examples of boilerplate.
10. Note that a task can have more than one customer and each might receive a distinct deliverable.
11. The primary reason why BPR failed to deliver dramatic improvements

is that it provides no practical test for whether a process is value-creating. Without insight into how processes impact a firm's productivity, even a well documented, logical, and efficient process may prove to be largely non-value-added.

12. More on seeking out the root cause of waste, and the "method of five why's" in Chapter 9.

13. Recall the story of the poor Greek, Sisyphus, who was given, as a punishment by the gods, the task of endlessly pushing a boulder up a mountain. Once he reached the top, the stone would immediately reappear at the bottom again, awaiting another grunting session by Sisyphus.

## Chapter 2

1. McGrath, M. E., Pg. 86. Discussion of QFD gone south, and the impact of analysis paralysis.

2. Dawes, R. M., Pg. 51.

3. Schuyler, J. R., Pg. 112.

4. Adams, S., Pg. 48. We all realize, of course, that Scott Adams has made a fine career of highlighting lunacy in the office environment. Fortunately, he has made enough money by now, because it is my mission to rob him of his source of material for the future. If we eliminate non-value-added waste from a firm, it may not be as funny, but it will be considerably more successful.

5. Smith, P. G. and D. G. Reinertsen, Pg. 166.

6. Reinertsen, D. G., Pg. 151.

7. Smith, P. G. and D. G. Reinertsen, Pg. 51.

8. Smith, P. G. and D. G. Reinertsen, Pg. 49. Imagine a "market clock" that begins ticking when a need for a product first arises, and stops when the product is no longer desirable.

9. Newbold, R. C., Pg. 29.

10. Reinertsen, D. G., Pg. 62. Phases and gates are one of the most obtrusive forms of time batch; they represent large batch transfers between low-batch-size activities. More will be said about why this is a bad thing in Chapter 7.

11. Henderson, B. A. and J. L. Larco, Pg. 63.

12. Widerman, R. M., Pg. 8–6.

13. Senge, P. M., Pg. 89. One of the highest leverage points for improving system performance is reducing system delays and accelerating feedback loops.

## Chapter 3

1. Results are derived from informal surveys of several dozen companies

spanning many industry sectors. The degree of time spent was driven by culture, the size of the firm, and the size of typical project teams. In no case have I found a firm that was even vaguely satisfied with time spent on e-mail.

2. Lipnack, J. and J. Stamps, Pg. 86.
3. Lipnack, J. and J. Stamps, Pg. 88.
4. Reinertsen, D. G., Pg. 113.
5. Note that I am using the concept of bandwidth in a figurative rather than a literal sense. Bandwidth actually is a technical term that describes the volume of data that can be transmitted per unit time at a specific noise level. Here I am using the term to describe the ability to communicate very complex concepts. A good way to think about this version of bandwidth is to compare the need for an in-person lecture / discussion by a physics professor, versus the ability to learn how to use your PC software through an on-line "help" function. Simple concepts can be transmitted through impersonal means, whereas abstractions require all the subtle nuance of an interpersonal, real-time interchange.
6. Haywood, M., Pg. 40
7. The recommendations in this table are derived from author experience merged with several sources, including Verma, V.K., 1996, Pgs. 22–25, Reinertsen, D. G., Pgs. 111–117, Lipnack, J. and J. Stamps, Pgs. 91–98.
8. Barham, K. and C. Heimer, Pg. 75.
9. For some additional ideas on reducing e-mail waste, see Haywood, M., Pgs. 36–42.
10. Pierce, J. R., Pg. 122.
11. This comment is referring to the "lost satellite" NASA evidently crashed into Mars in 2000. The reason for the crash appears to be a misunderstanding over whether some coordinates were in metric or English units.
12. Barnes, T., Pg. 127.
13. Leonard, D. and W. Swap, Pg. 126.
14. Cusumano, M. A. and R. W. Selby, Pg. 285.
15. Cusumano, M. A. and R. W. Selby, Pg. 73.
16. Senge, P. M., Pg. 80.
17. "Do unto others as you would have them do unto you." Or alternatively, "send nice, brief e-mails because you are sick of getting overlong, boring ones yourself."
18. Smith, P. G. and D. G. Reinertsen, Pg. 148.
19. Allen, T. J., Pg. 80.
20. Smith, P. G. and D. G. Reinertsen, Pg. 145.

## Chapter 4

1. Eden, C., et al (1998) Reference to learning curve applied to projects. Frequent change in a project environment can have a negative impact on learning curve (in addition to the *many* other negative consequences).
2. Some good references for standard work methods include: 1) Liker, J.K., Pg. 60, 2) Laraia, C., et al, Pg. 44, and 3) Imai, M., Pg. 54.
3. Mascitelli, R., Pg. 286.

## Chapter 5

1. Pierce, J. R., Pg. 23.
2. Reinertsen, D. G., Pg. 109.
3. Pierce, J. R., Pg. 79.
4. Pierce, J. R., Pg. 146.
5. A personal experience brought this home to me in a big way. I was assigned by my firm to serve as proposal manager on a major DARPA contract. The request for proposal, however, included a mandate that the technical write-up could be no longer than 100 pages (there was a similar Draconian limitation on the cost proposal). Previous proposals for projects of this size ranged from 300 to 500 pages, so we requested a waiver from DARPA. Their response was a firm no. Evidently, those rather forward-looking customers realized that most of the proposals they had received in the past suffered from far too little signal buried under vast quantities of noise. After much pain and suffering, my proposal team was able to meet the requirement, and afterward we agreed that this had been the best proposal generated in recent memory. We also won the contract.
6. Reinertsen, D. G., Pg. 16.
7. Senge, P. M., Pg. 35.
8. Schrage, M., Pg. 35.
9. Schuyler, J. R., Pg. 40.
10. Senge, P. M., Pg. 154.
11. Reinertsen, D. G., Pg. 71.
12. Reinertsen, D. G., Pg. 137.
13. Schuyler, J., Pg. 40.
14. Dimancescu, D., Hines, P. and N. Rich, Pg. 53.
15. Harry, M. J., 1994, Pgs. 22.1 and 22.7. See also, Lewis, J. P., Pg. 202.
16. Case, R. H. and J. Singer. This paper provides a humorous example of how team empowerment might work aboard Star Trek's Starship Enterprise.
17. Argyris, C.
18. Adams, S., Pg. 85.

19. Fleming, Q. W. and J. M. Koppelman, Pgs. 44 and 113.
20. Reinertsen, D. G., Pg. 137.

## Chapter 6
1. Reinertsen, D. G., Pg. 3 and 23.
2. Senge, P. M., Pg. 150.
3. Womak, J. P. and D. T. Jones, Pg. 176.

## Method #1
1. Lewis, J. P., Pg. 25. As this author suggests, the worst mistake a project manager can make is to assume that project stakeholders will value the outputs of their project as much as they themselves do.
2. Coy, P., 2000, "The Creative Economy," *Business Week*, August 28 Issue, Pgs. 77–82.
3. Christensen, C. M., Pg. 169.
4. I have chosen to use product case examples for this chapter since they will be more relevant to a larger audience than a project or industry-specific case.
5. This is not to say that in some very specific market segments, cell phone size may still be a value driver. Often markets contract in size as an attribute saturates, leaving only a few demanding lead users instead of a broad and profitable market.
6. Smith, P. G. and D. G. Reinertsen, Pg. 86.
7. Cusumano, M. A. and R. W. Selby, Pg. 43.
8. Cusumano, M. A. and R. W. Selby, Pg. 280.
9. Williams, T. M., 1999, "The need for new paradigms for complex projects," *International Journal of Project Management*, Vol. 17, No. 5, Pgs. 269–273.
10. Tatiknoda, M. V. and S. R. Rosenthal, 2000, "Technology novelty, project complexity, and product development project execution success," *IEEE Transactions on Engineering Management*, Vol. 47, No. 1, Pgs. 74–86.
11. Dimancescu, D., Hines, P., and N. Rich, Pg. 102.
12. Deschamps, J. P. and P. R. Nayak, Pg. 356–358.
13. Echikson, W., 2000, "Suddenly, PCs Are Falling Flat," *Business Week*, December 11 Issue, Pg. 66.
14. Wildstrom, S. H., 2001, "Sometimes, Less is More," *Business Week*, January 15 Issue, Pg. 23.
15. Smith, P. G. and D. G. Reinertsen, Pg. 94.
16. Reinertsen, D. G., Pg. 175.
17. For more on how to utilize QFD in this application, see: 1) Cohen, L., and 2) Terninko, J.

## Method #2

1. Berg, C. and K. Colenso, 2000. These authors consider the question of whether a project Work Breakdown Structure should consist only of project deliverables or should it include other activities. I believe that this is an easy determination to make: a WBS should consist of every task or activity that has a measurable deliverable, whether internal or external.
2. Dimancescu, D. and K. Dwenger, Pg. 73. Project teams should treat management as a customer for status reporting; management's requirements should be considered to be part of the project's overall deliverables list.
3. Smith, P. G. and D. G. Reinertsen, Pg. 165.
4. Dimancescu, D. and K. Dwenger, Pg. 46.
5. Reinertsen, D. B. Pg. 76.
6. McConnel, S., Pg. 569.
7. Schrage, M. Pg. 19.
8. Smith, P. G. and D. G. Reinertsen, Pg. 93.
9. Laufer, A., Pg. 56.
10. Dimancescu, D. and K. Dwenger, Pg. 74.

## Method #3

1. "Mired in Meetings," *Newsweek*, October 16, 2000, Pg. 52. I've noticed that the degree of waste associated with meetings can be dramatically different from industry to industry, and from firm to firm. As a general trend, the more complex, advanced, technically risky, or otherwise troublesome the industry, the more meetings will tend to dominate the typical worker's calendar.
2. Adams, S., Pg. 301.
3. Goldratt, E. M. and R. E. Fox, Pg. 87.
4. Leach, L. P., Pg. 85.
5. Smith, P. G. and D. G. Reinertsen, Pg. 177.
6. Henderson, B. A. and J. L. Larco, Pg. 58. Some of you more savvy readers may have noticed the similarity between the idea of daily work increments and the "TAKT Time" concept familiar to lean manufacturers. The word 'takt', which means musical meter in German, implies dividing up the overall work in a task into a series of bite-sized chunks to be performed at a daily pace. In production, the definition is literally, "available production time / number of units required per shift = minutes per unit."
7. McConnell, S., Pg. 405.
8. Cusumano, M. A. and R. W. Selby, Pg. 263.
9. Cusumano, M. A. and R. W. Selby, Pg. 268.

10. Smith P. G. and D. G. Reinertsen, Pg. 51.

## Method #4
1. Haywood, M., Pg. 7.
2. Jackson, T. L. and K. R. Jones, Pg. 35.
3. Grief, M., Pg. 48.
4. Dimancescu, D. and K. Dwenger, Pg. 51.
5. Sikes, D., 2000.
6. Lipnack, J. and J. Stamps, Pg. 28.
7. Bayles, D., Pg. 147
8. "Special Report: The Websmart 50," *Business Week*, September 18, 2000, Pg. EB 102.
9. "Opening the Spigot," *Business Week*, June 4, 2001, Pg. EB 17.
10. Blumenthal, D. and Y. A. Griver, 2000.
11. "A Revolution is Occurring," *Business Week*, October 2, 2000, Pg. 52.

## Method #5
1. Smith, P. G. and D. G. Reinertsen, Pg. 185.
2. Ichida, T., Pg. 13.
3. Dimancescu, D. and K. Dwenger, Pg. 107.
4. Leonard, D. and W. Swap, Pg. 69.
5. Ichida, T., Pg. 111.
6. Dimancescu, D. and K. Dwenger, Pg. 108.
7. Lewis, J. P., Pg. 258.
8. Harry, M. J., (1994), Pg. 23.1.
9. Bongiorno, J., 2001, "Use FMEAs to improve your product development process," *PM Network*, May Issue, Pg. 47.
10. Cooper, R. G., Pg. 196.
11. Rosenthal, S. R., Pg. 32.
12. Stamatis, D. H., Pg. 33.
13. Stamatis, D. H., Pg. 41.

## Method #6
1. Reinertsen, D. G., Pg. 176.
2. Dimancescu, D. and K. Dwenger, Pg. 143.
3. Clark, K. B. and S. C. Wheelwright, Pg. 301.
4. Thut, M., (2000).
5. McConnel, S., Pg. 425.
6. McConnel, S., Pg. 549.
7. Reinertsen, D. G., 139.
8. Smith, P. G. and D. G. Reinertsen, Pg. 87.
9. Galbraith, J. R. (2000), Pg. 285.

10. Lewis, J. P., Pg. 229.
11. Deschamps, J. P. and P. R. Nayak, Pg. 434.
12. Smith, P. G. and D. G. Reinertsen, Pg. 76.

## Method #7
1. Reinertsen, D. G., Pg. 112.
2. Clark, K. B. and S. C. Wheelwright (1995), Pg. 231.
3. Leonard, D. and W. Swap, Pg. 157.
4. Grief, M., Pg. 5.
5. Barnes, T., Pg. 17.
6. Tufte, E. R., 1983, The Visual Display of Information, Graphics Press. An excellent sequel by the same author should also be on your mandatory library list: Tufte, E. R., 1990, Envisioning Information, Graphics Press.
7. The following references will be helpful in implementing some of the ideas suggested in Figure M7.1. For a wealth of ideas on how visual communication has been successfully implemented on the factory floor, see Shimbun, N. K.. For graphical representation of the project life cycle: Dimancescu, D. and K. Dwenger, Pg. 81. Video or photographic "success stories" (such as those used by Hewlet Packard): Grief, M., Pg. 50 and Pg. 246. A visual checklist showing status of maintenance, procurement, or other project activity: Grief, M., Pg. 87. Use of wall schedules to communicate project status for a team's internal use (or management awareness): Grief, M., Pg. 106. Example of the use of "project symbols" or icons to identify documents or drawings that are specific to one project among many: Grief, M., Pg. 219. Use of yellow indicators to identify tasks or activities in a project that are critical to quality: Grief, M., Pg. 81. Display of monthly indicators of a firm's performance: Grief, M., Pg. 194. Visual indicator board that displays the level of training of employees: Grief, M., Pg. 183.
8. Harry, M. J., (1994), Pg. 22.41.
9. Grief, M., Pg. 152.
10. Henderson, B. A. and J. L. Larco, Pg. 144.

## Method #8
1. Senge, P. M., Pg. 42.
2. Barham, K. and C. Heimer, Pg. 260.
3. Waterworth, C. J., (2000).
4. Hayes, D. S., (2000).
5. Phillips, J. B., et al, (1999).
6. Wirth, I., (1996).
7. Lientz, B. P. and K. P. Rea, Pg. 111.

8. Cusumano, M. A. and R. W. Selby, Pg. 288.
9. Henderson, B. A. and J. L. Larco, Pg. 189.
10. Bicheno, J., Pg. 118.
11. Ichida, T., Pg. 186.
12. Stamatis, D. H., Pg. 321.
13. Dimancescu, D. and K. Dwenger, Pg. 36.
14. Reinertsen, D. G., Pg. 38.

## Method #9

1. Parkinson's Law states that the time that a task takes will grow to fill the time that is allowed. Since, by this law, a task will never come in early (which certainly matches with my general experience) then the only possibility when things don't go just right is a schedule slip.
2. Kidder, T., Pg. 131.
3. Uyttewaal, E., (1999).
4. There are a number of excellent books on critical-chain project management methods. Here are a few for those readers wishing to dig more deeply into this effective methodology. For a fictionalized account of critical chain by the "originator" of the concept, see Goldratt, E. M., (1997). More by and about the same seminal thinker includes: 1) Cabanis-Brewin, J. and 2) Goldratt, E. M., (1990). Some useful books and papers by other authors include: 1) Newbold, R. C., 2) Leach, L. P., 3) Rizzo, T. (#2), 4) Rand, G. K., and 5) Globerson, S..
5. Newbold, R. C., Pg. 84.
6. Lewis, J. P., Pg. 199.
7. Laufer, A., Pg. 49.
8. Newbold, R. C., Pg. 67.
9. Leach, L. P., Pg. 55.
10. Fleming, Q. W. and J. M. Koppelman, Pg. 32.
11. Newbold, R. C., Pg. 71.
12. Cusumano, M. A. and R. W. Selby, Pg. 190.
13. McConnell, S., Pg. 481.
14. Newbold, R. C., Pg. 59.
15. Leach, L. P., Pg. 92.
16. Leach, L. P., Pg. 169.
17. Laufer, A., Pg. 90.
18. Rosenau, M. D., Pg. 159.
19. Newbold, R. C., Pg. 76.
20. Newbold, R. C., Pg. 77.

## Method #10

1. Newbold, R. C., Pg. 21.

2. See, for example, 1) Dimancescu, D. and K. Dwenger, Pg. 13, and 2) Lewis, J. P., Pg. 166.
3. Dimancescu, D. and K. Dewenger, Pg. 13.
4. Leach, L. P., Pg. 115.
5. Lewis, J. P., Pg. 166.
6. Christensen, C. M., Pg. 82.
7. Carbno, C., (1999).
8. Cooper, R. G., Pg. 163.
9. Cooper, R. G., Edgett, S. J. and E. J. Kleinschmid, Pg. 134.
10. Lipnack, J. and J. Stamps, Pg. 126.
11. Graham, R. J. and R. L. Englund, Pg. 55.

## Method #11
1. Reinertsen, D. G., Pg. 44.
2. Graham, R. J. and R. L. Englund, Pg. 57.
3. Womak, J. P. and D. T. Jones, Pg. 53.
4. Newbold, R. C., Pg. 68.
5. Fine, C. H., Pg. 187.
6. Reinertsen, D. G., Pg. 49.

## Method #12
1. Reinertsen, D. G., Pg. 203.
2. Paquin, J. P., (2000).
3. Dimancescu, D., Hines, P. and N. Rich, Pg. 61.
4. Dimancescu, D., Hines, P. and N. Rich, Pg. 65.

## Chapter #7
1. Womak, J. P. and D. T. Jones, Pgs. 118, 140, and 211.
2. Each of these references describes how to effectively organize for new product development. Since these approaches differ considerably, we must conclude that either they are all wrong, all right, or only one is correct. Actually, parts of each strategy make sense for certain industries and products, but no one organizational structure and project control mechanism can work for every product in every industry. Use these references to broaden your options, but take none of them as gospel. See, for example, 1) Thomas, R. J., Pg. 95, 2) Shina, S. G., Pg. 104, 3) McGrath, M. E., Pg. 38, 4) McConnell, S., Pg. 142, 5) Gruenwald, G., Pg. 91, 6) Cusumano, M. A. and K. Nobeoka, Pg. 52, 7) Souder, W. E., Pg. 97, and 8) Galbraith, J. R., Pg. 247.
3. Smith, P. G. and D. G. Reinertsen, Pg. 154.
4. Cooper, R. and R. Slagmulder, Pg. 27.
5. Our current schedule calls for my lean product development book

to be available in early 2003. Please stop by our website at www.techper.com for availability announcements.

6. For a description of General Electric's "tollgate" process that has served as a model for many implementations of stage / gate NPD, see Clark, K. B. and S. C. Wheelwright, Pg. 289.

7. Cooper, R. G., Pg. 110.

8. As Don Reinertsen would say, "Concurrency will tend to reduce the average batch-transfer size in new product development." Big batch transfers (what I call time batches) are inherently wasteful, and concurrent engineering can help break down those big barriers to the flow of value. See Reinertsen, D. G., Pg. 135.

9. Souder, W. E., Pg. 146.

10. Cooper, R. G., Pg. 118.

11. Reinertsen, D. G., Pg. 63.

12. Davidson, J. M., et al, (2000).

13. Smith, P. G. and D. G. Reinertsen, Pg. 155.

14. Barnes, T., Pg. 74.

15. This terminology has become part of the lexicon of project work. A "Heavyweight" team leader has almost complete autonomy to execute his or her project. Once resources are assigned to their project, they become the primary manager for those resources, at least for the time periods that employees are working on their effort. See Clark, K. B. and S. C. Wheelwright, (1993), Pg. 293.

16. Smith, P. G. and D. G. Reinertsen, Pg. 138.

17. Clark, K. B. and S. C. Wheelwright, Pg. 90.

18. Laufer, A., Pg. 177.

19. The main body of work on this important lean topic has been performed by Dr. Durward K. Sobek II of the University of Montana and Dr. Allen Ward of Ward Synthesis. For some readable references, see: 1) Ward, A., et al, 2) Sobek, D. K., et al, (1998), and 3) Sobek, D. K, et al, (1999).

20. Reinertsen, D. G., Pg. 187.

21. "Attention Consumers: Creativity Never Comes Cheap," Business Week, October 2, 2000, Pg. 36.

22. Nonaka, I. and H. Takeuchi, Pg. 118.

23. Reinertsen, D. G., Pg. 36.

24. Deschamps, J. P. and P. R. Nayak, Pg. 57.

25. Smith, P. G. and D. G. Reinertsen, Pg. 60.

26. Mascitelli, R., 2000.

27. Reinertsen, D. G., Pg. 164.

28. Cusumano, M. A. and R. W. Selby, Pg. 361.

29. Deschamps, J. P. and P. R. Nayak, Pg. 256.

30. Mascitelli, R., 2000, Pg. 189.

31. Schrage, M., Pg. 187.

32. There are a number of approaches to prioritizing customer needs and homing in on an optimal value proposition for a new product. These include value engineering, value analysis, Kano diagrams, Pugh criteria, and of course, QFD. For more information on these methods, see 1) Deschamps, J. P. and P. R. Nayak, Pg. 90, 2) Terninko, J., Pg. 67, 3) Schonberger, R. J., Pg. 191, and 4) Terninko, J., Pg. 118.

33. For those readers interested in examples of products that have violated one or more of the three tests for value, see: 1) "The Cube: Looks Aren't Everything," *Business Week*, October 16, 2000, Pg. 29, 2) "Computers and Chips," *Business Week*, January 8, 2001, Pg. 94 – 95, 3) Smith, P. G. and D. G. Reinertsen, Pg. 66, 4) Anderson, D. M., Pg. 95, 5) "Windows ME: Not Worth the Trouble," *Business Week*, July 31, 2000, Pg. 26, 6) "Do One Thing and Do It Well," *Business Week*, June 19, 2000, Pgs. 94 – 96, 7) Christensen, C. M., Pg. 171, and 8) Cusumano, M. A. and K. Nobeoka, Pg. 8.

34. Cohen, L., (1995).

35. Fern, E. J., Pg. 3.

36. Smith, P. G. and D. G. Reinertsen, Pg. 93.

37. Hyman, B., Pg. 254.

38. Cooper, R. and R. Slagmulder, Pg. 171.

39. Smith, P. G. and D. G. Reinertsen, Pg. 99.

40. Pine, B. J. II, Pg. 47.

41. Bicheno, J., Pg. 48.

42. "IBM's Hottest Product Isn't a Product," *Business Week*, October 2, 2000, Pgs. 118–120.

43. "The Big Kahuna of B2B Exchanges," *Business Week*, October 9, 2000, Pgs. 166E2–166E4.

44. Anderson, D. M., Pg. 255.

45. Galbraith, J. R., (2000), Pg. 287.

46. To manage interfaces effectively, one must establish adequate design margins at each interface. Allow enough extra capacity at the interfaces to permit changes in the system to be contained within individual subsystem components. Reinertsen, D. G., Pg. 153.

47. "Visor: Versatility with a Vengeance," *Business Week*, December 11, 2000, Pg. 31.

48. Cooper, R. and R. Slagmulder, Pg. 84.

49. Tyndall, G., et al, Pg. 221.

50. Anderson, D. M., Pg. 117.

51. Boothroyd, G., Dewhurst, P., and W. Knight, Pg. 33.

52. Bralla, J. G., (1996), Pg. 23.

## Chapter #8

1. Verma, V. K., (1996), Pg. 172.
2. Verma, V. K., (1996), Pg. 183.
3. Clark, K. B. and S. C. Wheelwright, Pg. 542.
4. Cusumano, M. A. and K. Nobecka, Pg. 3.
5. Scotto, M., (2000).
6. Dinsmore, P. C., Pg. 68.
7. Kerzner, H., (1998), Pg. 125.
8. There are a number of sources for information on "value-stream organizations." Although the names used for these structures are different, the following resources provide insight into this powerful concept. See, 1) Dimancescu, D. and K. Dwenger, Pg. 35, 2) Womack, J. P. and D. T. Jones, Pg. 256, 3) Galbraith, J. R. and E. E. Lawler, Pg. 31, 4) Galbraith, J. R., (2000), Pg. 65, 5) Deschamps, J. P. and P. R. Nayak, Pg. 441, 6) Cusumano, M. A. and K. Nobeoka, Pg. 3, and, 7) Galbraith, J. R. and E. E. Lawler, Pg. 77.
9. Wenger, E. C. and W. M. Snyder, (2000).
10. Womack, J. P. and D. T. Jones, Pg. 156.
11. Senge, P. M., Pg. 234.
12. Graham, R. J. and R. L. Englund, Pg. 107.
13. Graham, R. J. and R. L. Englund, Pg. 14.
14. Dimancescu, D. and K. Dwenger, Pg. 196.
15. Kaplan, R. S. and D. P. Norton, Pg. 217.
16. Lipnack, J. and J. Stamps, Pg. 56.
17. See, for example, Hamel, G., Pg. 183. Clearly a great author and contributor, but in this work, Hamel recommends the kind of indulgence of chaos that I seek to banish. Outlaw projects are necessary only if your organization and system are not capable of promoting them in a "lawful" way. The only reason to condone such irregular measures is that you have basically given up on achieving a truly efficient operation.
18. Smith, P. G. and D. G. Reinertsen, Pg. 141.
19. See, for example, 1) Reinertsen, D. G., Pg. 37, and, 2) Cooper, R. G., Edgett, S. J., and E. J. Kleinschmid, Pg. 29.
20. Goodpasture, J. C. and D. Hulett, (Parts 1 and 2, 2000).
21. See, for example, 1) Groppelli, A. A. and E. Nikbakht, Pg. 78, 2) Groppelli, A. A. and E. Nikbakht, Pg. 69, and, 3) Reinertsen, D. G., Pg. 129.
22. See, for example, 1) Siegel, J. G. and J. K. Shim, Pg. 37, 2) Cooper, R. G., Pg. 193, and, 3) Cooper, R. G., Edgett, S. J., and E. J. Kleinschmid, Pg. 30.
23. Smith, P. G. and D. G. Reinertsen, Pg. 198.

24. Graham, R. J. and R. L. Englund, Pg. 37.
25. For more information on *Hoshin* Planning, see, 1) Akao, Y., Pg. 18, 2) Erhorn, C. and J. Stark, Pg. 130, 3) Cowley, M. and E. Domb, Pg. 19, 4) Bicheno, J., Pg. 35, and 5) Womack, J. P. and D. T. Jones, Pg. 96.
26. Senge, P. M., Pg. 275.
27. Womack, J. P. and D. T. Jones, Pg. 21.
28. Dimancescu, D. and K. Dwenger, Pg. 15.
29. Senge, P. M., Pg. 206.
30. Peiperl, M. A., (2001).
31. Senge, P. M., Pg. 274.

## Chapter #9

1. Lubianiker, S., (2000).
2. Dinsmore, P. C., Pg. 171.
3. Imai, M., Pg. 173.
4. For improvement blitz templates, under the guise of *kaizen* event worksheets, see 1) Imai, M., Pg. 319, and 2) Laraia, A. C., Moody, P. E. and R. W. Hall, Pg. 197.
5. Laraia, A. C., Moody, P. E. and R. W. Hall, Pg. 97.
6. Laraia, A. C., Moody, P. E. and R. W. Hall, Pg. 14.
7. For a *kaizen* event preparation checklist, see Liker, J. K., Pg. 237.
8. Liker, J. K., Pg. 65.
9. The book *Learning to See* is probably the easiest read on the planet, although it is focused on mapping manufacturing value-streams. The techniques are really the same, so you shouldn't have problems adapting the colorful examples in this book. See Rother, M. and J. Shook, Pg. 4. For some discussion of how to optimize a value-stream map, see Laraia, A. C., Moody, P. E. and R. W. Hall, Pg. 37.
10. Rother, M. and J. Shook, Pg. 21.
11. Rother, M. and J. Shook, Pg. 58.
12. Bicheno, J., Pg. 86.
13. Barnes, T., Pg. 162.

# References

*"The person who does not read good books has no advantage over the man who can't read them."*
—Mark Twain

Adams, J. R., 1997, *Principles of Project Management*, The Project Management Institute.

Adams, S., 1996, *The Dilbert Principle*, Harper Business.

Akao, Y., 1991, *Hoshin Kanri: Policy Deployment for Successful TQM*, Productivity Press.

Allen, T. J., 1997, *Managing the Flow of Technology*, MIT Press.

Anderson, D. M., 1997, *Agile Product Development for Mass Customization*, Irwin Professional Publishing.

Argyris, C., 1998, "Empowerment: The emperor's new clothes," *Harvard Business Review*, May-June Issue, Pgs. 98–105.

Barham, K. and C. Heimer, 1998, *ABB –The Dancing Giant*, Financial Times Publishing.

Barnes, T., 1996, *Kaizen Strategies for Successful Leadership*, Financial Times Publishing.

Bayles, D., 1998, *Extranets: Building the Business-To-Business Web*, Prentice-Hall.

Berg, C. and K. Colenso, 2000, "Work breakdown structure practice standard project – WBS vs. activities," *PM Network Magazine*, April Issue, Pgs. 69–71.

Bicheno, J., 2000, *The Lean Toolbox – 2nd Edition*, PICSIE Press.

Blumenthal, D. and Y. A. Griver, 2000, "Is building an extranet right for your company?," *PM Network*, October Issue, Pgs. 75–78.

Boone, L. E., 1999, *Quotable Business – 2nd Edition*, Random House, Inc.

Boothroyd, G., Dewhurst, P., and W. Knight, *Product Design for Manufacture and Assembly*, Marcel Dekker, Inc.

Bralla, J. G., 1996, *Design for Excellence*, McGraw-Hill, Inc.

Bralla, J. G., 1999, *Design for Manufacturability Handbook*, McGraw-Hill, Inc.

Cabanis-Brewin, J., 1999, "So . . . so what? Debate over CCPM," *PM Network*, December Issue, Pgs. 49–52.

Carbno, C., 1999, "Optimal resource allocation for projects," *Project Management Journal*, June Issue, Pgs. 22–31.

Case, R. H. and J. Singer, 1997, "Re: project team empowerment aboard the starship enterprise," *Research-Technology Management*, May-June Issue, Pgs. 13–15.

Christensen, C. M., 1997, *The Innovator's Dilemma*, Harvard Business School Press.

Clark, K. B. and S. C. Wheelwright, 1993, *Managing New Product and Process Development*, The Free Press.

Clark, K. B. and S. C. Wheelwright, 1995, *Leading Product Development*, The Free Press.

Clavell, J., 1983, *The Art of War by Sun Tzu*, Delacorte Press.

Cohen, L., 1995, *Quality Function Deployment*, Addison-Wesley.

Cooper, R. G., 1993, *Winning at New Products*, Perseus Press.

Cooper, R. G., 1995, *When Lean Enterprises Collide*, Harvard Business School Press.

Cooper, R. G., Edgett, S. J., and E. J. Klienschmidt, 1998, *Portfolio Management for New Products*, Perseus Books.

Cooper, R. and R. Slagmulder, 1997, *Target Costing and Value Engineering*, Productivity Press.

Cowley, M. and E. Domb, 1997, *Beyond Strategic Vision*, Butterworth-Heinemann.

Cusumano, M. A. and K. Nobeoka, 1998, *Thinking Beyond Lean*, The Free Press.

Cusumano, M. A. and R. W. Selby, 1995, *Microsoft Secrets*, Simon & Schuster.

Cusumano, M. A. and D. B. Yoffie, 1998, *Competing on Internet Time*, The Free Press.

Davidson, J. M., Clamen, A., and R. A. Karol, 2000, "Learning from the best new product developers," *IEEE Engineering Management Review*, First Quarter Issue, Pgs. 30–36.

Dawes, R. M., 1988, *Rational Choice in an Uncertain World*, Harcourt Brace College Publishers.

Deschamps, J. P. and P. R. Nayak, 1995, *Product Juggernauts*, Harvard Business School Press.

Dimancescu, D. and K. Dwenger, 1996, *World-Class New Product Development*, American Management Association.

Dimancescu, D., Hines, P., and N. Rich, 1997, *The Lean Enterprise*, American Management Association.

Dinsmore, P. C., 1997, *Winning in Business with Enterprise Project Management*, American Management Association.

Eden, C., Williams, T. and F. Ackermann, 1998, "Dismantling the learning curve: the role of disruptions on the planning of development projects," *International Journal of Project Management*, Vol. 16, No. 3, Pgs. 131–138.

Erhorn, C. and J. Stark, 1994, *Competing by Design*, Oliver Wright Publications, Inc.

Fern, E. J., 1998, *Time-to-Profit Project Management*, Time-to-Profit, Inc.

Fine, C. H., 1998, *Clockspeed*, Perseus Books.

Fleming, Q. W. and J. M. Koppelman, 2000, *Earned Value Project Management*, The Project Management Institute.

Fowlkes, W. Y. and C. M. Creveling, 1995, *Engineering Methods for Robust Product Design*, Addison-Wesley.

Galbraith, J. R., 1995, *Designing Organizations*, Jossey-Bass.

Galbraith, J. R., 2000, *Designing the Global Corporation*, Jossey-Bass.

Galbraith, J. R. and E. E. Lawler, 1993, *Organizing for the Future*, Jossey-Bass.

Globerson, S., 2000, "PMBOK and the critical chain," *PM Network*, May Issue, Pgs. 63–66.

Goldratt, E. M., 1990, *Theory of Constraints*, North River Press.

Goldratt, E. M., 1997, *Critical Chain*, North River Press.

Goldratt, E. M. and J. Cox, 1984, *The Goal*, North River Press.

Goldratt, E. M. and R. E. Fox, 1986, *The Race*, North River Press.

Goodpasture, J. C. and D. Hulett, 2000, "A balance sheet for projects: A guide to risk-based value – Part 1," *PM Network*, May Issue, Pgs. 68–71.

Goodpasture, J. C. and D. Hulett, 2000, "A balance sheet for projects: A guide to risk-based value – Part 2," *PM Network*, June Issue, Pgs. 63–71.

Graham, R. J. and R. L. Englund, 1997, *Creating an Environment for Successful Projects*, Jossey-Bass.

Grief, M., 1991, *The Visual Factory*, Productivity Press.

Groppelli, A. A. and E. Nikbakht, 1995, *Finance: A Streamlined Course for Students and Business People*, Barron's Educational Series.

Gruenwald, G., 1995, *New Product Development, 2nd Edition*, NTC Business Books.

Hamel, G., 2000, *Leading the Revolution*, Harvard Business School Press.

Harry, M. J., 1994, *The Vision of Six Sigma*, Sigma Publishing Company.

Harry, M. J. and R. Schroeder, 2000, *Six Sigma*, Currency Press.

Hayes, D. S., 2000, "Evaluation and application of a project charter template to improve the project planning process," *Project Management Journal*, March Issue, Pgs. 14–23.

Haywood, M., 1998, *Managing Virtual Teams*, Artech House.

Henderson, B. A. and J. L. Larco, 1999, *Lean Transformation*, The Oaklea Press.

Hyman, B., 1998, *Fundamentals of Engineering Design*, Prentice-Hall.

Ichida, T., 1996, *Product Design Review*, Productivity Press.

Imai, M., 1997, *Gemba Kaizen*, McGraw Hill, Inc.

Jackson, T. L. and K. R. Jones, 1996, *Implementing a Lean Management System*, Productivity Press.

Kaplan, R. S. and D. P. Norton, 1996, *The Balanced Scorecard*, Harvard Business School Press.

Karlsson, C. and P. Ahlstrom, 1996, "The difficult path to lean product development," *Journal of Product Innovation Management*, Vol. 13, Pgs. 283–295.

Kerzner, H., 1998, *Project Management – 6th Edition*, Van Nostrand Reinhold.

Kerzner, H., 2000, *Applied Project Management*, John Wiley & Sons.

Kidder, T., 1981, *The Soul of a New Machine*, Avon Books.

Laraia, A. C., Moody, P. E. and R. W. Hall, 1999, *The Kaizen Blitz*, John Wiley & Sons.

Laufer, A., 1997, *Simultaneous Management*, American Management Association.

Leach, L. P., 2000, *Critical Chain Project Management*, Artech House.

Leonard, D. and W. Swap, 1999, *When Sparks Fly*, Harvard Business School Press.

Leonard-Barton, D., 1995, *Wellsprings of Knowledge*, Harvard Business School Press.

Lewis, J. P., 1998, *Mastering Project Management*, McGraw Hill, Inc.

Lientz, B. P. and K. P. Rea, 1999, *Breakthrough Technology Project Management*, Academic Press.

Liker, J. K., 1998, *Becoming Lean*, Productivity Press.

Lipnack, J. and J. Stamps, 1997, *Virtual Teams*, John Wiley & Sons.

Lubianiker, S., 2000, "Opening the book on the open maturity model," *PM Network*, March Issue, Pgs. 30–33.

Mascitelli, R., 1999, *The Growth Warriors*, Technology Perspectives.

Mascitelli, R., 2000, "From experience: Harnessing tacit knowledge to achieve breakthrough innovation," *Journal of Product Innovation Management*, Volume 17, Pgs. 179–193.

Maslow, A. H., 1998, *Maslow on Management*, John Wiley & Sons.

McConnell, S., 1996, *Rapid Development*, Microsoft Press.

McGrath, M. E., 1996, *Setting the PACE in Product Development*, Butterworth Heinemann.

Mintzberg, H., Ahlstrand, B., and J. Lampel, 1998, *Strategy Safari*, The Free Press.

Nadler, D. A. and M. L. Tushman, 1997, *Competing by Design*, Oxford University Press.

Newbold, R. G., 1998, *Project Management in the Fast Lane*, St. Lucie Press.

Nonaka, I. and H. Takeuchi, 1995, *The Knowledge-Creating Company*, Oxford University Press.

Paquin, J. P., Couillard, J. and D. J. Ferrand, 2000, "Assessing and controlling the quality of a project end-product: The earned quality method," *IEEE Transactions on Engineering Management*, Vol. 47, No. 1, Pgs. 88–97.

Peiperl, M. A., 2001, "Getting 360 degree feedback right," *Harvard Business Review*, January Issue, Pgs. 142–147.

Phillips, J. B., 1999, "Management of modular projects: A templating approach," *Project Management Journal*, December Issue, Pgs. 33–41.

Pierce, J. R., 1980, *An Introduction to Information Theory – 2nd Edition*, Dover Publications, Inc.

Pine, B. J., 1993, *Mass Customization*, Harvard Business School Press.

Project Management Institute, 1996, *The Project Management Body of Knowledge (PMBOK) Guide*, The Project Management Institute.

Rand, G. K., 2000, "Critical chain: the theory of constraints applied to project management," *International Journal of Project Management*, Vol. 18, Pgs. 173–177.

Reinertsen, D. G., 1997, *Managing the Design Factory*, The Free Press.

Rizzo, T., 1999, "Operational measurements for product development organizations – Parts 1 and 2," *PM Network*, November / December Issues, Pgs. 42–47 (Part 1), and Pgs. 31–35 (Part 2).

Rosenau, M. D., 1998, *Successful Project Management, 3rd Edition*, John Wiley & Sons.

Rosenthal, S. R., 1992, *Effective Product Design and Development*, Irwin Professional Publishing.

Rother, M. and J. Shook, 1999, *Learning to See*, The Lean Enterprise Institute.

Schonberger, R. J., 1982, *Japanese Manufacturing Techniques*, The Free Press.

Schrage, M., 2000, *Serious Play*, Harvard Business School Press.

Schuyler, J. R., 1996, *Decision Analysis in Projects*, The Project Management Institute.

Scotto, M., 2000, "The project office: A common-sense implementation," *PM Network*, September Issue, Pgs. 94–96.

Senge, P. M., 1990, *The Fifth Discipline*, Currency Doubleday.

Shimbun, N. K., 1995, *Visual Control Systems*, Productivity Press.

Shina, S. G., 1991, *Concurrent Engineering and Design for Manufacture of Electronics Products*, Van Nostrand Reinhold.

Siegel, J. G. and J. K. Shim, 1991, *Barron's EZ-101 Finance*, Barron's Educational Series.

Sikes, D., 2000, "Using project websites to streamline communications," *PM Network*, June Issue, Pgs. 73–75.

Smith, P. G. and D. G. Reinertsen, 1995, *Developing Products in Half the Time*, Van Nostrand Reinhold.

Sobek, D. K., Liker, J. K., and A. C. Ward, 1998, "Another look at how Toyota integrates product development," *Harvard Business Review*, July-August Issue, Pgs. 36–49.

Sobek, D. K., Ward, A. C., and J. K. Liker, 1999, "Toyota's principles of set-based concurrent engineering," *Sloan Management Review*, Vol. 40, No. 2, Pgs. 67–83.

Souder, W. E., 1987, *Managing New Product Innovations*, Lexington Books.

Stamatis, D. H., 1995, *Failure Mode and Effect Analysis*, Quality Press.

Terninko, J., 1997, *Step-by-Step QFD – 2nd Edition*, CRC Press.

Thomas, R. J., 1993, *New Product Development: Managing and Forecasting for Strategic Success*, John Wiley & Sons.

Thut, M., 2000, "Accelerating time to market with technology building blocks," *PRTM Insight*, Volume 7, Number 1.

Tufte, E. R., 1983, *The Visual Display of Quantitative Information*, Graphics Press.

Tufte, E. R., 1990, *Envisioning Information*, Graphics Press.

Tyndall, G., Gopal, C., Partsch, W., and J. Kamauff, 1998, *Supercharging Supply Chains*, John Wiley & Sons.

Utterback, J. M., 1994, *Mastering the Dynamics of Innovation*, Harvard Business School Press.

Uyttewaal, E., 1999, "Take the path that is really critical," *PM Network*, December Issue, Pgs. 37–39.

Verma, V. K., 1995, *Organizing Projects for Success*, The Project Management Institute.

Verma, V. K., 1996, *Human Resource Skills for the Project Manager*, The Project Management Institute.

Ward, A. C., Liker, J. K., Cristiano, J. J., and D. K. Sobek, 1995, "The second Toyota paradox: How delaying decisions can make better cars faster," *Sloan Management Review*, Vol. 36, No. 3, Pgs. 43–61.

Waterworth, C. J., 2000, "Relearning the learning curve: A Review of the derivation and applications of learning-curve theory," *Project Management Journal*, March Issue, Pgs. 24–31.

Wenger, E. C. and W. M. Snyder, 2000, "Communities of practice: The organizational frontier," *Harvard Business Review*, January – February Issue, Pgs. 139–145.

Wideman, R. M. (ed.), 1992, *Project and Program Risk Management*, The Project Management Institute.

Wirth, I., 1996, "How generic and how industry-specific is the project management profession?," *International Journal of Project Management*, Vol. 14, No. 1, Pgs. 7–11.

Womak, J. P. and D. T. Jones, 1996, *Lean Thinking*, Simon & Schuster.

Womack, J. P., Jones, D. T., and D. Roos, 1990, *The Machine that Changed the World*, HarperCollins.

# Index

*"It is a good thing for an uneducated
man to read books of quotations."*
*—Winston Churchill*

# Spread the Lean Word!

To order additional copies of
## *Building a Project-Driven Enterprise*

or to learn more about
Ron Mascitelli's workshops on:

## *Lean Project Management*
and
## *Lean Product Development*

Please visit our website at:

## **www.techper.com**

or contact:

**Renee Winett**
Marketing Director
Technology Perspectives
techper1@att.net
(888) 366-7488
(toll-free in the U.S.)